MAKING
PEACE *with*
YOUR PAST

Other books by Harold Bloomfield, M.D.
(authored and coauthored):

Healing Anxiety Naturally

The Holistic Way to Health and Happiness

How to Enjoy the Love of Your Life

How to Heal Depression

How to Survive the Loss of a Love

Hypericum (St. John's Wort) & Depression

Inner Joy

Lifemates

Love Secrets for a Lasting Relationship

Making Peace in Your Stepfamily

Making Peace with Your Parents

Making Peace with Yourself

*Surviving, Healing and Growing:
The How to Survive the Loss of a Love Workbook*

The Power of 5

Think Safe, Be Safe

TM: Discovering Inner Energy and Overcoming Stress

MAKING
PEACE *with*
YOUR PAST

The Six Essential Steps to
Enjoying a Great Future

HAROLD BLOOMFIELD, M.D.,

with Philip Goldberg

HarperCollins*Publishers*

MAKING PEACE WITH YOUR PAST. Copyright © 2000 by Harold Bloomfield, M.D. All rights reserved. Printed in the United States of America. No part of this book may be used or reproduced in any manner whatsoever without written permission except in the case of brief quotations embodied in critical articles and reviews. For information address HarperCollins Publishers Inc., 10 East 53rd Street, New York, NY 10022.

HarperCollins books may be purchased for educational, business, or sales promotional use. For information please write: Special Markets Department, HarperCollins Publishers Inc., 10 East 53rd Street, New York, NY 10022.

FIRST EDITION

Designed by Lindgren/Fuller Design

Printed on acid-free paper

Library of Congress Cataloging-in-Publication Data

Bloomfield, Harold, 1944–
    Making peace with your past : the six essential steps to enjoying a great future / Harold Bloomfield with Philip Goldberg.—1st ed.
        p. cm.
    Includes index.
    ISBN 0-06-019528-2
    1. Self-realization. 2. Autobiographical memory. I. Goldberg, Philip, 1944–
    II. Title.

BF637.S4.B574 2000
    158.1—dc21   99-089719

00 01 02 03 04 ❖/RRD 10 9 8 7 6 5 4 3 2 1

Dedicated to the teachers of the heart
who helped me make peace with my past, especially
my beloved wife, Sirah.

. . . and to you, dear reader, my deep respect for
your desire to heal, love, and be more.

The Past—the dark unfathom'd retrospect!
The teeming gulf—the sleepers and the shadows!
The past! the infinite greatness of the past!
For what is the present after all but a growth out of the past?

—WALT WHITMAN

The terror that scares us from self-trust is our past act
or word. But why should you keep your head over your
shoulder? Why drag about this corpse of your memory?
Bring the past for judgment into the thousand-eyed
Present, and live ever in a new day.

—RALPH WALDO EMERSON

CONTENTS

PREFACE

We must make peace with our past; our lives may literally depend on it. In 1998 the prestigious *American Journal of Preventative Medicine* published a landmark study by a team of researchers at Kaiser Permanente Medical Care Program working with epidemiologists from the Centers for Disease Control (CDC) in Atlanta.[1] The survey of nearly 20,000 people found that those with "adverse childhood experiences" were, as adults, far more likely to suffer from cancer, heart disease, chronic lung disorders, and other leading causes of death.

The researchers asked questions such as, "Did a parent or other adult in the household often or very often swear at, insult, or put you down?", ". . . often or very often act in a way that made you afraid that you would be physically hurt?", and other queries pointing to significant childhood adversity. Those who had encountered abuse (physical, psychological, or sexual), or were raised in dysfunctional families (with violence, substance abuse, mental illness, or criminal behavior), were far more likely to develop life-threatening illnesses. In fact, an adverse childhood proves to be as powerful a predictor of subsequent illness as smoking.

Mental health professionals have always known that a painful childhood can contribute to significant emotional problems in adulthood. Studies have shown that childhood abuse and neglect increase the risk of personality disorders, addiction, anxiety, depression, and other psychological problems.[2] Now, with this groundbreaking study, there is hard data linking adverse past experiences with increased morbidity and mortality.

Why should there be such a link? For one thing, people whose early years are marked by emotional injury are far more likely to have high health risk factors. The study found a strong correlation between childhood adversity and obesity, physical inactivity, and smoking, as well as depression and suicide attempts. "High levels of exposure to adverse childhood experiences would expectedly produce anxiety, anger, and depression in children," the researchers concluded. "To the degree that behavior such as smoking, alcohol or drug use are found to be effective as coping devices, they would tend to be used chronically." And those risk factors, of course, would jeopardize their health.

There are additional plausible explanations as well.[3, 4, 5] A large number of research findings indicate that prolonged psychological adversity has a destructive impact on the physiology, making the person much more vulnerable to illness. It is well established by more than two decades of neuroscience research that the suffering of the past becomes emblazoned in the neural circuitry of the nervous system. A large body of evidence indicates that the very structure of our brains is dramatically impacted by adverse experiences such as shame or terror.

From a psychiatric perspective, the pain we try to suppress or repress doesn't just go away; unless these experiences are acknowledged, expressed, and resolved, emotional pressure continues to build, producing suffering and distress. Every day of the year, for instance, marriages break up because of still-unresolved pain from past love relationships.

Many people who have been through trauma or prolonged emotional hardship are hypervigilant, going through life continually on guard against any possible repetition of previous horrors. This hypervigilance bombards the body with waves of adrenaline and cortisol. Among other things, excess adrenaline can cause the overcontraction and eventual rupture of heart muscle fibers, increasing the risk of cardiac arrythmia and sudden death. Excess cortisol is known to lower immune response, raise cholesterol levels, and even kill brain cells.

Overall, the chronic stress of unresolved emotional pain wreaks havoc on your immune and circulatory systems, cardiac function, hormone levels, mood and memory, even your physical coordination and metabolic rate. In addition, the cascade of free radical cell damage produced by chronic stress is thought to contribute to as much as 80 percent of all illness.

The good news is, our brains and bodies have remarkably plasticity; we are capable of fully healing old emotional wounds, breaking self-defeating habits, and consciously transforming the way we think, feel, and act.[6, 7, 8] We can actually change the molecules, neurons, and even the operant genes that determine our physical, mental, and spiritual well-being. Through modern imaging technology such as PET scans and MRIs, we can see the limbic system, where emotional memories are stored, begin to be rewired for happiness and inner peace through specific techniques such as those used in this book. We can heal ourselves—and stop passing on emotional pain and suffering to future generations.

In a sense, I have known about the effects of painful early experiences my entire life. I was raised by Holocaust survivors. My mother had been so traumatized by the brutal murder of her parents during Hitler's reign of terror that my early years were marked by the constant chaos of what we now call "adverse childhood experiences." I remember thinking at a very tender age, "I am being wounded now, but I will heal later." I made a sacred vow to find the means to heal myself and share that knowledge with others. I was seven years old when I decided to become a psychiatrist. Later, my wounds led me to become an ardent seeker of psychological and spiritual truth. My personal and family life has benefited greatly from my effort to make peace with my past, and my professional work has been dedicated to helping others make peace with theirs.

Making Peace with Your Past is a systematic program based upon 30 years of work with tens of thousands of clients and seminar participants. Combining scientific research and recent breakthroughs in psychotherapy, I have developed a series of easy-to-follow guidelines and practical, powerful exercises that can rapidly reduce suffering and bring deep, lasting peace of mind. *This book will not only show you how to come to peace with an adverse childhood, but with the still-burning wounds of adolescence and adulthood as well.*

You *can* heal yourself. The runaway train that carries the wounds of past adversity hurtling toward a future of illness and sorrow can be stopped in its tracks. You may have known violence, shame, fear, turmoil, and despair. You may carry with you the lonely torment of guilt, regret, and self-doubt. Your heart may have been broken repeatedly and your spirit many times crushed. Still, you can heal; your past is not your destiny. You can transcend the boundaries of past circumstances, for life always seeks to surpass itself.

Making peace with your past is not about fixing yourself, but changing yourself. This book will help you release the residue of the past that no longer serves you. It will also open new vistas and grand possibilities. No longer dragging the weight of a painful past behind you, you will be free to love and thrive, not just survive; free to create yourself anew, and march into the future confident, open hearted, and joyful. What was once the source of suffering can now become a great resource for spiritual evolution and personal maturity. With a strong commitment here and now, *you will make peace with your past.*

Healing a Painful Past

HURT WAS INEVITABLE,
SUFFERING IS OPTIONAL

Those who cannot remember the past are condemned to repeat it.

— GEORGE SANTAYANA

The three most profound questions in every person's life are: Who am I? Where did I come from? Where am I going? This book will help you explore and answer all three. As you unravel the tangled web of your past, you will be able to extract from it the golden thread that is your essence and weave your future into a bold, brilliant tapestry.

Scientific research, depth psychology, and the great wisdom traditions of every culture all strongly concur that the root cause of human suffering is the accumulation of unprocessed experience from the past. In my 30 years as a psychotherapist and seminar leader, I have learned that no one can experience true love, or a joyful presence, or create an optimal future until he or she makes peace with the past. People come to therapy to deal with an immediate crisis or persistent problem. They are often depressed about the present or anxious about the future. But without exception, they soon discover that the pain and chaos of the present have origins in the past. To understand themselves and move forward with confidence and freedom, they must reflect on what brought them to this moment. Aspects of their personal history that are holding them back must be confronted and resolved; aspects that can rejuvenate their creativity and strength—the fun and wonder of childhood, for instance, or the visionary enthusiasm of adolescence—need to be rediscovered and resurrected.

Without a doubt, many of the here-and-now conflicts people have with their spouses, lovers, bosses, or children are, in part, reenactments of incidents that happened earlier in their lives.

Here are some examples from the people I'm currently seeing in my practice:

- Mary feels resentful and ashamed because her husband ran off with her best friend three years earlier. Beautiful, rich, and a well-known dermatologist, deep down she still can't get over the shock of having her charmed life torn apart. She is so mistrustful that she can't allow herself to get really close to any man or woman.

- James torments himself for squandering his inheritance in day trading and high-risk investments. Seeing his business school classmates build their fortunes and start their families fills him with self-contempt, regret, and jealousy.

- Now 38 and unable to conceive, Carol is plagued by feelings of guilt and regret for two abortions she had in her teens.

- A model in her thirties, Helen feels insecure around other women and is sure that any man she loves will leave her for someone prettier and smarter. She needs to see the connection to her childhood, when she was taunted, and sometimes tortured, by her older sister, who never let Helen play with her and her friends.

- An underachieving supermarket manager, Mark is a loner who complains of being bored with his life. Ever since he was twelve and saw his father die suddenly, he has been a self-declared hypochondriac and can't let anyone or anything become important to him.

- Deeply in love for the first time in her life, Janice is troubled because sex with her fiancé has become boring. Her basis of comparison is the wild, forbidden sex she had with "bad boys" when she was younger—and with her boyfriend when they first met and he was still married. She needs to find acceptable

ways to bring the excitement of her sexual past into the peaceful, long-term intimacy she also desires.
- At age 50, Peter is torn by competing desires: to stay with his wife of 20 years or start a new life with another woman with whom he is having an affair. He is repeating the same pattern he witnessed when his dad ran off with a young woman at the age of 50. At the time, Peter hated his father for leaving his mother, but also admired that he had "the guts to go for it" despite intense social disapproval.

As the great novelist William Faulkner once said, the past is not dead, it is not even past. Indeed, the past lives on in everything we think, feel, say, and do. The cells in our bodies may die and replace themselves every seven years; we may change jobs, spouses, addresses, even our names; but the imprint of every experience—large and small, pleasant and unpleasant—remains with us, each one adding to the sum of who we are, like the bricks and mortar in a house or the words on a page.

The past does not just sit there like an obedient child, waiting to be called upon when we want to remember things. It is a full participant in our lives. A painful past can haunt us, stirring up rage, regret, sorrow, shame, and other bitter feelings. The emotional residue of that pain—a background buzz of self-punishment, fear, and anger—can quite literally control us, turning us into victims of memory and drowning the more delicate emotions of love, joy, and compassion. Positive memories haunt us, too, making us long for the freedom and excitement of days gone by. But it's not just the past we remember that influences the present. To a large extent, the unremembered past shapes the feeling tone of our lives, sometimes calling forth confidence, generosity, and exuberance, and at other times unexplained anxiety, despair, and physical illness.

What echoes of the past are disturbing your peace in the present? To assess the extent to which you can benefit from this book, please answer yes or no to the following questions:

- Do you harbor guilt, gripes, or grudges from a past relationship?
- Are you plagued by thoughts like "If only I had ...," or "I wish I didn't ... "?

- Are you afraid of rejection, disapproval, or abandonment?
- When personal problems arise, do you sometimes think, "Oh, no, not again!"?
- Are you ashamed of things you've done?
- Do you wish you could apologize to someone you wronged and be forgiven?
- Do you wish you could set the record straight—and finally be vindicated?
- Does thinking about the way you were (beautiful, carefree, popular, athletic, etc.) leave you dissatisfied with who you are today?
- Do you frequently feel disappointed by, or bitter about, your relationships, work, or life in general?
- Are you fearful of the future?
- Has life not lived up to your expectations?

If you answered yes to even one of these questions, you've come to the right place. It's time to make peace with your past—now!

ENDING THE PAIN

One important order of business will be to take a close, penetrating look at the crises and catastrophes whose impact on your life have been most profound. The word *crisis* derives from a Greek root meaning "to separate" and from the Latin *krei*, from which we also get words like *recriminate*, *critic*, and *cry*. Those roots capture what it feels like when you go through an emotional crisis: separated, as if a chasm has cut you off from your usual sources of safety and security; as if your spirit is splitting under the weight of inner and outer forces you can't control.

Physically, crises and catastrophes can be devastating; the hormones, enzymes, and neurotransmitters that govern the immune system get depleted, making your body susceptible to incapacitating or life-threatening disorders. Emotionally, you feel as though you might be—or actually are—falling apart. Mentally, your old beliefs no longer make sense, and your old coping mechanisms no longer seem to work. Socially, you feel alienated and alone. Spiritually, you feel cut off from the larger forces of the universe or abandoned by God, as if staring into a frightful abyss with a sense of dread.

Old traumas don't die, but unlike old soldiers, they don't fade away, either. Unless you take steps to undo them, they stick with you like wallpaper. The deep, gaping wounds from violence, abandonment, betrayal, crippling injury, the death of a loved one, and other cataclysms can create a spiral of perpetual crisis and turmoil. Like pulling a scab off a sore, any similar hurts or losses in the present can reopen the wound, compounding the pain and making it harder to heal. Many wounded souls walk through life in a state of chronic fear and hypervigilance, waiting for the next shoe to fall, or living under adverse conditions for fear of change. They have a subtle but gnawing apprehension that becomes a self-fulfilling prophecy, breeding ever-new crises, conflicts, and catastrophes.

To dull or mask the pain of past traumas, we use a variety of painkillers: physical balms such as alcohol and drugs; emotional anesthetics such as shame and blame; intellectual analgesics such as denial, rationalization, and excuse-making; social palliatives like enablers, co-dependents, and fellow "victims"; and spiritual sedatives such as, "It was God's will," or "Everything serves a purpose," along with armored postures like cynicism, martyrdom, bitterness, and existential despair. The numbing effect of these anesthetics makes them appealing, but their effect is only temporary; the suppressed painful feelings persist and perpetuate.

It's not just major upheavals that can poison the present. Most of us are powerfully affected by the accumulation of insidious, commonplace losses, sorrows, and disappointments—a college or business setback, for example, a falling-out with a friend or relative, or the loss of a home or cherished pet. We have unhealed wounds inflicted by others—lovers who tormented us, parents who ignored us (or didn't really know us), teachers who belittled us, friends who let us down, enemies who humiliated us. And we have self-doubt, from decisions that didn't work out, choices we regret, words and actions we wish we could take back, grudges we hold, or love we've been pushing away. Even positive turning points—the birth of a child, a financial windfall, buying a home—can register as crises if they force you to make major adjustments in your life or stir up interpersonal conflict.

If you are wading through midlife, you might be painfully aware of such haunting memories. When you realize that the number of years you have left may be fewer than the years you have already lived, the impulse to look back and reflect becomes irresistible. "What has my life stood for?" "Where do I go from here—downhill?" You contemplate mistakes, question your choices, ache over lost opportunities, wistfully recall past glories. You may feel that life has not worked out as you expected it to. You may feel that you don't quite measure up to the vision you had for yourself—or that others had for you. You may feel like you've parked your potential at some fork in the road and, as darkness starts to descend, you can't find the keys. Whether you come out of this phase with fear and dread or with a spirit of renewal and passion hinges in large part on whether you make peace with your past.

Open wounds, old habits, and outworn attitudes cause what I call *psychosclerosis*, a hardening of the spirit. But we are all wounded healers. If you let old wounds stimulate a search for deeper truth and growth, you can unclog the arteries of your soul. This book offers a genuine opportunity to loosen the grip of the persistent, undigested pain from past adversity, take your spirit in your arms, and give it new life.

PAST AS PRELUDE:
THE REPETITION COMPULSION

Sigmund Freud observed that past emotional traumas, undigested feelings, and repressed memories have a tendency to reappear with awful precision if left unexamined. He called this the *repetition compulsion*. Simply put, we tend to recreate what we have not worked through. We each have a backlog of painful memories: times in the past when we were belittled, ignored, abandoned, attacked, or in other ways psychologically traumatized. The events that tend to repeat are those to which we attribute significance and meaning over time. They are like tiny emotional abscesses—

pockets of hurt and venom that won't stay safely tucked away, and find ways to restrict and diminish our presence.

Our emotional memories are stored in a portion of the brain called the *amygdala*. The experiences that frighten us the most produce high arousal in this alarm center, leaving behind an indelible imprint in the nervous system. The amygdala, which responds to threats to our survival, compares the present to what occurred in the past. If the new experience is even remotely similar to an old trauma, an emergency response is triggered in the amygdala, activating automatic thoughts, feelings, and behavior patterns conditioned by the past. Based on recent research findings, neurobiologist Robert Pollack suggests that the mind functions by continual reference to the past and that current emotional conflicts are rooted in repressed memories stored in neural networks associated with the amygdala.[1] Unfortunately, these old emotional survival mechanisms may be hopelessly out of date, inappropriate to the current situation and person you now are— or wish to be.

Harriet was a 44-year-old nurse who never had a relationship that lasted more than 13 months. Every man she got involved with eventually ran for his life because Harriet was possessive, jealous, and clingy. The only difference between a week-long affair and a one-year affair was how long she could keep her neediness under wraps. At the first sign that the man was starting to back off, Harriet would panic. She would try to hold on for dear life, but the more desperate she got, the faster the man ran.

Harriet's pattern was rooted in a debilitating sense of insecurity and worthlessness that began in childhood. Her mother was an unhappy, acid-tongued woman who spent her days complaining and blaming others for her fate. Among those she targeted was her only child. Little Harriet could do nothing right in her mother's eyes. She was even blamed for the boredom and bitterness of her marriage: "Everything was fine until you came along." Harriet's father was no help. She described him as a nonentity, a moody presence who was absent emotionally and then literally, fleeing when Harriet was seven. Her mother blamed her for that, too. Eight years later, just before Harriet's 15th birthday, her mother committed suicide. Harriet blamed herself.

She had absorbed her parents' negative messages about herself and had come to see herself as unlovable. Throughout her adult life she kept repeating the pattern established in her youth: desperately seeking love from someone who was destined to disappear. Even her choice of nursing specialties reflected that pattern: she worked in Intensive Care, where many of the patients she grew attached to would die. It was only when Harriet used the techniques in this book to thoroughly examine the roots of her insecurity and self-loathing that she was able to begin changing her behavior. As I write this, she is approaching her second anniversary with a man who loves her.

As Harriet came to understand, when people and situations in your current life resemble people and situations from your past—no matter how remotely—stressful memories are reactivated and negative patterns are repeated. An argument with a colleague may arouse long-buried feelings of rage toward the adolescent peers who humiliated you. You may become ill and need others to care for you, only to find that old fears of abandonment suddenly reemerge. You may fall in love with someone who seems different from all the rest, only to recreate the same predicaments that have marked every romance since high school. You can expect such patterns to continue until you make your peace.

For another illustration of the repetition compulsion in action, consider Tim. Independently wealthy from a sizable inheritance, Tim was a banking executive and philanthropist who came to therapy because he was having major conflicts with his wife over money. In addition to spending large amounts on clothes and furnishings, Carmella was taking care of 19 members of her family back in Mexico in lavish style. When Tim discovered the extent of his wife's extravagance, he hit the roof—and the panic button. The problem was not just a disagreement over financial priorities. He was tormented by the thought that his wife didn't really love him but was only using him for his money.

As we delved into his past, it became clear that Tim was acting out an old pattern. Raised in a small town where his father owned the textile plant that employed most of the local citizens, Tim was the rich kid from the side of the tracks where very few lived. Early on, he learned to use his privileged status to attract friends. He would throw parties at his home, buy expensive gifts for other kids, and let them use the pool and tennis court when his parents were away. But he always felt lonely and isolated. Unable to reciprocate, the other kids tended to shun Tim and stick with peers whose circumstances were more like their own. He could never be sure whether or not someone who was nice to him was actually trying to manipulate him for selfish ends.

When he left his hometown as a young man, Tim was careful to avoid ostentation and any outward display of wealth. But the pattern remained: he used his resources and position to attract people to him, and as soon as he succeeded he became insecure and suspicious about their motives, eventually driving them away. He had reenacted the same drama with friends to whom he was excessively generous; with business associates who took advantage of him; with two fiancées who never made it to the altar; and now with a wife who fit the role of suspected gold-digger to a T. Before he could resolve his conflict with Carmella, Tim had to look squarely at his own past and come to terms with the pattern that kept on getting him in trouble.

In contemporary language, we think of the repetition compulsion this way: what you resist, persists. That which you consciously try to avoid, whether fear, shame, anger, or any other painful feeling, will return, and the more you try to avoid it, the harder it will hit. Also, if you keep resisting feedback from your past, the past will persist unaltered in your subconscious mind and reassert itself repeatedly—often in unexpected, unwanted ways. That's when you find yourself groaning, "Here we go again," because you're repeating the same old thoughts, feelings, and behaviors, like a vending machine that spews out the same brand of candy when the same button is pushed. Perhaps you go from one relationship to another, only to once again feel dominated, controlled, unappreciated, or manipulated. Or you switch jobs only to feel unsatisfied, criticized, and dead-ended all over again. Or you find the same depression or bodily aches and pains cropping up each time you feel stuck in your life. Under stress, we revert to form.

You don't have to be a prisoner of the repetition compulsion. You can stop feeling victimized by the past and create a new, more fulfilling reality. Work carefully with the material in this book and you will find the results to be powerful, profound, and durable.

SHINING LIGHT ON YOUR PAST

An essential part of the peacemaking process is learning to see your life story in a new light, to expand your vision of who you were so you can think truly original thoughts and reshape your destiny.

The past is not just a saga of pain, shame, and blame. Your history is not just a cauldron of hurt. The creatures that lurk in the shadows of your unconscious are not all monsters. The memories you need to connect with to heal and grow are not just the ugly ones. Your past is also a treasure trove of unique strengths, talents, and wisdom. So, while we'll be viewing nightmares you'd rather forget and getting in touch with feelings associated with painful memories, we'll also be locating the immense beauty that's been locked away inside you.

We'll relive the times when your soul winked at you. We'll see what called you to adventure and purpose, what aroused your passions and sparked your enthusiasm. We'll listen for the voice of your soul, which may have been muffled by layers of negative feelings such as worthlessness, humiliation, and despair. As the songwriter Leonard Cohen put it, "There is a crack in everything, that's how the light gets in." Peeking through the cracks of the past to find the light will add vital balance to your vision of where you've come from and who you are.

ORIGINAL BLISS

We'll also peer through the cracks in existence itself and find the purest light of all. Each of us is born to this life in what I call Original Bliss. Before the moment of birth, we exist in a blessed state of oneness. Depending on your belief system, that can mean union with a transcendent realm of infinite peace—what the wisdom traditions call God, Brahman, Allah, the Void, the Absolute, and so on—or perhaps what Freud and other pioneers of psychology described as the supreme safety and security of the womb. At birth, we descend through a tunnel of contraction and emerge localized in time and space. We remain to some extent in a unified, blissful state, but now our needs are not always met instantaneously. There is greater separation between self and surroundings. Over time, the world becomes less and less magical, less and less an extension of our wishes and desires. And as we develop our individual identities and experience life's friction, blisters form over the Original Bliss.

But deep within our core lives the primordial memory of that blissful state. We get occasional glimpses of it in moments of grace, or during peak experiences—in the throes of creative passion, for example, in the silence of the woods, or during orgasm—and the mystics and meditators among us are often lucky enough to have sustained contact with it. But even when it's dormant, that deep, wordless memory creates in us a self-transcending drive to return to that original state in which mind, body, spirit, and all of Creation are one. That part of our past, while usually far from conscious awareness, is every bit as real as the past of trial and tribulation. Making peace with the past brings you closer to that eternal reality—and the more you attune to your sacred soul, the easier it is to peel away the blisters and reveal the bliss.

If we were to limit ourselves to the psychological arena, we would end up with an incomplete and tenuous peace, like the "peaceful coexistence" of the Cold War with all its tension and threats and wasted resources. If the peace you seek is more than the absence of war—if it is to be a deep and lasting peace—it can be found only by addressing *all* aspects of the self, including the soul's yearning for metaphysical meaning. Whatever your belief system may be, it's important to realize that you are more than a personality trying to avoid pain, more than a stimulus-response machine, more than a seething stew of unresolved conflicts. You are also a courageous mapmaker linked to a larger cosmic design.

THE QUINTESSENTIAL SELF

Man is his own star.
— JOHN FLETCHER

Your past has left its imprint on each aspect of what I call the Quintessential Self: mental, emotional, physical, relational, and spiritual. The self can be envisioned as a five-pointed star, with each component radiating out from a central core to form a unique whole.

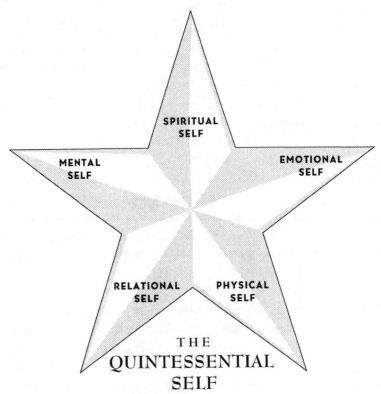

Our goal is to make peace in each of these five areas, and also among them, so you can shine brightly as a human star. All too often, attempts to make peace with the past focus on only one or two aspects of the Quintessential Self. Talk therapy, for example, usually involves primarily the mind in its search for insight, with the emotions and body as secondary beneficiaries. Such partial approaches can have great value, but they leave out vital aspects of healing. To truly make peace with the past and create the conditions for the self to shine brightly in the future, each point of the star needs to be addressed. For this reason, you will find exercises and suggestions throughout the book aimed at the quintessential healing of all five components of the Self.

THE MENTAL SELF

Gaining a more complete understanding of the past and its influence on you is, by itself, healing. We will also change the context of the past, so you come to see it from a deeper, fuller, more enlightened perspective, neither romanticizing nor demonizing it, neither denying painful truths nor wallowing in them. You can't change the facts of the past, but you can change the pictures of it that you carry in your head. This is important because your view of the past tends to reappear in the present: If you feel victimized by the past, you are likely to feel victimized in the present; if you feel sorrow about the past, you are likely to feel sorrow in the present.

Making peace with the past will help you learn valuable life lessons that may have been obscured by tragedies and traumas, and bring deep insights into your soul's unique path.

We'll also bring to light aspects of your past you may have suppressed; by courageously bringing those concealed truths to awareness, you can transform your subconscious from your worst enemy to your best friend. This work may be uncomfortable at times, but it's indispensable: The truth shall set you free. When the intellect can work with truth instead of illusions, it is better equipped to make effective decisions.

THE EMOTIONAL SELF

Every significant line and verse of your history is reflected in your emotional makeup. Making peace with the past entails letting go of the hurt, anger, shame, guilt, sadness, and other undigested feelings that have been festering inside you, creating a toxic buildup of resentment, cynicism, and mistrust.

Letting go does not mean denying, ignoring, or discrediting the past; it means resolving, releasing, and healing it. This may entail forgiving some people who have terribly wronged you. If you find yourself resisting that notion, remember that the main reason to forgive is not to give something to those who hurt you, but to enhance your own peace of mind. To open a place for forgiveness—and *self*-forgiveness—we'll perform some emotional heart surgery. We'll also do some emotional liposuction, to siphon off excess deposits of noxious feelings—and lighten up.

We live in a world that provides very few acceptable ways to express difficult emotions. This forces us to hold everything in, creating a state of emotional agitation. Through writing and other techniques that provide a safe outlet for long-unexpressed feelings, you will have the opportunity to cleanse your system of accumulated psychic sludge. You will also have what therapists call "corrective emotional experiences." These are essentially ways to give to yourself the emotional nourishment you did not receive earlier in your life.

THE PHYSICAL SELF

We'll also work with the residue of past traumas, tragedies, and triumphs that is deposited in your muscles and sinews and lodged in the very chemistry of your brain and nervous system. Research has found that every experience alters the chemistry of the brain and its intricate network of neuronal connections. Brain change is inevitable, but we can take control over the direction of change because we create our own reality. This remarkable neural plasticity—to literally rewire the brain and therefore our perceptions and memories—is what physiologically enables us to make peace with the past.

Thirty years ago, Dr. Elmer Green and his colleagues at the Menninger Clinic formulated what they called the *psychophysiological principle*. "Every change in the physiological state," they wrote, "is accompanied by an appropriate change in the mental-emotional state, and conversely, every change in the mental-emotional state, conscious or unconscious, is accompanied by an appropriate change in the physiological state."[2] To appreciate the truth of that insight, you need only to observe how you feel and think when you're tired, sick, or sexually frustrated and compare that to how you feel and think when you're rested, healthy, or sexually satisfied. Not only your moods but your very perception of what is true and what is false changes as the machinery of consciousness changes. Peace brings clarity, equanimity, and steadiness of vision.

Since every state of mind has a corresponding state of physiology, our bodies as a whole—not just our brains—carry the scars of the past. As described in the Preface, this principle has been dramatically demonstrated in medical studies showing that adverse childhood experiences are a major risk factor in the development of life-threatening illnesses. Through a number of powerful, proven techniques, you'll learn how to heal and repair the subtle and not-so-subtle wounds that adverse experience has etched into your body.

THE RELATIONAL SELF

Unfinished business from significant past relationships—whether with parents, siblings, friends, or an ex-spouse or lover—can undermine the quality of your current and future relationships. An important part of the peacemaking process, therefore, is to resolve old tensions and conflicts, and to transform the significant relationships in your life. Guidelines for doing so safely and productively will be offered. We'll be tapping the most powerful healing energy of all—love—along with its noble cousin, compassion. Love is the magic force that enables you to forgive. Most of us try very hard to get love; making peace means learning to accept the love we're offered and to be more *loving*.

We'll also suggest ways in which current relationships can facilitate the healing process. You suffer more when you're alone with your pain. Sharing your experiences and feelings with those who can offer love, respect, understanding, and acceptance is profoundly healing to that aspect of the Quintessential Self that has been hurt by others in the past. Reaching out *to* those in need is another key to achieving peace within yourself; helping others not only feels good, it is good for your well-being.

THE SPIRITUAL SELF

The past also influences how you relate to the sacred dimension of existence and whether you heed the urgings of your soul, for while the soul is immortal, the spirit can die. Like Job in the Bible, you may be one of the good and decent people who have suffered more than your share of pain. It may have seemed at times that the larger forces at work in the universe, however you define them, were conspiring against you. You may have raised questions like, "How can a loving God allow me to suffer this way?" "I've led a righteous life. Why have I been dealt such a rotten hand?" There are no easy answers to these mysteries, of course, but this book will help you align realistically with God, Goddess, Spirit, Christ, Nature, or whatever you call a higher power.

We will call upon a variety of spirit-based practices—prayer, meditation, visualization, and so on—to heal old wounds, expand your perspective, and create deep peace in the present. One of the great fallacies of psychology is that you have to work through all your "stuff" before you have a chance of finding inner peace. In truth, the process works in reverse as well: cultivating inner peace can help to heal the past. Some of the practices in the book will help you quiet your emotions, silence your restless mind, and resonate with your highest self.

The book will help you come to terms with the darker forces as well. To one degree or another, the way you've lived your life has brought out aspects of yourself you wish did not exist. In coming to terms with your past, you have to be willing to look at your dark side fearlessly and release the burdens of shame and guilt. Your shadow follows you wherever you go; you might as well make peace with it.

WHAT YOU CAN EXPECT

You *can* make peace with your past. You *can* continue to evolve and grow; to learn the vital lessons you missed out on before. You *can* resolve deep-seated conflicts and tie up loose ends. You *can* rediscover parts of yourself you left behind to your detriment—the vigor, the optimism, the capacity for joy, passion, and ecstasy. You *can* defuse the land mines that were planted in the soil of your psyche and walk fearlessly into the future. You *can* weave together a hand-crafted life from past devastation, misery, and upheaval. The first step is to look at the past—all of it, the good, the bad, and the ugly—and accept the complete truth about it.

The corollary to "What you resist, persists" is "What you accept, lightens." The minute the unseen is dragged from the shadows, it begins to lose strength. When the curtain of the unconscious is lifted and the truth is exposed, the past, like the Wizard of Oz, loses its ability to intimidate and control. And, like Dorothy, you can free yourself to come home to your authentic presence.

There are six essential steps to making peace with your past and enjoying a great future. The next six chapters are devoted to these steps:

Step 1. Experience the source of deep peace within you.
Step 2. Break the shackles of shame.
Step 3. Stop the slow acid drip of regret.
Step 4. Resolve the grief that will not end.
Step 5. Heal the wounds of love and sex.
Step 6. End the bitterness of blame and move on—and up.

The first step will undo some of the effects of past adversity and give you tools for maintaining inner peace and balance as you move through the subsequent steps. In the last five steps you will be working directly with the most common emotional weights that hold us back. It is important to remember that the purpose is not to dwell in past suffering but to recognize and release it. These are steps to be taken, transcended, and then transformed. They will enable you to put the painful past behind you—not with suppression, repression, or depression, but consciously, deliberately, and compassionately. Finally, you will be free to live, love, and be loved as you always dreamed possible.

As we proceed, you will find a variety of powerful techniques that can open the doors to positive, growth-enhancing change. Be assured that the exercises are time-tested, effective, and safe; they have proven to be healing and transformative. If you work with them diligently, the seeds of pain and sorrow can burst into blossoms of peace and happiness, and you will:

1. REAFFIRM YOUR SACRED WORTH—AND STOP FEELING AS THOUGH YOU'RE NOT GOOD ENOUGH

Many of us look back on our lives and find evidence that we are unworthy. This causes us to feel flat, stagnant, and sometimes panicky. It makes us don masks to hide the perception that we don't deserve or will never get, the good things in life. This book will help you re-own your true magnificence. You will come to realize that you are truly deserving. Then, when you look back, you will find courage for the times you felt afraid, compassion for the times you felt misunderstood, and forgiveness for the times you felt tormented. Your energy will be free to attend to the highest possibilities for your future. With the insights and tools that you glean from this book, you will be able to shape your life according to your own visionary blueprint instead of the blind habits of the past.

2. REAWAKEN TO THE MAGIC AND FUN OF BEING ALIVE

Many of us have gotten too serious, particularly about our past issues. Part of making peace is to look squarely at the monsters that have hurt you and the prisons and gutters you've been stuck in—and then put them in perspective, say good-bye to them, and perhaps even laugh at them. This will help you recapture the innocence, joy, and cosmic wonder of childhood, the curiosity and capacity for pleasure that are the hallmarks of adolescence, and the faith and idealism of young adulthood.

3. DISCOVER THE TREASURE THAT YOU BURIED

By resolving the painful aspects of your past and rediscovering its positive qualities, you will restore and replenish the gifts you misplaced; recapture the talent and imagination that may have been stifled; rekindle the passions that once burned brightly in your chest; and reclaim the trust, romance, and optimism that got buried under self-limiting beliefs and a false notion of maturity.

More specifically, the book will help you:

- Love and accept yourself as you are, not as you wish you could be.

- Come to grips with lingering sorrow, anguish, and hurt.
- Free yourself of envy and hostility.
- Update outworn attitudes and limiting beliefs.
- Rediscover the passion to live your highest destiny.
- Stop feeling ashamed and regain your spiritual dignity.
- Heal your sexual past and love more fully.
- Make peace and, if appropriate, reconcile with parents, siblings, and ex-lovers.
- Stop punishing yourself and learn to forgive and be forgiven.
- Feel truly grateful for what you have and who you are.
- Generate unparalleled success.
- Have a lot more fun and high adventure.
- Consciously direct your evolution and growth.
- Transcend past struggles and experience quintessential peace.

YOUR PEACEFUL INTENTION

Making peace with the past is, first and foremost, a choice, and intention is the most powerful tool of your consciousness. It marshals your personal power, sets your priorities, and mobilizes your will in the service of your deepest desires. By picking up this book, you have declared your intention to make peace with your past. Stating your wish deliberately and precisely can strengthen the power of intention; it signals your brain to direct its energy toward fulfilling your goal.

Here is a list of intentions. Choose the one—or more than one—that feels right for you, or compose a similar statement of your own. Write the sentence on some index cards or Post-its and place them where you will be sure to see them during the course of everyday life—the refrigerator, the bathroom mirror, the night table, the dashboard of your car, your desk, and so on. The idea is to reinforce the intention by placing your attention on it at various moments throughout the day.

DECLARE YOUR PEACEFUL INTENTIONS

- I will make peace with past adversity and embrace new possibilities.
- I choose peace and let go of my suffering.
- I release my past and create my life anew.

REMEMBRANCE OF THINGS PAST

Now let's get ready to explore what St. Augustine called the "vast mansions of memory." You are about to produce "This Is Your Life," with you as the honored guest. The purpose is to begin examining your relationship with the past.

The first step is to write your life story. Please take your time with this. Don't just dash it off. It may take an hour, or five, or several days. Let yourself sink into the process and give it whatever time it requires, and give yourself as many breaks as you need. Don't pay any attention to grammar, spelling, or punctuation. Don't censor yourself in any way. If you feel blocked, try beginning with the words, "I remember . . ." and write whatever comes to mind, letting memories flow into and out of one another. Don't worry about chronology, and don't let logic interfere; later on, if you wish, you can go over what you wrote to correct facts and edit for clarity. If you feel yourself getting carried away by emotion, go ahead and let yourself lose control. The mechanism involved in crying neutralizes hormones associated with stress. If you feel unable to have a good cry and sense that you need one, try peeling a couple of onions to prime the pump.

THE TIMES OF YOUR LIFE

To begin at the beginning, what happened prior to your birth, when you were floating in your mother's womb? To the best of your knowledge, write down what your environment was like: Was your mother healthy? Were your parents apprehensive? Were they ecstatic with hope and anticipation? Were there older siblings around? How did they feel about your imminent arrival? Reconstruct your prenatal experience as best you can, then proceed to the moment of your emergence: Was it a difficult birth? Did joy reign supreme? Were your parents and other family members glad to see you? Were you made to feel welcome? Was anyone jealous, fearful, or resentful because of your arrival on the scene? When you were taken home, were you enveloped in love and comfort? Were your needs met consistently?

Continue this process by describing each major period of your life, up through the present. Begin with your infancy and move forward through early childhood (ages 1 through 5), later childhood, puberty, early adolescence, your high school years, your college years or early job experience, your twenties, thirties, and so on. List the most important occurrences, beginning each period on a separate page so you can add other items as new information and fresh memories come to light. The idea is to create a chronology of your life. You'll refer to this many times as you work through the material in the book.

Please keep the following points in mind as you journey through time:

1. *What we believe to be so becomes so.* We look at our past like we look at the night stars, without realizing that we're seeing an illusion. The star we see may have died light years ago. In a sense, so has our past. We observe it through the telescope of memory, but what we see is filtered through needs, defenses, and emotional trickery, just as the light from a star is distorted by cosmic dust. We tend to block some painful events from our minds out of self-protection; other things we recall quite well, but over time the details grow fuzzy; some things we merely imagined take on the vivid character of memory, and we come to believe they actually occurred. Don't worry about the distortions, just get it down.

2. *Remember with your heart, not just your head.* Note the feelings and attitudes you associate with each episode of your life; how you felt is as important as what actually happened. We're after the truth—not just historical truth, but emotional truth as well. For example, see if you can identify the hopes, wishes,

dreams, and expectations that were projected onto you by your mother and father, and whether that supported or repressed your true self and individuality.

3. *Look for the light, not just the dark.* There is a tendency in exercises like this to emphasize the hurts, tragedies, mistakes, and other negative aspects of the past you wish to make peace with. An important part of the process, though, is to see the past in its entirety and appreciate all that was positive, nourishing, and life-enhancing as well. So be sure to give proper credit to all the people who enriched your life with love, protection, support, and guidance. Note the good times, the joys, the pleasures, the victories large and small, your favorite memories: your first crush, a family vacation, a friend who always made you laugh.

Write down the funniest thing that ever happened. Describe the sublime moments—the first book, work of art, or piece of music that truly moved you, the times you experienced the miracles of creation or felt the awe and wonder of God's presence.

Above all, give yourself the appreciation you deserve: record your contributions to the lives of others, the times you stood up for principle or defended yourself or others from mistreatment, the hard work and sacrifice that led to your achievements, the lessons you took pains to learn, the ways in which you rebounded from loss, defeat, and self-destructive behavior.

4. *Fill in the blanks.* To compensate for the distortions of memory and the tendency to remember only what you *want* to remember, I suggest you do some research. Take out your school yearbooks. Read the letters you've saved. Listen to songs from times gone by. Peruse newspapers and magazines in the library archives. Use any tool you can think of to spark your recollection and fill in the blank spots in your memory.

Perhaps the most revealing memory-joggers are old photographs and home movies. Dig up as many as you can from family members and loved ones. Study the pictures of yourself: Do you remember what that boy or girl was feeling at the time? What did he or she think about life? What was going on in your family at the time? Look at the facial expressions and body language of the people in the photos. What pressures and conflicts are reflected in their demeanor? What triumphs and tragedies? What love? What pain? What struggles? What masks are being worn on those faces, and what do they conceal? How do the images of you and your family members change over time? What do later photos reveal of the dramatic sweep of your life?

5: *Enlist the help of people from your past.* Interview family members, neighbors, friends, classmates, and anyone else who might have a different perspective. Find out what various events looked like from their point of view. Get their perspective on stories you were too young to remember, or weren't present for, or that contain mysteries they might be able to shed light on. This process can be extraordinarily valuable. One of my clients, for example, grew up watching his parents argue a lot and always thought his father felt trapped in his marriage. During his life review, he interviewed his father and was astonished to hear him say that despite the bickering and some difficult times, he loved his wife and was at peace with the choices he had made. It altered profoundly my client's view of his parents and his childhood.

When you interview people, ask probing questions and give them complete permission to be honest. Ask questions such as: What was I like when I was seven? What do you remember about my mother? How did you feel when so-and-so passed away? Did my parents really love each other in those days? What really happened that day we went to the circus?

YOUR LIFE AS A NARRATIVE

When you've finished writing down your story, step back and read it as if it were a novel; bear witness to yourself. You may come to see that there is profound meaning to the sequence of events you recorded. Ask yourself the following questions:

- Are there persistent themes running through your story?
- What patterns are repeated?
- What are the major plot points?
- Is your character portrayed as a hero or as a victim?

- Is he or she a sympathetic character? Would an audience root for him or her?
- Besides you, who are the other main characters?
- Are there any antagonists in your story—characters who thwarted your goals or stifled the expression of your gifts?
- Who are those antagonists and what did they do to you?
- How did you respond to them?
- Who were your allies—those who were there in time of need and provided consistent support?
- Which genre best characterizes your story? Is it a tragedy? Comedy? Farce? Drama? Melodrama? Romance? Fantasy? Satire? Some combination of these?
- If your life were a movie, who would direct it? Martin Scorsese? Steven Spielberg? Alfred Hitchcock? Woody Allen? Mel Brooks?
- Which actual movie is most like yours?
- How would the audience leave the theater? Depressed? Uplifted? Deeply moved, with a lump in their throats? Smiling? Bored? Can't wait for the sequel?
- If you were an objective reader of your life story, what would you say were the aspects of your past that you most have to make peace with?

PERSISTENCE OVERCOMES RESISTANCE

At the end of the way is freedom. Till then, patience.
— BUDDHA

I urge you to commit 100 percent to the journey we've just embarked on. The material in this book is powerful and practical; it can yield tremendous results if you approach it with sincerity. When you do the exercises in each chapter, please be as honest and specific as possible, for it's in honesty and specificity that the greatest healing takes place. When my patients begin therapy, I tell them, "You are in a safe, protective, loving atmosphere in which you can be completely open." To the greatest extent possible, that's what I would like you to create for yourself with the process this book will initiate.

I also urge you to be patient and persistent. This journey will be mostly pleasant, deeply moving, and at times great fun. But growth moves in cycles of rest and activity. You may experience a tremendous burst of change right out of the starting block only to feel, later on, that you're in a rut, apparently getting nowhere. Or you may feel like you're moving backward, only to be stunned by a sudden acceleration of inner growth. At times you might find that an issue you thought you'd already resolved has come back stronger than ever. That just means that this particular demon has been drawn into the open, where it can be managed or vanquished. At other times, some old painful feeling arises anew, which simply means that you're finally ready to feel and heal at your depths.

I recommend that you give each chapter its proper due. You may identify immediately with one or two of the topics and be eager to get to it. You may think that the other subjects don't apply to you. But the past often affects us in ways we're unaware of. In reading a chapter you don't relate to immediately, you might discover unanticipated treasure. Also, I suggest taking a break after you do the work in each chapter. A rest phase can be very valuable not only in refreshing your mind so you get more out of the next chapter, but also in giving the previous material a chance to take hold and solidify. The subconscious keeps working even when you're not paying attention.

As the Chinese say, a journey of a thousand miles begins with a single step. In an emotional journey, the first tentative steps are especially important because they must pass through your own resistance and apprehension. When that resistance crops up, look at it objectively and honestly. See it for what it is and keep moving ahead.

Resistance is likely to appear in one of several forms, depending on the issue you're dealing with at the time. You might, for example, hear yourself saying, "It's too late. It's been so long, I can never resolve that now." Or, "I can't bear to think of that again." Or, "I'm not smart enough to succeed with this book." All these are nonsense. It is never too late and no hurt is too deep, and you are certainly strong enough to do the necessary work—if you sincerely want to heal. Resistance may also come in the form of guilt: "What I did was so awful, I don't deserve to be at peace." Or it might be rooted in hostility so strong you don't want to let it go: "I'll deal with those other issues, but I'd rather rot in hell than forgive her," or, "I'll make peace after I get revenge. Someday I'll be vindicated!" Rage is no excuse to back off from the process. On the contrary, it is the best reason to proceed, because otherwise the poison will destroy you. Making peace is primarily for *you*, not those with whom you're in conflict.

Another source of resistance is an addiction to feeling victimized. Subconsciously, you might fear that resolving certain issues from the past would leave you with nothing to complain about. Don't be afraid to lose your identity as a victim, or your need for sympathy and self-pity. You may also be attracted to the adrenaline rush of conflict. Like an arms manufacturer, you might find yourself apprehensive about life after the hostilities end and a peace treaty is signed. Trust me, there are better ways to find meaning and purpose in life. For every aspect of your identity that's dependent on making war with your past, there are other, better aspects waiting to be discovered.

You may also be afraid that sorting through the flotsam and jetsam of the past will make it cling to you even more. It's true that if you wallow in past miseries they can get locked into your identity and make your progress toward peace as glacial as that of the Israelis and Palestinians. But we're delving into your past to cleanse it. The process is designed to help you move from realization to resolution to a profound inner release in which you finally let go of what needs to be discarded.

Resistance can come from other sources as well: impatience, self-deception, stubbornness, denial, pride, pessimism, procrastination, and so on. Whatever form it takes, when you notice yourself resisting a certain exercise or wanting to skip over a certain section, take a careful look at what's going on. Chances are you've come upon issues that are difficult to face. It's natural to want to close the book and turn on the TV. But that's the very time to draw on your commitment to growth and your determination to heal. What you've turned up is probably something you'll benefit greatly from resolving.

Here is a practical way to resist your resistance and make this book not only more productive but more fun: Find a partner or partners. Line up one or more Making Peace buddies and agree to monitor each other's progress. Call one another when you run into a wall of resistance, discuss the experiences that arise along the way, and give each other the necessary support to see the process through to completion. I know of no better way to get the most out of this journey than to help someone else get the most out of it.

As you do the work ahead, you will find that confusion is replaced by wisdom; incompleteness by closure; bitterness by gratitude; imprisonment by freedom; heavy burdens by a lightness of Being. Where pain was, there shall love be. Along the way, give yourself the kindness, warmth, and unconditional love of a divine mother. You are in charge of your own nurturance now. You may never have received the kind of love you deserved from birth—a love that has no outcome in mind other than to hold, cherish, and protect. You can give it to yourself now. Let yourself receive it. It will help you put the past to rest in a place of forgiveness, acceptance, and respect—not to be forgotten, but rather integrated with the present and future in a healthy way.

Be prepared to give up a lot as you make peace with your past. You may have to give up feeling sorry for yourself. You may have to stop straining to be someone you are not. You may have to quit hiding parts of yourself that you erroneously think are unacceptable or inadequate. You may have to give up your sorrow, your guilt, your grudges, and your self-loathing. Instead, you may have to learn to appreciate your life's journey just as it has unfolded, even if it did not turn out quite the way you hoped it would. And you might have to put up with a future so fulfilling that you'll no longer be able to agonize about the past.

IMAGINE!

Once dismissed as the language of art and the creator of all that is ephemeral and unreal, imagination is coming to be seen as the queen of our mental faculties. Research shows that the images, thoughts, and feelings that originate in the mind are experienced by the brain as very real indeed. The direct effect of mental imagery on physiology has been well documented: it can stimulate changes in heart and respiratory rate, oxygen consumption, blood pressure, the temperature and flow of blood in local areas, gastrointestinal motility and secretions, the levels of certain hormones and neurotransmitters, sexual arousal, and the rhythms and patterns of brain waves.

As an inner representation of a flow of thoughts you can envision, hear, feel, smell, and taste, imagery has a powerful effect on the way your brain codes, stores, expresses, and recalls information. Some of the brain's reactions to vivid images are virtually identical to those that occur when the actual events are experienced. For that reason, guided visualization has been quite effective in preparing athletes and others for maximum performance, modifying unwanted habits, and training the mind to replace negative thought patterns with positive, life-enhancing alternatives.

We will be using guided imagery a number of times throughout the book. The following principles apply in every case:

1. For some people, mental pictures come clearly and vividly. For others, they are hazy and vague. You will benefit from the process no matter how clear or vague your images are. Don't strain to visualize with the clarity of a movie screen. If your mind wanders, just gently bring it back to the visualization.

2. You may wish to make a tape recording of each visualization process—using your own voice or someone else's—rather than reading it each time or relying on memory. This allows you to close your eyes, listen, and focus your attention fully on the imagery. The voice on the recording should be gentle and the pace should be calm. Feel free to modify the script to make it more personal.

3. Give yourself 15 or 20 minutes to do the process. It might not take that long, but you don't want to feel rushed or worry about being interrupted. Put a "Do Not Disturb" sign on the door and turn off the ringer on your telephone.

4. Comfort is crucial. Take off your shoes, loosen your belt and collar, and make yourself as comfortable as possible. Sit in an easy chair or lie down on something soft. Keep the room warm

and cozy (cover yourself with a blanket if you'd like) and dim the lights. Many people find soft, soothing background music to be a welcome addition.

Now we're ready to begin. Every visualization starts with a period of relaxation. (We'll be using the same procedure each time.)

Once you're situated in your comfortable position, gently close your eyes. Take five slow, deep breaths. Breathe in through your nose, retain your breath for a second or two, and exhale through your mouth, making the sound "Aaah" to sigh away any tension. Notice the soothing calm that comes over you as your body begins to settle down.

You are now going to invite each part of your body to release, relax, and let go. Gently direct your attention to your feet and toes, feeling the muscles relax. Slowly, let your attention glide up your body, allowing each area to settle into a state of deep relaxation. Linger extra-long where you notice tension, giving that area time to soften. Move up to your ankles . . . your calves . . . your knees . . . thighs . . . hips . . . buttocks. Feel the deepening sense of relaxation fill the lower half of your body.

Now invite all the organs in your pelvis to relax. Take your time and let your attention rise to your abdomen and belly . . . chest . . . shoulders . . . and across your lower back . . . the midback . . . the muscles across and between your shoulder blades . . . and up to your neck . . . your jaw . . . your mouth . . . your face . . . your muscles around your eyes . . . your forehead and scalp. And the relaxation flows down your upper arms . . . your elbows . . . forearms . . . wrists . . . hands . . . and each of your fingers. Your whole body is now relaxing more easily, more comfortably, more deeply.[3]

YOUR SANCTUARY OF PEACE

In your state of deep calm, begin to visualize yourself as you embark on a great adventure in search of inner peace, love, and truth. You're in a wooded area at the foot of a green, mist-shrouded mountain. Before you is a trail leading into the forest. You don't know exactly what you'll find along that path, but you know you must take it, for you are determined to get to the mountaintop to find a greater source of wisdom for your life.

Feeling the firm earth underfoot, you enter the forest with a spring in your step. The woods are alive with the sounds of birds and other creatures. Shafts of light pour through the tall trees. A light breeze caresses your skin. You breathe the bracing air and take in the scent of pine and cedar. The trail climbs steadily upward.

As you ascend the mountain, the landscape varies. The trail is pleasant and easy in places. In others, it is arduous. Now the climate is warm and sunny. Then it is icy cold, and storm clouds threaten. Here the footing is sure; there it is tenuous, and you have to tread carefully. You stumble and fall, but you pick yourself up and continue your climb. The ascent is steady and gradual, and you walk at a steady clip. Then it gets steep, and you struggle to find the energy and strength to proceed. You climb and climb, becoming more and more exhausted. You wonder if you'll ever get to the top, where a higher vantage point awaits you. You gather your strength and forge ahead.

Now you have to squeeze through a narrow fissure in the mountainside. You're showered by rocks and dirt falling from the canyon walls. Bruised and sore, treading delicately on unsure footing, you struggle through the cold, dark passage. And finally, you emerge into the light. You have come at last to the end of the trail.

You find yourself in a beautiful lush meadow. The sun is strong and the air is clean and perfumed by the magnificent carpet of wildflowers that paints the meadow in colors of red and yellow and purple and white. Above you, the needles of the stately pines rustle in the breeze, as if welcoming you home. You can hear the sounds of the wind and the birds, but overall the effect is one of pure, primordial silence. A waterfall beckons. You strip off your filthy clothes and step into the cool, refreshing water to cleanse the dirt and grime off your weary body. You emerge feeling cleaner than you've ever felt in your life.

As you put on new, clean clothing, you see before you a beautiful structure—a golden dome nestled in a large five-pointed star (like the diagram of the Quintessential Self). You know that this is a holy place, a temple. You see a door leading inside. You enter, and immediately you are overcome by a feeling of reverence. Deep peace permeates the inside of the dome, which is filled with a radiant luminosity. You sit or kneel in the center of the room, feeling peace and light pervade every atom of your body.

Suddenly a figure appears before you. It is the physical embodiment of perfect wisdom, unconditional love, and pure compassion. You may envision this figure as a real man or woman who represents those qualities to you. Someone in your life or someone long gone. A historical person, a religious figure whom you revere, or a deity. It might be a persona you create right now. Or you may prefer to think of him or her as your best or highest self. However you choose to visualize this figure, he or she represents the source of healing, nurture, and insight you've always yearned for. He or she speaks to you now, in a voice that is as gentle as a dove and as strong as a lion:

"I am your spiritual guide. I know who you are. I know the depths of what you have been through. I know what you can become. I know that you can make peace with your past. I know you can find the truth. I know you can heal the pain and end the suffering. I know you can love and be loved. I know you can find the strength, courage, and wisdom to create the life you've always wanted.

"You are about to embark on a great and wonderful journey. I will be here to help you. You can return to this sanctuary any time you need a safe haven. Or simply look for me in the corner of your mind's eye. I'm always with you and I always know what you need. You can trust me completely, for I love you unconditionally. You can say anything that needs to be said, ask anything that needs to be asked, and know that what you'll hear back will be the truth, for I know the deepest secrets of your heart."

Deeply moved, you reach out to your spiritual guide in gratitude. He or she holds your hands. You look deeply into each other's eyes. You bask in the radiant love and absolute safety of this divine mentor, knowing that he or she represents the best and purest aspect of your Quintessential Self. Soon your guide signals that it is time to go. He or she embraces you, filling your body with pure cosmic energy and your heart with infinite love. You feel the safety and protection you've always yearned for. With a smile that says, "I'm always nearer to you than your breath," your spiritual guide gestures that it is time to say farewell and resume your journey.

You leave your sanctuary feeling bold and confident, knowing you can return to your temple of peace and communicate with

your spiritual guide any time you want. Outside, it is just as luminous and fragrant as before. You see before you the edge of a cliff.
You know that from this height you will be able to see where
you've come from. You walk to the edge and look out. The clouds
that fill the valley below dissolve. Now you can see the entire
sweep of your life with crystal clarity. With your expanded awareness, you can see things as you've never seen them, find answers to
questions that have plagued you, and gain a vision of the truth
that had been hidden from you. You are truly ready to look back
on your life with honesty and compassion, knowing that the truth
shall set you free.

Take two or three minutes to ease off your guided imagery.
When you are ready, slowly open your eyes. Rest for as long as
you need to before returning to regular activities or the next section of the book.

2

Quintessential Peace

TRANSCENDING THE STRUGGLES
OF THE PAST

Deep peace of the running wave to you.
Deep peace of the flowing air to you.
Deep peace of the quiet earth to you.
Deep peace, deep peace.
— ANCIENT IRISH PRAYER

In her first therapy session, Beth was agitated and impatient as she plunged into a heart-rending litany of sorrow, regret, and rage about her troubled past. Like a gale wind stirring up the mud and debris in a pond, a broken engagement had aroused long-suppressed traumatic memories and painful feelings of abandonment.

Jumping back and forth in time, she poured out fragments of her story: the workaholic father who numbed his discontent with martinis; the mother who wore her misery on her sleeve and spoke the language of complaint; the older brother who tormented her relentlessly and, as a teenager, twice tried to rape her. She recalled with bitter tears her parents saying she'd only imagined the rape attempts and dismissing her brother's aggression with, "Boys will be boys." Writhing in embarrassment, she alluded to her early promiscuity and drug use. Dropping out of college, dead-end jobs, disastrous love affairs, abortion, her brother's suicide, a failed marriage—she tossed out the pieces of her past in random fashion, like fragments of a jigsaw puzzle.

When she stopped to catch her breath, Beth looked at me expectantly. To her surprise, I did not ask any questions. I did not ask her to elaborate on any aspect of her story. I did not interpret the dream she mentioned or wrap her life into a neat psychological category. Instead, I asked her to close her eyes. I led her through a breathing exercise to ease her turmoil. Then we were able to have a calm discussion about her goals in therapy and my approach to the process. When the time was up, I reached for my pad, but not to write the prescription she expected. I jotted down the phone number of where to learn Transcendental Meditation as an adjunct to therapy.

As I explained to Beth, recounting the story of your life, exploring long-buried emotions, and working through unresolved issues are often essential for making peace with your past. But the reverse is also true: Finding peace in the present can help you to more effectively make peace with your past. To do the work well, you need to feel safe. That means not only feeling safe to speak your heart and mind, but also creating a zone of security within you. The deeper and more durable your inner peace, the more quickly and smoothly the process of resolving past issues will go. That is why this chapter comes early in the book. It will help you build a strong foundation of calmness and clarity for delving into the details of your past.

When the lights go out unexpectedly and we're plunged into darkness, it makes sense to trace the root of the problem, find out what caused it, and take steps to remedy the damage. In medicine, when illness appears, the most effective course of action may be to determine the cause and eradicate it—as when we prescribe an antibiotic to kill disease-producing bacteria. At the same time, it is often wise to strengthen a patient's immune system and overall wellness to prevent future infections. Making peace with the past can be seen in much the same way. Part of the work may involve probing the darkness and eliminating old emotional bacteria that are poisoning the present. We can, in addition, turn on the light and find peace right here, right now, where it always is—deep within us.

QUINTESSENTIAL PEACE

Accessing inner peace is its own reward. It also changes your relationship to the past, altering its impact on all five aspects of the Quintessential Self. As the following diagram illustrates, the core of peace inside you is the unchanging, transcendent center from which all aspects of the Quintessential Self radiate, and around which the stages of life revolve.

It is important to make one crucial distinction: The peace I'm referring to is not the listless placidity of indifference or the sedated repose that comes from tranquilizers, alcohol, or drugs. It is not a sleepy peace, nor a dull, lethargic peace, nor a "can't be bothered" peace. Rather, it is a vibrant peace marked by a serene but responsive nervous system, steady but spirited emotions, and a centered, focused, fully attentive mind. I call this state *restful alertness*—deep physical rest accompanied by a clear, alert mind. There are almost infinite gradations of restful alertness, ranging from ordinary relaxation to the exalted state of illumined serenity described by the world's spiritual and religious traditions. The deeper you penetrate the core of perfect peace and pure awareness within you, the more clearly you think, the more accurately you perceive, and the more balanced you feel emotionally—and the more you are freed of the negative impact of the past.

On the level of the physical self, deep peace helps to alleviate the deadly impact of past trauma, pain, and distress. A huge body of research indicates that emotional and psychological stress has profound long-term consequences on the body, eroding the very foundation of health. That is why children who suffer abuse are more likely to develop life-threatening illnesses as adults, and why men and women who undergo prolonged distress are more susceptible to disease and shortened lifespans. Deep relaxation can help undo the damage of past stress and build a stable foundation to fend off subsequent blows when the repetition compulsion stirs things up again.

Deep peace also creates a refuge for the emotional self. The pain of the past may have eroded your trust in life and in other people, causing you to be guarded, like someone with an open wound who's afraid to bump into the furniture. With peaceful presence you feel more secure, more open, more confident. Old emotional wounds lose some of their sting, and painful memories are less likely to overwhelm you when they arise. Inner peace also serves as a protective shield, preserving your emotional integrity when issues from the past resurface in the present.

Quintessential peace creates a core of silence for the mental self. If, like Beth, you have a tendency to ruminate or obsess about the past, the ability to steady your mind is an invaluable asset. Like slowing down a film or freezing the frame, steady mental clarity enables you to evaluate complex situations more accurately and discern the truth with greater reliability. It shifts you to a higher mental vantage point, expanding your frame of reference.

Things start to make more sense from that perspective. You see what really is, not what you fear and not what you've been conditioned to expect. When viewed from a place of contentment and ease instead of tension and turbulence, the past takes on new meaning—not necessarily a rosier one, although that may be the case, but certainly a clearer and more balanced one. Restful alertness enables you to find deeper meaning in the incidents of the past, no matter how painful they were, and to see them with more of the informed detachment of a biographer.

In addition, a restfully alert mind makes for easier access to the intuition of inner wisdom. When you dwell in the reservoir of peace at the core of your being, insights arise more clearly and dependably, feeding you fresh answers to nagging questions. At its deepest level, quintessential peace puts you in touch with the universal creative intelligence that directs the flow of atoms and galaxies and nerve cells alike. "We live in the lap of an immense intelligence," wrote Ralph Waldo Emerson, "which makes us receivers of its truth and organs of its activity. Whenever a mind is simple, and receives a divine wisdom, old things pass away—means, teachers, texts, temples fall; it lives now, and absorbs past and future into the present hour."

Deep peace also alters the relational self's link to the past. Past conflicts lose their ability to keep on causing pain when their memory—or their repetition in the present—is received by a calm, centered nervous system. You also become less susceptible to the way others have defined you in the past and less constrained by the roles you were forced to play. By bringing contentment in the present, quintessential peace reduces the tendency to compare yourself to others and base your self-perception on where you stand on various social ladders.

With repeated dips into the well of deep peace, the identity you derived through pain and suffering further loses its grip. Like the "back story" in drama, the past is what happened before the curtain went up. It has explanatory value, but it is not what's onstage in the present. The false self, the masks, and the predictable behavior patterns I call "rolebots" come to be seen for what they are—only one of an infinite number of possibilities for what you can be.

Having a stable interior enables you to rectify old rifts between you and others with greater skill. And because the core of peace within you is also the place where the spark of divine love resides, regular contact with it brings a higher level of compassion, appreciation, and generosity to damaged relationships. When you connect to the common source that binds us to one another, said the Chinese sage Lao-Tzu, you become "kindhearted as a grandmother, dignified as a king."

THE PEACE WHICH PASSETH UNDERSTANDING

It is in the realm of the spiritual self that quintessential peace finds its highest meaning. One of the central tenets in the mystical strains of every spiritual tradition is that within each person is a shared source of eternal wisdom and perfect peace—the peace which passeth understanding, in biblical terms. The sacred teachings also tell us that connecting to that source—whether you call it God, Allah, the Tao, or Being—also brings the power to transform your relationship to the past by transcending its grip.

The Jewish tradition speaks of attaining peace in the present by reaching for the light. "Every spot where a person raises his eyes to heaven is a holy of Holies," proclaims a Hasidic teaching. A passage in the Talmud reads, "A single moment of awakening in this world is eternity in the world to come. The inner peace of the world to come is living in this world with full attention." This sense of divine radiance in the moment is, perhaps, why the Old Testament refers to God's true name as I Am, and why verses like this one appear in Psalms (139): "Darkness is no darkness for thee, and night is as luminous as day; to thee both dark and light are one."

The Hebraic tradition of transcendent peace continued with Jesus, who told his disciples, "My peace I leave with you, my peace I give unto you: not as the world giveth, give I unto you. Let not your heart be troubled, neither let it be afraid" (John 4:27). In the Gospel According to Thomas, Jesus adds these instructions to find the deep peace that comes when the individual soul merges with the Divine: "When you make the two one, and when you make the inner as the outer and the outer as the inner, and the above as below . . . then shall you enter the Kingdom" (22:25–35). The location of that kingdom is made clear in Luke 17:21: "Neither shall they say, Lo here! or, lo there! for, behold, the kingdom of God is within you."

In the Vedic tradition of India, which gave rise to what we know as Buddhism and Hinduism, the purpose of spiritual disciplines is even more explicit. They aim to put us in touch with the cosmic Self that we share with all beings—as distinct from the small self of the individual personality, which is something we *have*, not the essence of who we *are*. "The heart and mind can find peace and harmony by contemplating the transcendental nature of the true self as supreme effulgent light," said the seer Patanjali in the *Yoga Sutras*. The Self is referred to as *sat-chit-ananda*, or absolute bliss consciousness, and when it is fully realized it confers a peace that is immovable. At the highest levels of spiritual attainment, the peace to be had is said to transcend mere happiness or contentment. One doesn't just *feel* peace at that level, one *is* peace.

By putting you in touch with your timeless, transcendent core, spiritual disciplines alter your relationship to the past. Ever since you were an innocent child, impression upon impression has been piled onto your nervous system. The effect of these countless layers of imprints has been to condition your responses to the world, restricting the full expression of your spirit. Freed from the prison of conditioned responses, you can enjoy the present moment more richly and fulfill your highest destiny.

At the furthest reaches of quintessential peace, where the individual spirit meets the divine, you don't just become a better person, you become a *different* person—not one who wears a better mask but one who discards masks entirely. In Eastern philosophy, detachment from one's past persona is sometimes referred to as "killing the ego," although it seems kinder and more accurate to think of it as redefining the ego and taming it in the service of the soul. For many Christians, this sense of dying to the past and awakening to life anew is captured in the term *born again*. And Jews pray on the High Holy Day of Yom Kippur, "Purify me, revive me, uplift me. Forgive my past and lead me into the future."

The direction to which the wisdom teachings point is inward, toward the non-changing I-ness that remains constant in the midst of our varied life experiences. That's where one must turn to find the deep peace and effulgent light that lightens the negative residue of the past.

Transcending the past, it must be emphasized, does not negate the importance of working *with* the past when necessary—confronting it, understanding it, and coming to terms with it, as we will do in subsequent chapters. Some spiritual teachers have considered the psychotherapeutic exploration of an individual's past to be useless or even harmful. Why demoralize people by dwelling in the muck and mire of the past, the thinking goes, when they can bypass the darkness and head straight for the light? The criticism might reflect a limited view of modern psychotherapy. The older psychoanalytic schools do tend to wallow in the darkness of the past, but most contemporary therapeutic practices are grounded in the present and delve into the past only enough to understand it, resolve it, and heal it so the person can focus more effectively on moving forward. I have personally treated many spiritual seekers who thought they could ignore the unpleasant baggage of their pasts and make a beeline to the light. They found, sometimes years later, that while spiritual practice transformed their lives and opened a window to the divine, it was still necessary to make peace with specific aspects of their pasts.

With quintessential peace, the present attains a new luster, and the past loses some of its ability to narrowly define you. You come to see how the shifting dance of life throws us into temporary roles, like actors going from script to script: today a saint, tomorrow a sinner; today a prince(ss), tomorrow a pauper. But, as Mother Teresa learned when she discovered the Hitler inside her, the saint is just the sinner in another cosmic guise. As you come to see yourself as a spiritual being in human form, you begin to answer the question "Who am I?" not by your family origins, your heritage, or the trials and tribulations of your past, not by your occupation and titles, but by your status as an eternal soul. In that realization lies the truest, deepest peace.

WAGING PEACE

Part of making peace with your past is learning new habits of self-care. Chances are that your parents did not know how to nurture their own inner peace. They may have been preoccupied, tense, or agitated much of the time. This simple fact would help explain—but not excuse—why you were sometimes treated poorly or even harshly as a child. It may also explain why you, like most of us, were not bathed in peace when you were young or taught how to find serenity within yourself. You can make up for that now by becoming a beacon of peace.

The following suggestions will help you create inner peace in the midst of everyday life. They will keep your body tranquil yet responsive, adaptable, and energetic, while your mind is focused, clear, steady, and highly aware. Valuable under any circumstances, you will find the recommendations especially helpful as you work through the material in the rest of the book. At times you may catch yourself ruminating endlessly about days gone by. You may feel overwhelmed by memories of pain, shame, and loss. Feelings of blame, guilt, rage, or regret may create distress. These techniques are tools for regaining your quintessential peace. But their purpose is not just to provide temporary relief or an island of calm in which to take refuge. They will also free up your energy and expand your awareness so you can see the past clearly, resolve old emotional issues, and chart a new course with bold, creative, flexible vision. (Remember, in addition to the practices that follow, you can always return to your peaceful sanctuary and the comfort and wisdom of your spiritual guide, described in chapter 1.)

REFRAMING THE PAST

It is through being wounded that ... power grows and can, in the end, become tremendous.
—FRIEDRICH NIETZSCHE

To the extent that you can make sense of past adversities, you can neutralize their harmful effects. This means actively seeking value in having experienced traumatic circumstances. *How can this terrible experience make me stronger, wiser, more compassionate, more tolerant, or more grateful for each moment from now on?* You may not have been able to control the hurtful events that happened in the past, but you now have power over how you continue to experience those events.

Learning to reframe experiences that prey on your mind can bring peace where there had been turbulence. When you dwell on old miseries or complain repeatedly about the trajectory of your life, you drive the negativity deeper into your being and strengthen its hold. You are, in fact, giving whatever hurt you the power to destroy you. There is great freedom in being able to shift your awareness, even slightly, from destructive, poisonous thoughts to constructive, supportive thoughts. Even while looking squarely at the painful aspects of your past, you can choose to see them differently. Doing so not only gives you more peace in the present, it helps you do the work of healing.

When the sting of painful memories disturbs your peace, or when old patterns reappear and cause problems in the present, pause and take a few deep breaths. Instead of letting the disturbance overwhelm you, take control of your reactions and reframe the associated images.

When you become upset, notice if you are repeating an old negative thought pattern. You can stop that pattern by mentally or subvocally saying to yourself, with conviction, "I choose peace and let go of my suffering." Then distract your mind by vividly bringing to awareness the memory of a loving, joyful experience from your past. Repeat this practice as often as necessary.

In addition, look at the source of the pain, conflict, or trauma and ask yourself how the same experience might start creating value for you in a fresh context. For example, if you're resentful toward someone who deceived you, ask yourself what the incident may teach you about trust, faith, and betrayal. If you're kicking yourself over a failure or mistake, shift the energy of regret to that of curiosity and view what happened in a larger context. Perhaps it was a necessary aspect of your experience, without which you would not have had certain successes.

ACCEPTING WHAT IS AND WHAT WAS

Yesterday is history.
Tomorrow a mystery.
Today is a gift—that's why it's called the present.
— ANONYMOUS

There is great peace in accepting what is for what it is and what was for what it was. In and of itself, acceptance defuses the past and loosens its grip on your life. What was done can't be undone or wished away. You have accumulated pain during your journey, but you have also acquired the awareness and determination to break free of the past. Everything that happened to you before has brought you to this moment of healing. If you can find peace right here, right now, the past could not have been—and indeed was not—100 percent bad.

Needless to say, reframing should not lead to denial. I am not suggesting that you brush aside the negative aspects of your past or make excuses for those who caused you harm. Acceptance does not mean you can't take a stand or work to correct the wrongs of the past. Quite the contrary: Bemoaning your fate and refusing to accept reality do not help you heal the past; they keep you stuck at the starting gate spinning your wheels in the mud. Rather than make you a naïve Pollyanna, acceptance gives you a more realistic, balanced perspective. That very well might include accepting what you must do to change things. Essentially, acceptance means not wasting time and emotional energy wishing things were different—or had been different.

AN ATTITUDE OF GRATITUDE

If the only prayer you ever say in your entire life is
Thank You, it will be enough.
–MEISTER ECKHART

One giant step beyond acceptance is gratitude. On one level, gratitude is the ability to appreciate the blessings you have been given.

On a higher level, it is the ability to not only accept whatever life offers you, but to receive it thankfully, knowing that there is something to be gained even from the tribulations.

As you sort through the events of your life in later chapters, see if you can begin finding gratitude not only for your obvious blessings but even for some of the hardships. The pain may have deepened you. The anguish may have ignited a spiritual search, forcing you to question the nature of good and evil or your place in the universe. The mistakes you regret may have brought self-knowledge that would have otherwise eluded you. Surely it would be false to suggest that suffering is necessary for growth. But it is certainly true that we can use suffering as a fertilizer to stimulate growth. There is value in looking for the gain in the pain—if you can do it without creating an artificial mood or whitewashing the horrors of the past.

In his poem "The Guest House," Rumi, the 13th-century Sufi mystic, compares the thoughts and feelings that rise and fall in the mind to unexpected visitors. "Welcome and entertain them all," he implores, and treat each guest honorably, "even if they're a crowd of sorrows." The poem concludes:

> *The dark thought, the shame, the malice,*
> *meet them at the door laughing,*
> *and invite them in.*
> *Be grateful for whoever comes,*
> *because each has been sent*
> *as a guide from beyond.*

Try doing Rumi's exercise right now. While challenging, the gratitude Rumi writes of profound peace and transformation.

SEEK OUT INSPIRATION

An indispensable way to reframe the past is to seek out sources of wisdom and inspiration. You may want to turn to your religious tradition or your own personal spirituality. A number of studies have found a strong correlation between lifelong well-being and the sense of meaning and purpose that derives from faith. A spiritual perspective, however you interpret that, enables you to stand back and see your troubles in a larger context. No matter how much you've suffered, knowing that problems are an inevitable part of a soul's journey and that you are connected to aspects of existence beyond the boundaries of your physical presence can lend a measure of peace and faith in tomorrow. A healthy spiritual perspective accepts that what you experienced is real and must be dealt with—and also that there is a higher, nobler way of seeing that can add purpose to your healing.

Another good source of inspiration is the biographies of exceptional people who were able to overcome hardship to achieve greatness. Helen Keller, Jackie Robinson, Franklin Roosevelt, Mother Teresa—history is filled with remarkable lives that were raised from the ashes of impairment, oppression, tragedy, and brutality. Reading about such individuals not only puts your own burdens into perspective, it also helps to cultivate a sense of your own life as a narrative whose ending has yet to be written. Consider, for example, the tormented soul who wrote these words: "I am now the most miserable man living. If what I feel were equally distributed to the whole human family, there would be not one cheerful face on earth. Whether I shall ever be better, I cannot tell. I awfully forebode I shall not." The author was Abraham Lincoln.

You may also find inspiration in nature, poetry, or art. You may find it in a scientific description of the vastness of the universe or the realization that the laws governing the hum of electrons in every atom of your body are the same that drive the engine of the stars. Whatever moves you to feelings of awe, wonder, and connection can give you the peace that comes from knowing you are part of a master plan that is greater and grander than your private tale of woe.

However you achieve it, enlarging your vision of your place in the universe is both humbling and elevating. There is something wonderfully peace-producing about realizing that you are at the same time ordained and ordinary. The Talmud advises us to walk through life with two messages, one in the left pocket and one in the right. One message says that you are but a speck of dust in the wind. The other says that you are the center of the universe and all of creation was designed just for you.

THE PRECIOUS PRESENT

The Buddha was once asked what practices he and his disciples engaged in. "We sit, we walk, and we eat," he replied.

"But isn't that what everyone does?" asked his inquisitor.

Said the Buddha, "When we sit, we know we are sitting. When we walk, we know we are walking. When we eat, we know we are eating."

In the act of becoming fully aware of the present moment, not ruminating about the past or pondering the future, you can immediately start to suffer less. "When we are mindful," writes the Vietnamese monk Thich Nhat Hanh, "deeply in touch with the present moment, our understanding of what is going on deepens, and we begin to be filled with acceptance, joy, peace, and love." Obviously, there are times when thinking about the past or planning the future is appropriate. But all too often we obsessively repeat the same old mental routines, like tape recorders on automatic replay, or we rummage through our emotional attic for no purpose other than to make ourselves miserable once again. When your mind is flooded with futile or useless thoughts of the past, the simple act of grounding yourself in the present moment can be remarkably peace-producing. At times, it can even evoke delight and wonder, for we have at every moment the potential to see, as William Blake put it, "a world in a grain of sand, and a heaven in a wild flower."

When you're feeling *nowhere*, you can break the spell by being *now here*. Being fully mindful is a simple act, but it is not always easy when the mind is in overdrive or the heart is burdened by negative feelings. Here are some techniques to help you return to the peace of presence, whether you're washing the dishes or driving to work:

FOCUS ON YOUR BREATH

Put your attention on your breathing and simply follow its natural in-and-out movement. Notice the sensations in your nostrils, your chest, your diaphragm, and your belly as you inhale and exhale.

RECITE A WORD OR PHRASE

Mentally or sublingually repeat a comforting sound on the in breath and another on the out breath. For example, you might use the words "peaceful" and "presence."

NOTICE WHAT YOU PERCEIVE

Especially if your mind is racing, it can be helpful to notice what your senses are experiencing and articulate it inwardly: "I see the red Toyota changing lanes." "I hear the howling of the wind." "I feel the hot soapy water and the sponge in my hand." "I smell the coffee brewing." "I taste the sweet crunchy cereal as I slowly chew." You might also articulate what your body is doing as you move through space, for example, "I'm walking through the gate to the backyard. I step from the concrete onto the soft grass...."

REACH OUT AND TOUCH SOMETHING

Touch whatever is within reach and focus your attention on the feeling. It could be the arm of your chair, the steering wheel, the person next to you, your fork, or something in your pocket. Shifting your attention to the immediate sense of touch will ground you in the moment. You might even want to create a peaceful presence amulet. Choose a small object—a crystal, a seashell, even a Cracker Jack toy—that can be carried in your pocket or purse. Whenever you need to bring your attention to the moment, simply hold that object and focus on the sensation.

ANCHOR IN A PEACEFUL HARBOR

An anchor is a nervous-system cue that can elicit from memory the sensation of deep peace. Here's how to create a personal anchor to trigger peaceful presence at any time: Set aside 10 to 15 minutes when you won't be disturbed and follow the relaxation instructions for visualization exercises in chapter 1 (see page 29). When you are completely relaxed, gently bring to mind the image of you standing before your temple of peace. You enter the golden dome and immediately feel the deep peace of your sanctuary. Your spiritual guide is there to remind you that you are safe and secure. Allow yourself to rest there for a few minutes, relaxing more and more deeply.

When you are as calm as you can be, make a unique sensory signal with the sense of touch. For example, press your thumb against the tip of your index finger, applying a specific amount of pressure. The memory of this sensation combines with the image of you in your sanctuary and the peace you feel at the moment to create a kind of homing beacon for the nervous system. Anytime you need to ground yourself in the present, you can use the signal of thumb to index finger to evoke deep peace. If your anchor does not seem to be effective right away, repeat the meditative practice to reinforce the signal.

With practice, grounding yourself in the present becomes easier and easier, and eventually routine. The habit can alter your relationship to the past and future. "As you begin to live in the present moment, you will experience a subtle but profound change," writes Douglas Bloch in *Words That Heal.* "A deep peace will enfold you, a peace that says, 'All is well. There is nothing to fear. Everything is unfolding according to plan, and you are being guided each step along the way.'"

THE TRANSCENDENT PEACE OF MEDITATION

When the entire nervous system comes to a completely peaceful state, it reflects Being, and this gives rise to Bliss consciousness.
— MAHARISHI MAHESH YOGI

In 1972, I was completing my psychiatric training at the Yale University School of Medicine, but I felt miserable. My personal life was in turmoil. I saw several respected therapists on the faculty, none of whom seemed to understand the soul-searching I was going through. This only added to my confusion. Then, on the recommendation of a friend, I went to a lecture at Yale on Transcendental Meditation (TM). It changed my life.

The speaker was a young, well-educated American much like myself, only he radiated a peace and tranquillity I had only dreamed of. Because I wanted whatever he had, I was instructed in TM. When I sat to meditate for the first time, within 10 minutes, my mind, which had been a whirlpool of constant agitation, fell quiet, and my body sank into a stillness I had not even been able to achieve in sleep. Every fiber of my being felt bliss. It was as if I'd come home at last. When my instructor signaled the end of meditation, I did not want to stop. Tears of gratitude were streaming down my cheeks.

It is no exaggeration to say that my personal and professional lives were transformed that day. Soon I became the first American psychiatrist to be trained as a TM teacher, and I had the great privilege of appearing with Maharishi Mahesh Yogi, the founder of the TM movement, at many public events where I spoke about the therapeutic value of meditation. In the years since I have seldom missed the opportunity to meditate twice a day. Everyone in my family and thousands of my patients and workshop participants have learned TM. The great majority have had experiences much like my own. It is with great conviction, therefore, that I recommend it as the centerpiece of any regimen for achieving peaceful presence.

My endorsement of TM is in no way meant to disparage other meditative practices. There is, of course, a broad array of techniques that have come to us from the great spiritual traditions—Buddhist mindfulness and breath awareness, Christian contemplative practices, and so forth—as well as variations developed by my colleagues in medicine and mental health. But TM has been thoroughly researched in more than 500 scientific experiments conducted over the last three decades. The research shows that TM produces a unique combination of deep physiological rest and alert mental coherence, and significantly reduces all recognized indicators of stress. It is also easy to practice, is taught in a precise, systematic fashion, and requires no changes in lifestyle.

Meditation is also a technology for unlocking mental capacities to which you may have been denied access, thus enabling you to work more effectively with troublesome issues from the past. "I have no doubt whatever that most people live, whether physically, intellectually or morally, in a very restricted circle of their potential being," wrote the pioneering psychologist William James nearly a century ago. James suggested that yogic disciplines such as meditation might be "methods of getting at our deeper functional levels." TM research on learning ability and other indicators of enhanced functioning would seem to have proven him prophetic indeed.

Another reason meditation is an important tool for making peace with the past is what psychologist Arthur Deikman called "deautomatization." By providing access to levels of awareness previously untapped, meditation can rewire the mind, freeing it from the layers of conditioning and habit that have piled up since childhood. It can open up fresh lines of thought, feeling, and perception for a mind that has been mired in ruts.

The research on TM has legitimized meditation in the public mind as a valuable tool for relaxation and, to a lesser extent, enhancing mental capacity. That alone stands as a major contribution to the West. It is, however, somewhat unfortunate, because it limits our perception of what meditation is and can be. There is a point at which relaxation ends and higher consciousness begins. Every spiritual tradition considers some form of inner practice as the principal engine for cultivating the transcendent peace that comes from union with the infinite ground of being. Certainly, that's what TM has always been about for most long-term practitioners, even while they appreciate its mental and physical benefits on an everyday basis.

In my very first meditation, I experienced not only deep peace but also the realization that I was not just the hubbub of thoughts and feelings that had been creating such chaos in my mind. It is because that state of awareness brings with it the deepest and purest kind of peace that I consider meditation essential to anyone wishing to come to terms with, and at the same time transcend, his or her past.

There is a great deal of haphazard advice in the marketplace, much of which fails to take into account the nuances of meditation and can keep you from receiving the full range of benefits. I urge you to find a qualified TM teacher for personalized instruction rather than trying to learn from a book or tape. To learn more about the technique, call 1-888-LEARNTM or go to the Web site at www.tm.org.

MOVING INTO PEACE

Scientific research clearly shows that men and women who move their bodies on a regular basis are healthier and more resistant to stress than their couch potato counterparts. It does not take much to get enough exercise to burn off tension and restore your physiology to a state of equilibrium. Joining a gym and working with a qualified trainer are excellent choices, but not the only ones by any means. Competitive sports, jogging, bicycling, swimming—the fitness options are plentiful and ubiquitous. There are also venerable and medically proven exercise forms such as yoga and tai chi, which help to cultivate inner peace in the midst of outer activity. And don't forget the easiest, most convenient, and possibly the most effective peace-producing exercise of all: walking.

The research of Dr. Robert E. Thayer, a biological psychology professor at California State University, Long Beach, indicates that the fastest and best way to improve your mood is to take a brisk 10-minute walk.[1] Other studies show that walking is an effective way to defuse anger, reduce tension, lighten a mild depression, and stimulate creative thinking. And the nice thing is, walking can be done virtually anytime, anywhere. The value of that convenience in our busy lives is pointed up by another research finding: Three 10-minute exercise sessions a day produce essentially the same fitness gains as one 30-minute session.

Try to build as much walking time as possible into your daily routine:

- Walk to and from work, if not all the way, at least part of the way.
- If you take public transportation, get off a stop or two early and walk.
- Take the stairs up and down instead of the elevator.
- Park farther from your destination instead of looking for the closest parking space.
- Choose a more distant restaurant for your lunch break—or get takeout and walk to a park to eat it.

- After supper, take a walk with your family instead of immediately plopping down in front of the TV.

WALKING WITH PRESENCE

Walking briskly to burn off tension and strolling to your various destinations both have great value. For a different kind of peace, take a walk with mindful presence.

Set aside periods of time to just walk aimlessly with no goal in mind, not even the goal of inner peace. A nature trail, a beach, or a tree-filled park are ideal locations, but you can also walk around your lawn, your office, your neighborhood, or any other convenient place. Walk slowly, letting your shoulders relax and your arms hang loosely. To keep your back and neck straight without straining, lift your gaze to the horizon as opposed to staring at the earth immediately in front of you.

As you walk, try to be effortlessly present. Put your attention on the soles of your feet. Notice how the weight shifts from heel to toe and from one foot to the other. Notice the firmness or softness of the ground beneath your feet. Notice how your skin feels as it touches the grass, the sand, or the fabric of your shoes. As you walk, you may want to shift your attention to the sights, sounds, and smells around you. Verbalize inwardly what your senses are experiencing as you move through space.

You may also want to put your attention on your breathing, taking two to three steps for each inhalation and two to three for each exhalation. If it helps to keep you present, you can also count each step silently. Alternatively, you can recite a word or phrase, one with the in breath and another with the out breath.

Please do not strain with any of these practices. If trivial thoughts or disturbing feelings intrude, treat them with indifference, like the noise of the street or gusts of wind, and gently return your attention to your object of focus.

One final suggestion for your aimless walk: smile. Studies show that the physical act of smiling, even when it's intentional as opposed to spontaneous, produces positive biochemical changes. "Smiling as you practice walking meditation will keep your steps calm and peaceful," says Thich Nhat Hanh, "and give you a deep sense of ease."

THE DEEP BREATH OF PEACE

In the midst of turmoil, peace is as close as your breath. When you're tense or upset, your breath tends to be shallow and rapid, delivering less oxygen to your cells. When you're at peace, you breathe slowly and deeply. A vital component of your repertoire, therefore, is simply to reverse the stress response by taking slow, deep breaths.

Get into the habit of breathing from your abdomen, not from your upper chest as many of us do. Breathing by expanding the chest prevents the lungs from filling up completely, leaving stale air unexpelled and the oxidation of tissues incomplete. The result is increased tension. Try this instead: Breathing through your nose, push your abdomen out as you inhale. This moves your diaphragm downward, allowing oxygen to enter the lower portion of your lungs. As the breath continues, expand your chest, filling the rest of your lungs. When you exhale, draw in your abdomen. This makes the out breath slightly longer than usual, allowing more used air to leave your lungs.

Research shows that people who practice breathing exercises daily cut their levels of stress and tension in half. Here is a simple yogic breathing exercise that can be practiced regularly to restore equilibrium to your system: Sit comfortably with your back relaxed but straight, and loosen your clothing so you can easily expand your abdomen. Close your right nostril with your thumb and inhale deeply through the left nostril to a count of three. Then hold your breath to a count of three. Now release your thumb and close the left nostril with your ring finger and pinkie. Exhale through the right nostril to a count of three. Hold for one or two counts, then inhale through the same nostril. Continue to alternate nostrils in this sequence: out—in—switch, out—in—switch for three or four minutes, allowing your attention to rest effortlessly on your breathing. You will find that this quickly restores peace to your Quintessential Self.

When my patients become agitated, I often have them do the following one-breath relaxation technique: Straighten your back, relax your shoulders, and take a deep breath. Vividly feel the sensation of peace-giving air filling your chest and permeating every cell in your body. Hold your breath for several moments as you imagine a bright light illuminating every corner of your mind. Exhale through your mouth with a sigh, releasing the darkness from your mind and the tension from your body.

Some people find it effective to use a word or sound to focus the mind as the breath goes in and out. For the in breath, words like *peace, one,* or *God* are often used. For exhalation, many like using the sound *hu* (pronounced like the name Hugh). It's an ancient sound for power and resonates with a number of good English words, such as *human, humor,* and *huge.*

The one-breath technique is simple but effective. Use it whenever you get jarred by circumstance, or when troubling emotions arise as you work through issues from your past.

SOOTHING THE SAVAGE BREAST

Music has charms to soothe a savage breast.
— WILLIAM CONGREVE

A number of scientific studies have documented that the right rhythms, melodies, and lyrics can calm, heal, and inspire. Research shows that music can alleviate tension, release pent-up emotions, and evoke a wide variety of feelings, from sadness to joy, from zesty enthusiasm to silent tranquillity. Music can reduce the level of stress hormones, blood pressure, respiratory rate, and contractions of the stomach and intestines—all signs of anxiety and tension.

The music does not have to be slow and soft to have that effect. Choose high-quality music that suits your needs at any particular moment. At times, something as soul-stirring as Beethoven's Ninth or a gospel choir might be just the thing to bring peace to your soul. At other times, pop songs that evoke poignant memories or happy times might do the trick. Whatever sounds you choose to bring peace to your presence, try to set aside time in which music is more than a background to your busyness. Dim the lights, close your eyes, and let it absorb you so completely that you become the music and the music becomes you.

INNER JOGGING

Laughter is the tonic, the relief, the surcease for pain.
— CHARLIE CHAPLIN

Laughter heals. This was recognized as far back as ancient Greece by Hippocrates, the father of medicine. More recently, in *Anatomy of an Illness*, Norman Cousins called laughing "inner jogging" because a robust 20-second yuck provides as much of an aerobic workout as the same amount of running—and the same release of endorphins, the natural painkillers that produce a sense of peace and well-being.

So, laugh. Play. Have fun. Goof off. You'll be doing some serious work on the road to peace with your past. You'll be dealing with painful memories and difficult emotions. All the more reason to take time along the way to enjoy the simple pleasures and give yourself the gift of laughter. Chances are that you've become, like most of us, too adultified. Part of the price you've paid for a difficult past may have been the stifling of your childlike capacity for joy.

You might want to think back to your childhood and remember the delight you took in eating an ice cream cone or splashing in water or watching a butterfly. Go ahead and do it now. Let yourself be a magical child once in a while. If you need help, go find a bona fide child to play with. As Jesus taught, "Except ye be converted, and become as little children, ye shall not enter into the kingdom of God."[2]

Use your imagination to think up fun things for each aspect of your Quintessential Self. Let your physical self frolic in the surf, roll around in grass, kick a ball, dance, spin, or ride a toboggan down a hill. Give your mental self puzzles to solve and novels to read for sheer escapism. Treat your emotional self to an amusement park, a comedy club, or a goofy movie. For your relational self, round up some friends you can just fool around with, who make you laugh, think up adventures, and remind you that life is as ridiculous as it is sublime. Lift your spiritual self with an infusion of wonder, innocence, and awe: Go to a planetarium, a natural history museum, an art exhibit, a zoo, a concert of sacred music. Don't fall into the trap of equating spirituality with solemnity.

"Humor is a prelude to faith," wrote Reinhold Niebuhr, "and Laughter is the beginning of prayer."

Keep fun and laughter in your life on a regular basis. Use a humorous desk calendar. Post cartoons on your refrigerator. Listen to tapes of great comedians as you drive. Make funny faces in the mirror. Above all, learn to laugh at yourself. Your problems are serious, your pain is real, but if you look hard enough—or light enough—you'll also find an element of absurdity in it all. There is a certain peace in not taking yourself too seriously. As G. K. Chesterton put it, "Angels can fly because they take themselves so lightly."

And spread the wealth. Don't just make yourself laugh, make others laugh as well. It's infectious. The Koran, the holiest text of Islam, states, "He deserves Paradise who makes his companions laugh."

PEACEFUL PAUSES

Remember the sabbath day, to keep it holy.
— EXODUS 20:8

The tides, the rhythm of the seasons, electromagnetic waves, the sleeping and waking of creatures great and small—everything progresses in cycles of rest and activity. For inner peace to flourish, all aspects of the Quintessential Self, not just the body, need rest. Traditionally, of course, one day a week was set aside to attend to the soul. If you can't take a full day, at least give yourself half a day. Don't work. Don't strain. Instead, spend time in contemplation and enjoying friends and loved ones.

Every religion has, in addition to some form of weekly sabbath, a tradition of extended getaways for silence and contemplation. They are usually called retreats. I prefer to call them advances. Take a weekend on occasion, or even a week, to sojourn in a formal spiritual context or by yourself, preferably in a quiet, natural setting. Nothing brings peace like nature unspoiled. As you gaze at an ocean or a river, contemplate the never-ending fluctuations of waves and ripples, which create a new ocean or river every nanosecond. In the stillness of the forest, notice the constant motion of the wind-blown leaves, the songs of the birds, the comings and goings of the creatures. Is it not like your own life? Hasn't your past been a ceaseless ebb and flow of change? Haven't you become a different person with every oscillation? Hasn't every obstacle on your journey been just a temporary detour, like the rocks that redirect the current of a stream? Great peace can be found in seeing your life as a reflection of the same eternal principles that regulate the natural environment.

If you're not inclined to extended solitude, allow yourself the time to lay around on a quiet beach or otherwise unplug and do nothing. Or treat yourself to a spa. Luxuriate in hot tubs, steam rooms, and mineral pools. Pamper yourself with facials and massages. In fact, make massage a regular stop on your making peace itinerary. Whether you massage yourself, get massaged by your love partner, or visit a professional massage therapist, take advantage of the healing power of touch. The need to touch and be touched is universal. Babies who are touch-deprived can suffer severe developmental disorders, and studies show that physiological signs of stress are reduced in adults who receive a calming touch. Massage is not only calming and soothing, it can, especially when deep and firm, help to release the physical residue of past stress and trauma.

A PRAYER FOR PEACE

The truth is, God talks to everybody.
— NEALE DONALD WALSCH

Medical research is validating what the religious have always understood: Prayer has healing power.[34] In *The Varieties of Prayer,* sociologist Christopher Ellison, Ph.D., and pollster George Gallup write that 90 percent of Americans pray from time to time; 88 percent of them say they usually experience deep peace and a sense of well-being when they do.

Definitions of prayer differ from one tradition to another, and the methods of prayer are numerous. There are prayers of praise, prayers of petition, and prayers of gratitude—and some spiritual leaders recommend combining the three: Praise God, ask for a blessing, and give thanks. However one defines it, prayer is an intimate encounter with the Divine. And whatever method one uses, there is peace to be found in surrendering to the human impulse to revere that which is eternal, omnipresent, and almighty, whether you understand that to be a deity or a force of nature.

You might want to set aside sacred time for prayer and create a sacred space to do it in. If you are so inclined, use the format of the religious tradition you follow and direct your prayers to the god, saint, or higher power whose presence you wish to invoke. Some feel most comfortable reciting a traditional prayer from a sacred text. Others prefer to speak their own words. You may find a prayer of your own already inscribed in your heart, or you may wish to let the rhythm of your soul make it up as you go along. If you are not religious and prayer as such does not appeal to you, consider finding a way of declaring your intention to heal the pain of the past and find quintessential peace within you.

The following prayers were adapted from each of the major religions:

From Judaism: *"Help us, O God, to lie down in peace, and awaken us to life on the morrow. May we always be guided by Your good counsel, and thus find shelter in Your tent of peace. . . . Guard us always and everywhere. Bless us with life and peace. Praise to You, O God of peace, whose love is always with us."*

From Christianity (Saint Francis of Assisi): *"Lord, make me an instrument of Your peace. Where there is hatred, let me sow love; where there is injury, let me sow pardon; where there is doubt, faith; where there is despair, hope; where there is darkness, light; and where there is sadness, joy."*

From Islam: *"Guide us, O God, on the path of perfect harmony, the path of those whom You have blessed with the gifts of peace, joy, serenity, and delight, the path of those who have not been brought down by anger, the path of those who have not been lost along the way."*

From Buddhism: *"May all beings be free of suffering. May all have happiness and contentment. May all be peaceful and at ease. May all be protected from harm and fear. May all be healed. May all awaken from their illusions and be enlightened. May all be free. May all beings abide in the great innate peace."*

From Hinduism: *"May there be peace in the higher regions; may there be peace in the firmament; may there be peace on earth. May the waters flow peacefully; may the herbs and plants grow peacefully; may all the divine powers bring unto us peace. The Supreme Lord is peace. May we all be in peace, peace, peace; and may that peace come into each of us."*

Breaking the Shackles of Shame

FROM THE FALSEHOOD OF HUMILIATION TO TRUE HUMILITY

We live in an atmosphere of shame. We are ashamed of every-thing that is real about us; ashamed of ourselves, of our rela-tives, of our incomes, of our accents, of our opinions, of our experience, just as we are ashamed of our naked skins.
— GEORGE BERNARD SHAW

You may be tempted to skip this chapter, thinking it does not apply to you. "Shame is not my issue," you may be thinking. "I'll just move on to the chapters I identify with." Please read on. You might be surprised to discover that this is the most important chapter in the book for you.

Of the many thousands of people I've seen in psychotherapy, only a small percentage present shame as their initial complaint. Initially, many say they don't relate to the word at all. But once they learn what it really means, most come to realize that deep-seated shame from the long-ago past exerts a strong influence in their lives, underlying or exacerbating the issues that brought them to therapy in the first place.

Shame is the cancer of the spirit. For some it's a raging malig-nancy. It can feel so bad that the victims become convinced it's ter-minal. They feel broken beyond repair, certain that their problems are hopeless and any remedy they could possibly try is doomed to failure. For others, shame is more like a localized tumor that causes deep-seated pain and discomfort; shameful memories rise up at certain times and stab them in the gut, all the while keeping them from functioning at full capacity. For most of us, shame is a small, undetected growth on the periphery of awareness, growing insidiously and gnawing away at the tissues of our psyche.

Everyone is affected by some degree of shame. We can hardly avoid it, since we swim in a sea of subliminal competition, comparing our looks to those of supermodels and movie stars, our cars and clothing to those of people more affluent than us, our skills to those of athletes and artists, our behavior to that of saints. Even if we know that our standards are absurdly high, on some deep level we're ashamed that we don't measure up. In our secret self-disgust, we imagine that others are not only more competent but kinder and more loving than we are. And in our secret discontent, we imagine that they are happier, too—and then we feel ashamed of our envy. In short, the voice of shame, perhaps the most painful of all the destructive voices in our heads, resounds to some extent in every human being. Even the healthiest among us can benefit from identifying that voice, seeing it for the fundamental lie that it is, and casting it out.

THE NATURE OF SHAME

Let's begin by defining exactly what shame is and what it is not. It's important to distinguish it from two closely related emotions: guilt and remorse.

The dictionary defines guilt as the "remorseful awareness of having done something wrong." Shame is a far more searing and durable emotion. We feel shame not for what we've *done* but for what we *are*. It's a sense that something is inherently wrong with us, that we are basically flawed, that we are a sham. In extreme cases, shame takes the form of a self-loathing so intense that the person feels totally worthless: "I am disgusting, I am despicable, I am unlovable, I don't deserve anyone's respect or concern." Ironically, people who are shame-based (or shame-debased, to be more accurate) sometimes have little capacity for guilt. How can you feel guilty for something you've done if you're so worthless to begin with that nothing better can be expected of you?

Shame is also quite different from remorse. Defined by the dictionary as "moral anguish arising from repentance for past misdeeds," remorse is a healthy emotion that enables us to feel and express genuine sorrow when we do something wrong. The capacity for remorse is a crucial ingredient of mature self-awareness. Without it we would not have the ability to recognize our mistakes, learn from them, and grow. Nor would we be able to apologize, make amends, and humbly accept the forgiveness of others—or ourselves. To a large extent, remorse is what teaches us compassion. It helps us to develop a strong sense of conscience and produces strength of character.

Shame has no such redeeming qualities. With deep-seated shame, you don't just make mistakes, you feel you *are* a mistake; you don't just feel sorry for what you've done, you feel sorry for *being*; you don't have self-respect, you have self-contempt; and you can't accept forgiveness because you feel you don't deserve it.

To understand how devastating shame can be, consider the difference between self-esteem and self-worth. We measure our self-esteem by our impact on the world through our deeds. It is basically something we earn, and it rises and falls depending on how we evaluate our actions and achievements. Self-worth is more basic; it's a measure of our intrinsic value. Many people suffer periodic blows to their self-esteem but still retain a healthy sense of self-worth. If they make a mistake, fail at something, cause pain to others, or do something shameful, they feel horrible about it, but their self-worth remains intact. People with a core of shame tend to lack that capacity. In severe cases, they feel fundamentally worthless.

Raised by his parents to feel insignificant and unimportant, Harry came to see every setback, big or small, as confirmation of his secretly held poor view of himself. He constantly compared his career achievements to more successful men and measured his success with women by the standards he imagined others attained. In psychotherapy he revealed that he felt totally worthless as a man. The distinction between self-esteem as something you earn and self-worth as God-given made a big impact on him. Once he accepted that worth was his birthright, he was able to start shedding the lies he was shamed with as a child. This freed him to be kinder, more respectful, and more loving to himself. By achieving greater self-acceptance, he was able to focus on becoming the best possible Harry instead of comparing himself to others and trying to be like them. He felt worthy for the first time in his life. As a result, he became more successful at work and was able to have a mature relationship for the first time in his life.

THE SUBTLE SIGNS OF SHAME

If you suffer from intense, pervasive shame, you don't have to be told that this is an important issue in your life. You feel it all the time. You feel alone and apart, cut off from all that sustains us on our journey through life: self-acceptance, the love of others, a higher power. A voice in your head is constantly reminding you that you are flawed, defective, and hopeless. That is the tragedy of shame.

But shame also has a voice whose treachery is much more cunning. What follows are the not-so-obvious signs of shame. As you read through them, ask yourself to what extent they might apply to you.

Do you:

- Feel that things are just not going to work out—that people will let you down and you're bound to be disappointed?
- Feel unsatisfied with how you look, no matter how many compliments you get?
- Fail to stand up for your own beliefs?
- Hesitate to express your wants and needs?
- Refuse to forgive yourself for minor mistakes and misdeeds?
- Allow yourself to be abused physically, sexually, or verbally?
- Feel like a failure no matter how successful you are?
- Constantly doubt your abilities, skills, and competence?
- Constantly feel that you have to apologize for yourself?
- Feel unsure of your opinions and reluctant to express them?

- Want to punish or humiliate others—only to feel ashamed for having such thoughts?
- Deny yourself sexual or sensual pleasures?
- Have negative thoughts like:
  - ❑ "Who do you think you are?"
  - ❑ "You'll probably make a fool of yourself."
  - ❑ "You'll only let them down."
  - ❑ "You're never going to really make it."
  - ❑ "You don't deserve it."
- Think of yourself in any of the following terms?
  - ❑ Unlovable
  - ❑ Useless
  - ❑ Ineffectual
  - ❑ Despicable
  - ❑ Pitiful
  - ❑ Insignificant
  - ❑ Worthless
  - ❑ Dishonorable
  - ❑ Defective
  - ❑ Disgusting

These are signs that shame may be hiding in the dark, secret crevices of your being, whispering that you are undeserving and unworthy. It's important to remember that shame exists on a continuum and that it attacks each of us with varying degrees of intensity. "Every one of us carries a deforming mirror," wrote Anaïs Nin, "where he sees himself too small or too large, too fat or too thin, even you who see yourself so free, blithe and unscarred."

On the surface, it may sound bleak to say that virtually all of us harbor some degree of shame. But recognizing our common condition is the beginning of freedom. Once you realize that *everyone* has felt ashamed at one time or another, that *everyone* has been humiliated, and that *everyone* thinks he or she is the only one who harbors shameful secrets, you can relax a bit and get on with healing the toxic shame that can destroy you. "One discovers that destiny can be directed," Anaïs Nin went on to say, "that one does not need to remain in bondage to the first imprint made on childhood sensibilities, one need not be branded by the first patterns. Once the deforming mirror is smashed there is the possibility of wholeness, there is the possibility of joy."

Shame may be a cancer, but once it is diagnosed it is a highly treatable condition. If you're willing to take on the work of healing, the prognosis is excellent. You can break the shackles of shame and reclaim your birthright as a free and radiant being.

Shame's Achilles heel is this vital truth: The sense of worthlessness that shame produces is nothing but a grand illusion. No one is worthless. We all come into this world with unconditional self-worth. In the eyes of God (or nature, the universe, or whatever term suits your view of a larger design), we all retain our innate worth regardless of our victories and defeats, our good deeds and bad deeds, our virtues and vices. Self-worth is a given; it is our birthright. Remembering that is the first step to undoing the erroneous belief that you are shameful.

THE ROOTS OF SHAME

Because it makes us feel as though a piece of us were missing, shame is the enemy of inner peace. To break its hold and restore our wholeness we have to first uncover the origins of our shame.

Shame is not something that happens once, like a trauma. In most cases, it is inflicted upon us over and over again—either maliciously or inadvertently—by parents, peers, and authority figures such as teachers and clergy. With each shaming incident, the sense of defilement is reinforced. After a while it becomes internalized. At that point, we become not only the target of shame but the source, not just the victim but the perpetrator, for we pick up where the others left off and start to shame ourselves.

Where does it begin? In a sense, it begins at the beginning. Earlier, we saw that we come into this life as a bundle of bliss, united with our source, only to experience the shock of separation. That primal experience sets the template for shame, for shame at its deepest level is a tear in the fabric of our being that separates us from all that is nourishing and sustaining.

As infancy progresses and we grow toward self-awareness, we become more and more capable of feeling the pain as well as the joy of separation. Even under the best of circumstances, our needs are not always met instantaneously. Sometimes we are not attended to. Sometimes we don't receive the unconditional, all-embracing love we deserve. As we move into early childhood, at around 18 months, we become conscious for the first time that we are unique beings with feelings and thoughts of our own. That experience is, at the same time, liberating and frightening, and the confusion it breeds is the root of what we call the Terrible Twos. It's around that time that we start to hear the word *no*. Now we start to have demands made upon us. Now when we do something wrong, we are told about it—and sometimes admonished, scolded, or punished.

If, during those early years, we are essentially well loved and our needs are consistently attended to, the pain of those moments of negation is slight. It can even be beneficial. It becomes what I call homeopathic shame. As in homeopathy, where minute doses of a potentially toxic substance are capable of inducing a healing response, small doses of naturally occurring shame can lay the foundation for remorse—which, as mentioned earlier, is important in developing character. Homeopathic shame becomes the bedrock of self-awareness, individuality, responsibility, compassion, and other positive qualities.

But if we are not loved unconditionally, if we are not welcomed and embraced, if the inevitable noes are dispensed with anger and resentment and the necessary lessons are administered with the tenderness of a sledgehammer or an electric prod, then we are wounded, not strengthened, and toxic shame infects the deepest parts of our personalities.

This is true even in the preverbal stage of life. Certainly, as infants, we are not capable of thinking about what's wrong or reasoning about its causes, but we feel it just the same. Just as we respond to the warmth of Mom's loving arms and Dad's delighted smile, we respond to the frowns, the scowls, the groans, the indifference, and the absence. We sense the difference between a parent who hears our cry as a summons to love and one who hears it as a factory whistle calling him or her to work. Just as we feel the bliss when our parents are thankful for our presence, we feel the blisters when they see us as a burden and wish we hadn't been born.

As children, we personalize everything. Our worlds revolve around our need for safety and security. We need love, constant attention, and concern. If our needs are not being met, we know something is wrong. And what could be wrong but *us*? Certainly not our parents. They brought us into this world. They protect us and provide for us. If they don't respond to us, it must be our fault. If they're unhappy, there must be something wrong with us. If they say no to us, it must be because what we want is wrong, and we must be wrong for wanting it.

When a parent scolds or scowls with disappointment, she or he may mean nothing more than, "You must not do this or you'll hurt yourself," or, "You can't have that because it's not good for you." But what the child hears is, "You're bad." At that age, we can't make the intellectual distinction between our behavior and our selves. And if the upset parent responds with rage, a child can't reason, "That's an inappropriate reaction and I don't deserve it." For a small, dependent child to realize that a parent is wrong for causing him or her pain would be unimaginable. "Those enormous creatures who protect and feed me can't be flawed. They can't be defective. If they are, then I'm in real danger. No, no, they're okay, in fact, they're perfect, it must be *me* who's flawed." Such feelings give rise to shame.

HOW SHAME GETS INTERNALIZED

If this occurs with well-meaning, well-adjusted parents, think of what can happen in cases of overt abuse. Put yourself in the place of a small helpless child. Imagine someone 25 feet tall and 900 pounds—the person you depend upon for your very existence— looking down on you from that towering position and shouting, "Shame on you!" Imagine being told, "I wish I never had you. My life is miserable since you came along!" Imagine needing that person and being ignored. Imagine being abandoned. Imagine being beaten. Imagine being used by that person for his or her sexual gratification. Even in the face of horror, a child can't think that his or her parents are doing something monstrous. The feeling sense that worms its way into the child's essence is, "They would never do anything like that if I didn't deserve it. I must be defective."

With enough repetition, the shame becomes internalized and self-induced. We feel ashamed not only of what we've done, but of who we are. Each time something goes wrong, we think and feel in our child's logic, "I'm screwed up, I'm no good, I'm worthless, I'm unlovable."

Those are the seeds of shame. They take root in the psyche as wordless pain and grow with constant feeding into the self-defeating thoughts, feelings, and behavior that keep us unfulfilled as adults.

As an example of how early shame can seep into the cracks and crevices of adult life, meet a client of mine named Tina. Tina's father had had two sons by a previous marriage and wanted a third. Her mother was thrilled to have a little girl, but felt so overwhelmed by circumstances that she could hardly show it. She was too busy finding ways to survive with a man who was demeaning, demanding, and sometimes violent. She was expected first and foremost to take care of her husband and stepsons. The little girl would have to wait.

Shortly before her third birthday, Tina's already wounded soul received a shattering jolt. Her mother gave birth to twin boys. Tina had not even been prepared for *one* new baby and now she was faced with two. Fifty-two years later, in therapy, the searing pain was visible on her face as she remembered the shock of seeing a strange infant in her mother's arms—and the horror of seeing her father's delight as he cradled the twin.

If Tina felt ignored before, now she felt abandoned. Her childhood was torn from her. At a ridiculously early age, she was expected not only to fend for herself, but also to help her mother. "I was basically a child laborer," she recalled. "At three I was picking up after my older brothers. By the time I was six I was in the kitchen, helping with meals and doing dishes for seven people." When she needed her mother's attention, she was scolded and made to sit in the corner until she could "be nice."

At this point in her story, Tina squirmed, averted her eyes, and revealed a secret she had kept all these years: She hated her twin brothers from the moment they were born. She'd even had fantasies of killing them. These ugly thoughts reinforced the feelings of shame and worthlessness that had already infiltrated her tender soul. Afraid of the rage she felt, she suppressed it as best she could and played the role of nice dutiful girl to the hilt. That pattern continued through her adult years. Always feeling inferior to others, disconnected from her emotions, Tina shied away from asserting herself. She got married twice, to men who disrespected her and ultimately walked out on her. And she denied herself the love of a child by having her tubes tied. Deep down, she was afraid her shameful feelings would suddenly rise up and make her do something awful.

WAVES OF SHAME

Some of us get through our early childhood years uninfected by toxic shame. The minute doses we receive are handled with love and emotional nourishment, helping us to define who we are and grow strong. But we're not out of the woods by any means. The onslaught of shame can come fiercely in later childhood and/or the perilous years of adolescence. Those attacks can have long-lasting impact, and if they follow on the heels of intense early childhood shame, their devastation is multiplied many times over.

At around age eight, as we spend less time with Mommy and Daddy and more with our friends, we begin to develop a healthy sense of individuality. But it's a precarious time, because now a lot more is expected of us. We want lots of things we can't have—at least not immediately and automatically. Now we have to earn them. Rewards and punishments are more explicit and exacting because we're capable of understanding right from wrong. We're scrutinized more thoroughly, as our parents start looking for signs that their expectations for us will be realized. Now our actions have real consequences for our future—and for our parents' self-image. Now we can make them proud—or disappoint them. Now they start comparing us to other kids to see how we measure up—and as a result, we start measuring ourselves.

If we're lucky, our parents are reasonable in their expectations, they allow us to make mistakes and suffer setbacks without compromising our worth, and they help us unfold our true selves instead of imposing an identity on us. But if they are perfectionists, holding us to unrealistic standards and treating every perceived impediment as a threat to their dreams, we internalize their disappointment. Parents whose own sense of worth is too wrapped up in their children's performance—"How can you embarrass me like that? How can I look the other parents in the eye?"—transfer their shame to us.

It is also at this time that a mother or father who wants out of the marriage is less likely to stay in it for the sake of the kids. They think you're less likely to be harmed now that you're old enough to understand and can visit them on weekends. In truth, it hurts even more because now you know what abandonment is, and now you can see that other kids still have both parents and you don't. Sad to say, it is also at this time that parents and other adults who have the capacity to abuse find excuses to let loose. Now, in their distorted eyes, your flesh and bones can withstand a beating and your mind can learn a lesson from it. And now, sadly, a sexual molester has a victim whose body is mature enough to do his or her bidding.

Needless to say, any of the above patterns delivers a devastating dose of shame because the child concludes that he or she must be fundamentally defective to have earned such treatment.

In these prepubescent years, shame also gets handed out by our peers. Janice, a 32-year-old single mom who is making ends meet as an office temp while getting a bachelor's degree at night, remembers vividly the cruelty of children. A slow student to begin with, Janice's trouble in school was magnified because her large, unruly family made it hard for her to get to sleep until late at night. She would sometimes fall asleep in class with her head on the desk, sucking her thumb. Her classmates teased her unmercifully. One rainy spring day, while walking home alone, she lost a shoe in the ankle-deep mud. She asked some kids for help, but they laughed and called her a retard instead.

Feeling that everyone was always watching her, just waiting for something to taunt her about, Janice retreated into a shell. The constant apprehension made it even more difficult to concentrate in class, and every time she answered a question wrong, the whispers and giggles added to her humiliation. Things at home were not much better. Eventually, she compensated for her shame by becoming a rebellious, arrogant teenager. She dropped out of school, took to drinking by herself, and tried to fill her lonely nights with anonymous sex. Years later, Janice discovered that she'd had Attention Deficit Disorder all her life. Medication is helping her with that problem, but the shame that led her to conclude that she was damaged goods will take a longer time to heal.

THE PERILS OF PUBERTY

As the engine of maturation drives us inexorably into puberty, fresh waves of shame come upon us. They can either lap the shores of our psyches, depositing fresh ground on which to stand, or they can crash heavily and relentlessly, pounding us to our knees and drowning us in pain.

Now the pressure to perform and the comparison to peers intensifies. Now we hear things like, "I sacrificed everything for you and this is the thanks I get?" "I paid through the teeth for private tutors and all you do is talk on the phone!" "You'll never attract a boy looking like that!" "How come Tom is the starting pitcher and you're sitting on the bench?"

And it is now, with the blossoming of our young bodies, that we become conscious—and highly *self*-conscious—of our sexuality. Now we start to notice what's happening to other kids' bodies. We're ashamed that we're checking out who has pubic hair and underarm hair, or which girls are menstruating and whose breasts are budding like ours—or like ours are *not*—or how big the other boys' penises are and whether they, too, get hard at inconvenient times. We think we're the only ones peeking up Ms. Smith's skirt or imagining what Mr. Jones looks like with his pants off, and we're absolutely certain we're the only ones touching ourselves *there*.

Such developments are, by themselves, shame-inducing, but most of us come through it okay as long as that's all there is to it.

If we enter puberty with a backlog of shame, however, it's harder to escape the feeling that we're basically flawed.

It is also now that sexual abuse is more likely to occur—not just from grownups close to home, but from strangers. And not just the unspeakable, subhuman forms of molestation, but less obvious shame-inducing behavior, such as teasing, whispering, and invasions of privacy. Parents and siblings open the bathroom door when we're peeing or getting out of the shower. They walk into our bedroom unannounced while we're getting dressed—or, heaven forbid, when we're exploring the wonder of our bodies. They stare at our awakening body parts and remark out loud or under their breaths about the size of our penis or breasts, or the sprouting of pubic hair. In all innocence, they make suggestive jokes. They express pride and wonder at how fast we're developing and how sexy we're becoming. "Girls won't be able to resist him," they mutter furtively, or, "She'll have to fight off boys with a stick." Or the opposite: "She'll never attract anyone the way she's turning out." Certainly, none of this comes close to the horror of rape or incest. But these seemingly harmless, ever-so-normal events can leave a mark of shame.

THE PSYCHIC PROMISES OF PAIN

Whether this fresh onslaught of shame enhances our strength and individuality or utterly destroys them depends on how the crisis of puberty is handled—and how the previous waves were dealt with. If the shame is severe, a child may attempt to alleviate the pain by forming "psychic promises" with those who are heaping it on. In essence, we make a sacred pact with ourselves, either consciously or unconsciously, that we think, in our innocence, will end the torment. See if any of these psychic promises ring a bell with you:

- I'll become a replica of my parents. *If I'm just like them, they'll treat me better.* (This is why alcoholics beget alcoholics, and abusers beget abusers, and perfectionists beget perfectionists.)
- I'll be the total opposite of my parents. *That'll teach them!*
- I'll do anything to win their approval and acceptance. *Then they won't abuse me or abandon me.*

- I'll turn out just the way they want me to. *If they want a superstar, I'll be a superstar. If they want me to be a doctor, I'll become a doctor. If they want me to marry a rich man, I'll marry a rich man.*
- I'll turn out just the way they're *afraid* I will. *They say I'll never be happy, okay, I'll be miserable. They say I'll never amount to anything, okay, I'll become a slacker. They say I'll become a big fat slob, okay, bring on the chips and fries.*
- I'll fulfill all their unrealized dreams. *They were losers, so I'll be a huge success. They were unpopular, so I'll have a zillion friends. They couldn't make ends meet, so I'll get rich.*
- I'll never surpass them. *I won't make them jealous by being thinner, or happier, or more successful.*
- I'll punish myself. *Then they won't have to punish me anymore.*
- I'll always be nice. *I'll never do anything to give them—or anyone else—a reason to be angry or upset.*
- I'll never do anything right. *I'll get revenge by giving them nothing to be proud of as parents. I won't give them a way to justify how they raised me. I'll shame them as they shamed me.*
- I'll shut off my feelings. *If I'm numb, I won't feel the shame. Of course, I won't feel love or joy or happiness, either, but at least I won't be in pain.*

Sometimes the vow we take is so binding that we essentially give up our lives to fulfill it, often transferring the agreement in adulthood to our lovers, employers, and other figures who replace parents in our lives. Unfortunately, we seldom get what we hoped for when we naïvely signed the contract: We don't get freedom from pain and shame.

Here are sections of a letter from a patient named Joe, describing his psychic promises:

> *I vowed that I'd never be violent like my father. That has kept me from ever showing anger appropriately.*
> *I promised that I'd always be there for those I love, unlike my parents. As a result, I have been a "rescuer" all my life, putting my own needs on hold.*

I vowed to have wealth and power to make up for the struggles of my family. That made me a perfectionist and a people pleaser.

I promised to always treat women with respect. This has meant that I was not sexually aggressive even when it would have been appropriate.

Keeping these promises requires enormous effort. It has made me weary of life. I feel like I've wasted much of my God-given gifts and that it is too late for me.

It took some time, but eventually Joe was able to give himself permission to start breaking those contracts and free himself from the decades-old shame that gave rise to them.

THE ANGST OF ADOLESCENT SHAME

In the teenage years, the opportunities for shame are limitless. Every day offers fresh possibilities for feeling lousy about yourself—your looks, your grades, your body, your competence, your personality, your taste in clothing or music, your friends (or lack of them), your parents . . . the list goes on. It's a virtual shamefest. Adolescents are constantly measuring themselves against various social ideals, and they invariably find themselves lacking. Even those who choose to rebel can't escape the feeling that something is wrong with them.

With the emergence of physical maturity comes pressure. Now the demands are more explicit and the disapproval is more in-your-face. Parents with high hopes for their children's future look at grades and test scores as if they determine who will live and who will die. Now you're expected to "act like a grownup." Now you're forced to think about the distant future when you can't see past Saturday night. Now you're expected to make big decisions about college and career when you can't decide what to wear and you're sure you'll absolutely *die* if you wear the wrong thing. Everything seems monumental. Every admonition—"You better shape up or you'll end up pumping gas the rest of your life," "You better watch your weight or no one will ask you out"—is felt with enormous poignancy. And if, on top of all that, you're hammered with contempt, ridicule, or physical abuse, or you're abandoned due to divorce, it can be absolutely devastating, because now you're old enough to understand what's going on but still as tender as a sapling.

It is also in the teenage years that peers become the principle purveyors of shame. It's a time of individuation and identity formation, with two powerful impulses waging war with one another—the desire to be unique and the equally desperate desire to fit in. Aching to figure out who and what they are, teens constantly compare themselves to others and to the prevailing image of what is cool. And they are the most judgmental of creatures, often capable of malicious cruelty to their compatriots. We all remember how shattering it was to be rejected, teased about our appearance, laughed at for goofing up in class, or whispered about because we couldn't get a date. Such experiences can make adolescents feel like they're flawed beyond repair, leaving an indelible mark of shameful inadequacy. And if their peers are not doing it to them, they're doing it to themselves. They may be the most popular, the smartest, the greatest athlete, the most beautiful, but in the gossip chambers of their brains they tell themselves they are really a sham and they might be exposed at any moment.

While all this is going on, stampeding hormones are sending wild, confusing, volatile messages to the brain. Teens have all sorts of thoughts they consider dirty, disgusting, and shameful— sexual thoughts, aggressive thoughts, selfish thoughts, hostile thoughts ("I wish she was dead!")—and fantasies that make MTV look like the Disney Channel. Unfortunately, what they need most is the one thing they almost always lack: someone with whom to bare their souls. Even teens who jabber constantly have no one to tell their deepest secrets to. Not their parents, from whom they are trying to separate; not the geeky guidance counselor, who couldn't possibly understand; not even their closest friends, because teenagers don't really talk to their friends, they *perform* for them. They think they'd be ostracized if anyone knew what was going on in their heads, when in fact they're all going through the same madness.

For those who have internalized a massive dose of shame in childhood, the ordinary humiliations of adolescence reactivate the pain and turn the teenage years into a torture chamber. Every sign that you don't quite measure up is proof that you're hopelessly defective.

I've had countless clients whose main task in therapy was to undo the effects of adolescent shame. Let's look at one example. Blake's parents got divorced shortly after he turned 13. Because he had been a rambunctious kid who was constantly being reprimanded, he convinced himself that he was the cause of the breakup. As he and his sister shuttled between their parents' new homes, Blake's sense of shame grew stronger. Shy by nature and somewhat gawky, he suffered by comparison to his sister, who was a knockout with a sweet, friendly disposition. She was showered with admiration and attention; Blake was either ignored or criticized. His most vivid high school memory is of his sister's friends gawking at him and giggling; he was sure they wondered how she could possibly be related to an ugly misfit like him.

Deep inside, Blake craved the kind of attention his sister was getting. Hurt, isolated, and lonely, he hid behind a wall of forced indifference, withholding his love from others—and from himself. To numb his feelings, he started using drugs. The pattern continued through his twenties. His only companions were the patrons and strippers in a bar he hung out in; the closest he came to intimacy was with his television and the occasional one-nighter. He avoided family functions, and when he found himself in a social situation he was awkward and uncomfortable. He would not allow anyone to hug him.

By the time he was 30, Blake got tired of drifting from job to job, going home alone, and waking up with hangovers. He went to AA and started therapy. It did not take him long to realize that he had internalized a shame-based voice that said, "There is something wrong with me. That's why I have to be alone in my sordid little world." It has taken a lot of work for Blake to realize he is not worthless, but he is finally emerging on the other side of shame.

Most adolescents develop a two-tiered personality. One part knows they're special. As Joseph Chilton Pearce observed, "Adolescents sense a secret, unique greatness in themselves that seeks expression." The other part knows they're flawed and jumps on every opportunity for self-deprecation. The lucky ones have friends and family who reinforce their worth, support the expression of their unique gifts, and escort them through the minefields of shame relatively unscathed. But for those who are forced to endure one explosion after another, the emotional shrapnel can penetrate to the very core of their soul.

THE LEGACY OF SHAME

We ride these successive waves of shame into adulthood. If they've taught us humility, self-awareness, and healthy remorse, we can take life's inevitable setbacks in stride. When we mess up, we see it as a sign that we have something to learn. When we hurt someone, we make amends and ask for forgiveness. When we do something unethical or immoral, we accept responsibility and resolve not to do it again. We can forgive ourselves and move on with our self-worth intact. But if we've internalized the shame, every bump in the road—a divorce or breakup, a business failure, a rejection, a misjudgment, a blunder, a repugnant thought, a lack of courage— reactivates the pain, and once again we embrace the delusion that we are worthless.

The residue of shame affects each aspect of the Quintessential Self:

PHYSICALLY
Even in infancy, the body responds to emergencies by pumping out adrenaline and other stress-related substances. That's bad enough for a developing body, but when the stress of abuse, abandonment, or humiliation is compounded by the massive stress of shame, the adrenal cortex floods the system with cortisol. Over the long haul, chronic or repetitive waves of shame alter the biochemistry of the body, leading to a variety of adverse conditions, including:

- Suppression of the immune system
- Elevation of blood pressure

- Chronic muscular tension, with increased chances of headaches and back pain
- Higher cholesterol counts and elevated low-density lipoproteins
- Calcium depletion
- Excess stomach acid
- Elevation of clotting elements in the blood
- Spasms of the gastrointestinal tract
- Decline in sex hormones

This is why, as mentioned in chapter 1, men and women who were abused as children are more likely to develop a life-threatening illness.

MENTALLY

That flood of stress chemicals affects the brain as well. It can interfere with the action of neurotransmitters, and contribute to the premature aging of brain function. Research shows that chronic distress can damage learning ability, memory, concentration, and IQ.

Deep-seated shame affects not only how we think but also *what* we think. Our minds react to shame with thoughts of vengeance, hostility, and bitterness—which only make us more ashamed. The voice of shame is cruel, relentless, and unforgiving. Shame-based thinking stands between us and all that we want and need, because it whispers, "You don't deserve it." It makes us see ourselves as deficient in every quality we value. If we value strength, we feel ashamed at any sign of weakness. If we value money, we feel ashamed when we can't afford something we want. If we value appearance, we feel ashamed when we don't look perfect. You name it, a shame-based person will feel it. When a wave of shame comes over us, everything we are and everything we've ever done seems worthless, and any happiness we may have experienced seems like a mistake, because we're sure we're inadequate, useless, and doomed to be miserable.

EMOTIONALLY

Internalized shame can numb our feelings, shutting us off from pleasure and happiness as well as the pain we seek to avoid—or it can make us hypersensitive, paranoid, and explosive. The emotional impact of chronic shame can be seen in this list of D words, any or all of which a shame-based person might feel.

- Depression[1]
- Distress
- Denial
- Demoralized
- Defeated
- Deprived
- Defective
- Divided
- Deficient
- Despicable
- Disgraceful
- Deserted
- Diminished
- Debased
- Defensive
- Desperate
- Devastated
- Diminished

Which of these apply to you? Can you think of other D words that fit?

RELATIONALLY

Shame-based people are extremely harsh in their self-evaluation. There is always someone to whom they compare unfavorably in success, intelligence, fame, fortune, beauty, and any other qualities that matter to them. They never think they are what they should be.

The relational aspect of shame is also expressed in how we evaluate our behavior toward others. Shame-based people see every social imperfection as proof of their worthlessness. An ethical lapse, a selfish act, an inappropriate remark, a self-protective lie—every minor transgression seems unforgivable. This extreme vulnerability can make them so cautious that they're afraid to stand up for themselves. Many become solicitous doormats. Or they become the opposite: They project their own self-loathing onto others and lash out in rage at the slightest provocation, often driving people away and becoming social pariahs. And shame-based people usually become shaming parents, perpetuating the cycle of shame generation after generation.

SPIRITUALLY

Shame is a buzz saw that severs the connection between us and all that is sacred, holy, and pure. Religious people who have internalized shame—sometimes thanks to shaming from the very religious institutions they revere—often feel ashamed in the eyes of God: "A deity who knows all must know how shameful I am. I am unlovable even to an all-loving God." Shame-based people who are not religious are nevertheless alienated from forces larger than themselves. Their capacity for awe and wonder, their ability to appreciate and commune with nature, their access to the deep peace and bliss that is our human birthright—all this is lost to those who feel worthless and undeserving. Shame has pulled the plug on their higher selves and poisoned their spirits.

In all these ways, shame does damage to each component of the Quintessential Self. It also creates gaping chasms *between* the five components, causing us to feel fragmented. But the hopelessness that shame makes us feel is an illusion. Shame *can* be cast out. The Quintessential Self *can* be restored to wholeness. The rest of this chapter is devoted to that transformative process.

NAME THE SHAME

For thou shalt forget the shame of thy youth.

— ISAIAH 54:4

The first step to overcoming the ravages of shame is to recognize and accept a fundamental truth: The shame you've internalized has caused you pain and despair, but *it is not who you are.* In the eyes of God—or, if you prefer, in the orderly design of nature—you are worthy. Yes, you're imperfect, just like everyone else on the planet, but your existence has value and purpose. You are here to grow and learn and become the best possible human you can be. You deserve love and all of life's blessings.

This may be hard for you to accept at the moment, but it's true at the deepest level of your being. Read that paragraph over and over; repeat it to yourself like an affirmation. Eventually, you will not only believe it, but come to live its truth.

Another important task is to identify your voice of shame: the one that whispers that you are shameful, despicable, or inadequate; the one that taunts you unmercifully, insults you, and uses every mistake and foible as evidence that you are worthless. Be vigilant. As you develop the ability to recognize that voice, you will find that you can stop it in its tracks and replace its destructive messages with life-affirming truths.

Upon the ruins of shame, you can build a mansion of self-worth. The exercises that follow will help you do that, regardless of the source of your shame or how deeply entrenched it is. However, if as a child or adolescent you suffered physical violence, sexual molestation, or other severe forms of abuse, no book can give you everything you need to heal your wounds. In addition to the work you do here, be sure to take advantage of psychotherapy, support groups, and other resources that address your specific set of experiences. We'll be discussing those resources in a later chapter.

Let's identify the sources of your shame. Think back to your childhood. Who were the shamers? Your mother? Father? Siblings? Other family members? Schoolteachers? Friends? Make a list of all those who shamed you and write down *how* they shamed you, mentioning specific examples. These questions will help jog your childhood memories.

- Did anyone abandon you?
- Were you neglected?
- Were you abused, physically, verbally, or sexually?
- In what ways were you humiliated, belittled, or demeaned?
- Were you made to feel unwanted? Unacceptable? Useless?
- Were you compared unfavorably to other kids?
- Were you made to feel wrong, bad, or stupid?
- Were you taunted or teased by other kids?

Now think back to puberty and adolescence:

- If you were a girl, did people comment on your figure or your chances of attracting boys?
- If you were a boy, did anyone remark on the size of your penis or your overall manliness?
- Did your parents get on your back to work harder, groom yourself better, or achieve more so they could boast to other parents?
- Did they say things like, "We gave up everything for you, and this is how you thank us?" and "You're such an embarrassment. Why can't you be like so-and-so?"
- Were you told you'd never amount to anything?
- Were you humiliated by your teachers—or embarrassed by being singled out for praise?
- Were you shunned or ostracized by your peers?

Be sure to list all the sources of shame, even if they seem trivial from your adult perspective. Don't let anyone off the hook.

SHARE YOUR PAIN

It is enormously healing to speak out your shame. I strongly encourage you to find a trusted person—a psychotherapist or pastor, perhaps, or a trusted friend, or, if appropriate, your significant other—to whom you can safely describe the shameful experiences of the past. You must be sure that the person or persons you choose will respect your privacy, honor your confidentiality, and never use what you say against you in any way. The person should be a good, patient listener who understands that you need him or her simply to be there, not to solve your problems or offer unsolicited advice. He or she should be someone who will give you a hug if you need one, and who won't be uncomfortable if you get emotional. You don't want to feel inhibited.

Here is a way to ask for what you need. Feel free to say it in your own words. "I need to share something very personal with you. I'll need an undivided hour of your time. If I ask for feedback, please give it to me honestly. Otherwise, please just listen and make it safe for me to share what I have to express. Afterward, if you would like the same opportunity, we can arrange a time for that. I'd be honored to listen to whatever you'd like to share."

Choose a comfortable, quiet, private place in which to tell your story. When you're finished, receive whatever comfort and understanding the other person can provide. Let it sink into your awareness that he or she loves, respects, and accepts you for what you've revealed. Then take some time to relax and nurture yourself, either alone or with that person.

THE WRITE STUFF

Researchers have determined that suppressing negative feelings requires such arduous physical effort that it takes a toll on your health. Those who confide their troubles in a private diary often experience marked improvements in their health, attitude, and immune function.[2] One study found that people who write about their past traumas heal faster from physical illnesses such as asthma and arthritis, visit their doctors less frequently, and have stronger immune systems.[3] In other studies, college students who wrote about distressing experiences had improved grades, and unemployed engineers were more likely to find new jobs than out-of-work colleagues who did not do the writing exercises. Such is the power of expressing your feelings in writing.

In this exercise, you're going to write a letter of outrage to each of the people who shamed you. *No one will read these letters but you.* The purpose is not to hurt anyone or get revenge. It is to let out the feelings of hurt and rage that have been festering inside you. So don't hold back. Don't censor yourself. Don't worry about spelling, grammar, or coherence. Don't worry about being redundant. Take as many pages as you need for each letter.

Imagine that you can separate out the negative aspects of the people you are addressing. Set aside the parts of them that you love and respect. You are writing only to the parts that shamed you. Of course you understand them better now. Of course they too had pain. Of course they didn't know any better. But for now, speak to them as the child and adolescent who was hurt by them. Give yourself permission to be forceful. Use words you would never speak out loud. Accuse them. Condemn them. Say what they did to you and how it made you feel. Tell them how their shaming affected your life—your self-esteem, your sexuality, your relationships, your career, your state of mind, and your physical health.

Make sure to use explicit language. Cite examples, describing specific scenes in detail. There is great healing in specificity. And make sure you tell them, in your own strong words, "I did not deserve to be treated that way. I do not deserve to have this burden. I refuse to carry this shame any longer. I'm giving it back to you!" Giving them back the shame they laid on you is the way to get rid of it.

Set aside ample time to write your heart out. You don't want to feel rushed and you don't want to be interrupted. Begin with the shamers you feel strongest about and work your way down the list. You don't have to write all the letters in one sitting.

HAVE A BASH

The value of catharsis has been understood ever since the word was coined in ancient Greece, when Aristotle wrote about the cathartic power of tragic drama. In modern times, we have come to realize that physical catharsis can be a crucial element in healing. Sometimes we need to purge our systems of the pent-up remains of suppressed emotions, and we need to do it in a more muscular way than writing permits.

Once again, separate out the negative aspects of the people who shamed you, putting aside their positive qualities and all you loved about them. In a private place, arrange some thick pillows, a mattress, or a soft punching bag so that you can smash it with your fists or a child's plastic wiffle bat. You're going to discharge your rage safely and constructively.

Imagine that the face of the shamer is on the striking surface (use a photo or something that reminds you of the person if you think that will help). Assume a balanced stance so you don't fall or injure yourself. Take a few deep breaths and then let loose. Pound away. Bash. Smash. Hammer. Don't hold back. And let out your rage verbally at the same time. Roar. Yell. Shriek. Curse. As each painful memory comes up, shout out what they did to you and how much it's hurt you. Scream out, "Shame on you!" and imagine giving back the shame they dumped on you. (If you're concerned about being heard by the neighbors, put on some loud music to drown out your voice.) You may be surprised by the feelings that come up or the sounds that pour from your mouth. Trust the process. Don't suppress it. Let everything out.

Continue bashing each shamer until you feel emotionally spent or physically fatigued. You don't have to go through every person on your list in one session, but it is important to get to all of them eventually. Do this as often as necessary. It may take a number of sessions to feel complete with those who shamed you most.

You may find yourself resisting this exercise. You may feel foolish. You may feel awkward. You may feel guilty. That's only natural. But I strongly urge you to put your self-consciousness aside. This is a tremendously healing process, and you'll feel better having done it. Remember, you're not harming anyone. It is something you do *for yourself*, not *to* anyone else.

If you're feeling emotionally unstable, do the exercise in the presence of a psychotherapist or a trusted friend. If you think it's going to be physically taxing—if, for example, you have a heart condition or back pain—try a less demanding outlet, such as squeezing a stuffed doll, tearing pages from a telephone book, or throwing something against a wall.

When you're done for the day, treat yourself kindly and gently. You might want to shower or bathe, take a walk on the beach or in the woods, and treat yourself to something special—a nice meal, perhaps, or some form of entertainment. Congratulate yourself for exorcising the demons of shame.

BREAKING THE SHACKLES

Receive the light with passive and loving attention.
—THOMAS MERTON

The visualization exercise that follows is designed to help you break free of the self-perceptions that shame has inflicted upon you.

Begin by following the relaxation instructions on page 27. When you are fully relaxed in your place of peace and tranquillity, you see a doorway. You walk toward it and enter. Inside is a narrow stairway leading down. As you descend the stairs, it gets darker and darker, colder and colder. You reach the bottom of the stairs and suddenly find yourself in a dungeon.

There sits the part of you that has been damaged and diminished by shame. It's so dark, you can barely see your own hands. The chill, damp air penetrates to your bones. It smells rank and foul. Your shamed self is all alone, bound to a post by thick, steel chains—the shackles of shame. You feel them slicing through your skin. You hear the shrill, mocking voices of all the people who ever shamed you, echoing like a demonic chorus through the dungeon, telling you you're doomed to an eternity of bondage. You feel the agony of long, relentless years of pain and frustration as you tried in vain to free yourself. You cry out to be released. You vow that if you are set free you will live a life of value to yourself and others.

And then, high up in the dungeon, you notice a crack in the wall. A ray of light shines through. It grows brighter and brighter, gradually spreading throughout the dungeon. Soon this pure white light surrounds you, embracing you with the soothing warmth of love and truth.

Now the light enters your body. It illuminates the energy center at the base of your spine, infusing you with a sense of safety and security.

And the light moves up to the energy center in your genitals, restoring your capacity for passion and pleasure.

It rises up to your solar plexus, strengthening your sense of worth and self-esteem.

Now the light reaches the energy center of your heart, reawakening your ability to give and receive love.

And it fills your throat, activating the authentic voice of your spirit.

The light continues to rise, up to your forehead, infusing you with the wisdom to see through the lies of shame and know who you truly are.

And now the light fills the crown of your head, awakening your highest self and illuminating your eternal bond with all that is sacred.

As the light radiates throughout your body, you are filled with power and strength. You take a deep breath, and as you exhale, you spread your arms and expand your chest, shattering the shackles of shame that have imprisoned you all these years. They burst into pieces and fall to the ground, where they disintegrate. The dust of those once-heavy chains blows away with a gust of wind.

You look around. The room is filled with white light. It's warm. The voices of torment have given way to a choir of angels. You feel cleansed, you feel safe, you feel whole. You breathe your first truly free breath. You are filled with the vibrant energy of freedom and joy. Focus clearly on this healing image. Affirm to yourself that you will allow this feeling to continue to work deep within you.

When you are ready, you stand up on strong, sturdy legs and walk back up the stairs. You see a door leading to the outside. You open it and boldly reenter the world, knowing that you are in the light and of the light, that you always have been and always will be, that you are worthy and deserving, and fully open to loving and being loved.

When you feel complete, take a few minutes to slowly and gradually open your eyes.

Now take some time to symbolically cleanse yourself of any remaining shame. Take a shower or immerse yourself in a bathtub or pool. You might also want to create a ritual to mark the end of shame. Let the cleansing power of water wash away whatever you need to let go of. Take the letters of outrage you wrote, or your list of shaming incidents, and ceremoniously destroy them: burn them, tear them into small pieces and cast them to the wind, toss them into an ocean or river, or bury them in the earth. Cast them out. (If you want to keep those written exercises, make copies to destroy, or use something else that represents your shame, perhaps a drawing or a photo of the people who shamed you.)

This should not be treated as a one-time exercise. It may take a while to purge yourself of deep-seated shame. Consider doing it daily for a week and then anytime thereafter when you feel the need. I also strongly recommend the audiotape series "Ending Shame" from Concept Synergy (800-678-2356).

You may want to recite a prayer or affirmation to honor your breakthrough from the darkness of shame into the light of self-worth. Use a suitable invocation from your own spiritual tradition, or write one of your own. For example, one of my clients wrote: "In the deepest roots of my awareness, I have the power to weave golden threads of love and healing into the torn places of shame and sorrow. Through love for my whole self, including the painful events of the past, doors of hope spring open, revealing a gift of intimate understanding. As I turn the pages of my days, I make the decision to forgive and be forgiven and move on. I am free of the lies of shame."

4

The Slow Acid Drip
of Guilt and Regret

ENDING THE PAIN OF SELF-PUNISHMENT

Footfalls echo in the memory
Down the passage which we did not take
Towards the door we never opened
Into the rose-garden.

—T. S. ELIOT

One of the most poignant moments in American film comes in *On the Waterfront*, when an anguished Marlon Brando cries, "I coulda been a contender. I coulda been somebody. Instead of a bum, which is what I am." The line "I coulda been a contender" has become part of our language because it resonates with something deep in the human psyche: regret. As the poet John Greenleaf Whittier pointed out, the saddest words of tongue or pen are, "It might have been."

In my 30 years as a psychotherapist I have listened to people complain that they coulda been contenders if only they'd worked harder to accomplish their goals—and highly successful people lament that they didn't stop to smell the roses or participate more actively in raising their children. I've heard people wish they'd never gotten married—and others weep over the man or woman who got away or failed to show up. I've had people kick themselves for not trying harder to save their marriage—and others declare that they should have gotten divorced sooner. I've seen people punish themselves for not taking more risks—and others wish they'd played it safer. The list goes on, and it often includes the regret that they did not come to therapy sooner.

Regret seems to be part of the human condition, the price we pay for the gifts of memory and imagination. Our minds are wired to think, "I should have . . . ," "Why didn't I . . . ?" and "I wish I hadn't . . ." It would be as unrealistic to think you can live regret-free as it would be to think you can undo the past. But the miracle of human memory becomes a curse instead of a blessing when we continuously rewind the tape of life and wish we could edit it so every past decision works out perfectly, every word we've ever uttered sounds golden, and every action is heroic. It's one thing to have an occasional wistful thought of what might have been—"It would have been nice if I had done such and such," or "I wish I hadn't done that, I'll know better next time"—and quite another to agonize compulsively over roads not taken and decisions irreversibly made. What's important is the degree to which you are tormented by regrets.

Are you stuck in the past, constantly wishing you could do things over again? Do you expend so much energy ruminating about regrets that you can't enjoy the present? Does regret inhibit your decisionmaking? Is it making you feel dejected or forlorn? These are signs of unhealthy regret.

THE MOMENTOUS GAP

"Between what one wishes to become and what one has become, there can be a momentous gap," wrote the novelist James Baldwin. Regret is the painful feeling that comes when you stare into that gap and compare what is with what might have been. Even if it seems like only a mild annoyance, like the steady drip of a faucet, regret can destroy your peace of mind because each drop sears like acid, carving a chasm deeper and deeper into your soul.

It has been said that we live the first half of our lives with unrealistic expectations and the second half with regret. That's a bleak assessment, of course, but not far off the mark. In our culture, it's as hard to escape regret as it is to avoid advertising. No society in history has afforded human beings as much freedom to choose their own lifestyle or values. But that freedom comes with a hefty price tag. When your possibilities are limited only by the borders of your imagination, so are your opportunities for regret. Dreaming impossible dreams can be a formula for magnificent achievement, but it can also create a downward spiral of desire, disappointment, and discontent. We look around and see that others have something we don't: They're thinner, richer, more powerful, more successful, better looking, happier; they have nicer cars, bigger homes, better spouses, perfect kids. And those are just the real human beings. Add the fantasy images in films and commercials, and you have a surefire formula for envy and regret.

This ongoing comparison between our real self and our fantasized self—between who we are and what we wish we could be—can keep us in a constant state of agitation. There is always something we haven't done, something we haven't accomplished, something we don't have. When we look back to see what went wrong, we recall certain turning points and think, "If only . . ." We are especially vulnerable to harsh assessments during midlife, when most of us compare where we are to where we hoped or assumed we would be. Baby boomers are especially vulnerable to this, having grown up believing that they can do it all and have everything.

Regret is the misery we inflict upon ourselves for not taking a more compassionate and forgiving look at our past. In many instances it amounts to self-punishment based on make-believe. Instead of fantasizing about the future, we fantasize a fairytale past: "If only I had done such and such, everything would have turned out great!" That sort of thinking invariably leads to self-blame and hating ourselves for what we did or did not do.

The punishment is compounded each time something happens that resembles the original regret: "There I go again! I should have known better by now! I'm so stupid, I'm so screwed up, I'm so [you name it]." The pain of that self-punishment can lead to a tragic timidity—a phenomenon known as *regret avoidance behavior.* Many regretful people enclose themselves in a box, limiting themselves to the safe areas of life, unwilling to take risks because they're afraid they will once again do something they'll regret.

They end up in a predictable rut. The irony is that they end up with *more* to regret: lost opportunities, stifled desires, and crushed dreams, not to mention the time they've spent wallowing in regret instead of enjoying their lives.

Regret avoidance can also lead to the opposite behavior: impulsivity and foolish risk-taking. People who feel that they've missed out on opportunities in the past will often go to extremes to make up for it, hoping to avoid similar regrets in the future. As the economic juggernaut of the 1990s rolled along and the Dow climbed inexorably toward the 10,000 mark, more and more clients told me how much they regretted not getting into the market earlier. Seeing others double or triple their investments was driving them crazy. Unfortunately, many were so eager to make up for lost time that they bought overvalued stocks or threw more money than they could afford into high-risk investments. The attempt to make up for regret has other expressions as well, like the middle-aged man who regrets getting married too young and working too hard, and suddenly leaves his family, quits his job, and plunges headlong into a foolish romance.

TAKING STOCK OF REGRET

"My past changes every minute according to the meaning given it now, in this moment," said the Nobel Prize–winning writer Czeslaw Milosz. The past is, indeed, mutable. You can change its meaning by changing your perception of it and the uses to which you put it.

Let's begin the process of resolving your regrets by making a complete inventory of them. Write down all the actions and decisions you wish you could take back, the significant turning points that you wish you could revisit and handle differently. Take your time with this. Include even those regrets that may now seem minor or trivial. And don't restrict yourself to the memories you think about frequently. Dig beneath the surface for regrets you may have suppressed because they're too painful to look at. Use the life story you created in chapter 1 to help you identify these.

Completing the following sentence fragments will help you articulate your regrets. Use whichever sentences fit your circumstances, and write as much as you need to complete your thoughts.

I wish I had never_____.

If only I had_____.

I didn't do the right thing when_____.

I failed to live up to my values when_____.

I wish I had taken better care of myself (physically, emotionally, financially, etc.) when_____.

I wish I had said_____.

If only I hadn't said_____.

A decision I wish I hadn't made is_____.

I wish I had spent more time_____.

I'm sorry I didn't listen to my intuition when_____.

I should have taken a stand when_____.

I could have done more to _____.

Look at every aspect of your life to make sure you don't leave anything out. Are there career or education decisions you wish you hadn't made? Risks you wish you had taken—or *not* taken? Do you think back longingly to a love affair you wish had never ended—or bitterly at one you wish had ended sooner? Are you sorry you rejected someone you were attracted to—or caused him or her to reject you? Do you wish you'd moved to another location—or hadn't moved? Do you wish you could take back things you said to a parent, boss, friend, or child? Can you remember moments when you wished you'd been more courageous? More generous? More aware? Did you ever betray your truest self for the sake of money or security—or turn away from an opportunity because of fear or a desire to please someone else?

A GAME OF "WHAT IF"

Once you've completed your list, contemplate each of your regrets and complete the sentence, "What I should have done instead is _____."

Now ask yourself how your life would have been different if you had done everything the way you wish you had with the benefit of

20–20 hindsight. Do you think those alternative scenarios are realistic? Would each story really have had a happily-ever-after ending?
Or is it possible that things might even have turned out worse?

It's important to be realistic about imagined outcomes. One of
the reasons regret is so corrosive is that our minds are capable of
utopian visions. We dream great dreams, and when they don't
materialize we dream of what might have been. But we can never
really be sure what would have happened had we done things differently. Life is far too complex for that. In most instances, it's
just as likely that the decision you now wish you'd made would
have set in motion a chain of events leading to disappointment or
disaster.

Remember the movie *It's a Wonderful Life*? In it, James Stewart
is about to commit suicide when an angel rescues him and shows
him what life would have been like for his family and his town if he
had never lived. This changes the character's attitude from despair
and regret to gratitude and determination. Try doing the same
now with your list of regrets. Ask yourself what *really* might have
happened had you done things differently:

> What experiences might you have missed out on?
> What people might you not have known?
> What opportunities might not have come your way?
> Who might have been hurt?
> How much love might you have lost or never found?
> What accidents, illnesses, or other tragedies might have
>   ensued?
> What jobs or opportunities might not have come your way?
> What life lessons might you not have learned?

Let yourself imagine the worst. Chances are, those scenarios
are no more unrealistic than the gratifying fantasies that fuel your
regrets. Can you accept that in many cases your life might not
have been appreciably better if you had done things differently—
and in some ways might even have been worse?

ALL GOD'S CHILDREN
GOT SHOULDS

Regrets are a way of punishing ourselves with what the eminent psychologist Karen Horney called "the tyranny of the should." As we grow up we internalize a set of rules and expectations from parents, teachers, and other authority figures: "I should never make mistakes," "I should always work hard," "I should always be the best," "I should never upset anyone." If these shoulds are rigid, demanding, or unreasonable, we grow up with a propensity for guilt and regret because they are extremely hard to live up to. One reason you might be burdened by regret, therefore, is that you feel you've let someone down—perhaps a father or mother who expected a great deal from you and piled a heavy load of shoulds on your shoulders. Maybe you've been judging yourself by someone else's impossible standards.

Look back over your list of regrets and ask yourself, "Who am I trying to please?" "Whose approval am I desperately seeking?" "Whose standards have I internalized?" "Which unreasonable and unrealistic rules am I trying to live up to?" To heal those regrets—and prevent similar ones from arising in the future— you have to give up straining to be someone you are not. You have to forgive yourself for not being perfect and stop expecting super-human feats from yourself. You have to accept yourself as you are instead of as you—or other people—think you should be. And you have to declare loud and strong that you don't owe it to any-one else, living or dead, to fulfill their dreams or live according to their rules.

One good way to take the edge off regrets that stem from unfair and unreasonable expectations is to rephrase the way you articulate them. Look at your list of "I should haves." Write down a lighter, more forgiving phrase instead: "It would have been nice if _____." Speak the new words aloud as you write them down. Then, with conviction and resolve, repeatedly cross out the shoulds until you can't see them anymore.

ACCEPTING YOUR MISTAKES

The only man who makes no mistakes is the man who never does anything.

— ELEANOR ROOSEVELT

I'm sure that some of your regrets are unequivocally regrettable. We've all done things whose outcomes can only be construed as negative. If, for example, you sold a stock whose value tripled the following week, or drove carelessly and wrecked your car, your regret is understandable. I know a defense attorney who wanted so badly to beat a particular prosecutor in court that he compromised the ethical principles of his profession to get his client off on a technicality. Within a week, the client killed two people. The lawyer has lived with that regret ever since and probably always will. But he turned it into something more than a painful memory: He lives and works by a rigorous code of ethics now, and works tirelessly for crime prevention and victims' rights.

To make peace with such regrets, it is vital to remember that the person you used to be was less mature, less wise, and less informed than the person you are. You could not possibly have known then what you know now. Everyone makes mistakes. In fact, highly successful, creative people make *more* mistakes than the rest of us because they're always trying new things and searching for better ways to do them. The difference is, they look their mistakes squarely in the eye, learn from them, and move on. So cut yourself some slack and accept that you are not perfect, because imperfection is the human condition and your curriculum on planet Earth is to learn and grow.

Try to look back at the actions you've come to regret and remember exactly who you were, what you knew and didn't know, what you reasonably assumed, and what your actual choices were. What needs, hopes, and dreams did you have? What influences were impinging on you? Replay the entire scenario in your mind and look for the things you did that were right instead of only your mistakes.

This reassessment can help you see the person you once were in a kinder, more compassionate, and more realistic light. Can you now say to yourself, "I made the best possible choice under the circumstances," or "I did the best I could under those conditions"? Give yourself the benefit of the doubt, as you would to anyone else who made a decision he or she regrets. You wouldn't tolerate a spouse or roommate who constantly reminded you of your past mistakes, so why tolerate it from yourself?

In this context, this familiar passage from Reinhold Niebuhr's "Serenity Prayer," is well worth remembering: "God grant me the serenity to accept the things I cannot change, the courage to change the things I can, and the wisdom to know the difference."

JEALOUSY: SLAYING THE GREEN-EYED MONSTER

Many of our regrets are caused by what Shakespeare called the "green-eyed monster": jealousy. That fire-breathing demon is so insatiable that many of us live with a feeling of perpetual deprivation. When you can always find someone who has something you don't, you can't help but look at some of your past actions with regret.

It is extremely important to realize that life is a series of trade-offs. No one has everything. The person you envy envies someone else—maybe you. The person who has something you wish you had wishes he or she had something, too—maybe something you have. My co-author, for example, was once extremely envious of a fellow writer he'd just met. Phil liked the man, but was so jealous of his success as a screenwriter with a stratospheric income and an Oscar nomination that he almost said no when the fellow invited him to lunch. He thought it would be too painful to hear about the guy's career. At lunch it was revealed that the screenwriter envied Phil! Why? Because Phil had published a novel and he had been unable to sell his own. He had invited Phil to lunch to ask his advice. This important lesson in the relativity of envy was driven home with even greater force when the conversation turned personal. The screenwriter's wife had just run off with another man and a big chunk of their savings.

Are any of your regrets rooted in envy or jealousy? One excellent remedy is to do what Phil did inadvertently: Get to know someone who has what you wish you had, or has done what you wish you had done. If you can't meet such a person, try to learn as much as you can about one by speaking to others or reading a biography. Make sure you look at *all* aspects of the person's life, not just the parts you envy. Chances are you will find ample evidence of pain and suffering, weaknesses and shortcomings, deprivations and hardships. You may still wish you had something he or she has, but you probably won't want the whole package.

There is another reason to study those you envy: to learn from them. One of the best ways to slay regrets based on jealousy is to get what you wish you had. And one way to do that is to learn how others did it. "Find out what skills or qualities enabled the person to attain what you envy, then see if you can emulate them," writes Mark Goulston in *Get Out of Your Own Way*.

LEARNING THE RIGHT LESSONS

"Mistakes are the portals of discovery," said James Joyce. Look honestly and carefully at your biggest regrets and try to extract from them the most important lessons you can—not just the obvious or easy lessons, but the subtle and difficult ones as well. Here are two examples of learning the wrong lessons. A client of mine had deep regrets because her husband had walked out on her. When I asked her what lessons she could derive from the experience, she said, "I shouldn't have provoked him into leaving." Her ex-husband had openly cheated on her and beat her up numerous times. The more constructive lesson would have been: It was not my fault, I deserve better, and I must not tolerate physical and emotional abuse. Another client had been caught cheating on his income taxes and owed the IRS a great deal of money. What was his regret? That he should have done a better job of not getting caught. Wrong lesson!

"A man who makes a mistake and doesn't correct it," said Confucius, "is committing another mistake." By deriving the wrong lesson from regrettable experiences, you run the risk of repeating the same mistake and ending up with something new to regret. What are the most valuable lessons you can derive from your past regrets? Which lessons will best help you prevent future recurrences? For each of your major regrets, fill in the blanks in the following statement:

> If I ever [describe the event] again, I will not [describe the regrettable behavior]. Instead, I will [describe the preferred behavior].

When your energy is consumed by regret, you lose the power to enjoy the present and make your dreams come true. By looking at your past actions in the light of your present understanding, you can convert regret into wisdom, reduce the negative charge attached to those memories, and strengthen your ability to create a regret-free future.

TRANSMUTING GUILT INTO GOLD

Guilt is never a rational thing. It distorts all the faculties of the human mind, it perverts them, it leaves a man no longer in the free use of his reason, it puts him in confusion.
— EDMUND BURKE

Guilt is to ordinary regret what imprisonment is to probation. It is a far more brutal punishment: The spirit is incarcerated, the agony is severe, and the stigma is hard to erase. All of it is self-inflicted, of course. You've put yourself on trial, prosecuted yourself, and sentenced yourself to a long period—perhaps even a lifetime—of self-contempt. That's what guilt is: self-inflicted punishment for something you've done—or believe you've done—to betray or harm another person, or to violate a sacred principle (for religious people, this amounts to feeling guilty in the eyes of God).

THE ORIGINS OF GUILT

Our parents are the primary architects of conscience. They supply us with our basic sense of right and wrong. Very early in life we learn to trust the signals they use to let us know when we've lived up to their expectations and when we haven't. When they say we did something wrong, we listen—not just because we don't want to be punished, but because we sense that their disapproval is rooted in a deep concern for our welfare. However, many parents go overboard, using guilt as a teaching tool, a means of control, and a form of discipline. They use statements like, "I sacrifice everything for you and look at how you treat me," and "You'll be the death of me," as well as an arsenal of sighs and moans, expressions of hurt, and gestures of exasperation, all intended to induce the desired behavior through guilt.

Parents are also the guardians of our family and cultural traditions, representing social roots that may extend far back in history. In many cases, they use guilt to encourage offspring to perpetuate those traditions. I've heard therapists say, "Thank God for the Catholic Church and Jewish mothers, they count for ninety percent of our clients." It's a joke, of course, but children of certain ethnic backgrounds *are* taught that not doing exactly what they're told amounts to punishing their parents, their ancestors, or their religious leaders. How can children not feel guilty for punishing those who love and protect them?

As with shame, a small degree of guilt can be healthy. Early in life, a proper dose of homeopathic guilt can help instill the capacity for remorse. It leads to the development of a moral structure that encompasses respect for other people's needs, feelings, and welfare. It provides a language for the voice of conscience and establishes moral guideposts for the future. The capacity for guilt enables us to know when we've done something wrong, motivates us to seek a remedy, and inspires us to do better in the future. For example, if you break your word, a dose of medicinal guilt can move you to own up to your misconduct and take steps to make amends.

Healthy guilt can also serve as a warning system. Like the dashboard lights that tell us the car door is open or the gas tank is low, a twinge of guilt can warn us that we're about to do something we shouldn't do. It can stop us in our tracks before we do something we'll truly regret. You start to tell a lie, and guilt feelings tell you to alter the sentence. You're attracted to a sexy stranger, and guilt buzzes you like a pager and reminds you that you're married.

For all these reasons, nature wired us with the capacity to feel guilt. The problem is, there is a dark side to guilt, as there is with so many other aspects of our humanity, and that dark side is irrational, cruel, and relentless.

When parents use guilt excessively or inappropriately, they lay the groundwork for excessive and inappropriate *self-imposed* guilt. In their constant search for love and approval, children internalize the voice of the guilt-inducing parent. Even where guilt is not applied blatantly, too much disapproval and criticism can create a habit of self-blame because children always feel guilty when they don't meet their parents' expectations.

One of the most difficult tasks of adulthood is to come to terms with the values and expectations imposed by our parents and to some extent the rest of society. The seminal stages of this struggle occur during adolescence, but the challenge of declaring our independence can continue well into middle age. It is almost impossible to go through this process without suffering some guilt pangs: "I'm letting them down." "What would they think?" We want to do right by our parents' wishes, but we also have to assert our own power and respect our own values. If this conflict remains unresolved, the propensity for guilt becomes a permanent feature of the psyche, triggering guilt feelings at the slightest provocation. Guilt-prone people convict themselves of crimes they didn't commit and punish themselves excessively for the things they did wrong.

In many cases, the guilt-prone imagine that their behavior had tragic consequences when there is no evidence that it actually did. This is essentially a reverse form of delusions of grandeur. You exaggerate your power to do harm and believe you can control situations that in fact you have no control over. Take, for example, an otherwise rational and fact-driven biologist named Karen. One stressful day she lost her temper when she was inconvenienced by her dentist's receptionist. Two weeks later she learned that the receptionist no longer worked at the clinic, had moved out of her rented apartment, and removed her child from the day care center where Karen sent her own child. Without even considering other explanations, Karen concluded that she had cost the receptionist her job, which led to her eviction and her inability to pay for day care. She wracked herself with guilt for three months. One day, she spotted the former receptionist on the commuter train. Summoning up her courage, she went over to apologize for what she had done and see if she could make up for it somehow. But before she could speak, the other woman told her happily that she'd left her job because a terrific opportunity had come along and she had moved to another town with her son. She didn't even remember Karen's temper tantrum.

Particularly vulnerable to guilt are those who were raised to have the self-image, "I am a good person." Always be good, always be nice, always be kind and thoughtful and generous—wonderful virtues to cultivate, certainly, but when goals like that become an absolute imperative, it's a surefire formula for guilt. Whenever such people deviate even the slightest from their saintly image of goodness, they feel as though they've betrayed something sacred. They can never accept the basic truth that even good people sometimes mess up, act selfishly, and hurt people inadvertently. Then, to prove to themselves how good they *really* are, they punish themselves with guilt. It's as if by feeling guilty, they are declaring, "I'm a good person after all because I can inflict this punishment on myself for doing wrong."

Sometimes guilt-prone people can't win for losing because they've internalized conflicting messages. A client named Arthur, for example, had a free-spending father whose philosophy was, "Enjoy what you have while you have it." His mother was a pennypincher who was always trying to rein in her husband and get him to salt away money for a rainy day. Arthur grew up hearing loud arguments over the family budget, absorbing contradictory lessons from his parents. As an adult, he was doomed no matter what he did. If he spent money, he felt guilty for violating his mother's principles. If he denied his family the things they wanted in order to save, he felt guilty for negating his father. It took a lot of work to get Arthur to a point where he could hear the voice of his own truth instead of his parents' contradictions.

Another important cause of guilt is clinical depression. Depression is incapacitating. Like other illnesses, it leads to a certain amount of self-absorption, which makes it harder to be there for other people. That can create situations that leave you feeling guilty for letting someone down. Depression erodes your self-image because it plainly reveals your dark side and renders you unable to function effectively. This can lead to the irrational notion that you are the cause of everything that goes wrong, not only with your own life but also with your family, your job, and your circle of acquaintances. Finally, when you are depressed everything seems worthless, hopeless, and bleak. This makes you extremely vulnerable to existential questions like, "What did I do to deserve this? What have I done to bring this misery upon myself?" As a psychiatrist I have had countless occasions to see people view the exact same incidents from their past in a totally different light once their clinical depression lifts. (We'll discuss ways to treat depression in chapter 8.)

As you can see, guilt has many roots, some healthy and some unhealthy. What's important is to distinguish between the two now. When guilt is the product of a mature conscience, it prompts us to take action, whether to make a situation better, to make amends to someone we hurt, or to change our behavior in the future. Unhealthy guilt is a form of self-punishment that leads to inhibition, self-defeating behavior, and unnecessary pain.

THE RAVAGES OF GUILT

Guilt is the Mafia of the mind.

— BOB MANDEL

Innocent until proven guilty may be a fundamental premise of our justice system, but you'd never know it by the way guilt-prone people treat themselves. As with shame, habitual guilt-tripping can eventually lead to feelings of worthlessness. You might sentence yourself to an emotional chain gang because deep down you feel that anyone who has committed the sins you have does not deserve happiness. You might deny yourself love or success for the same reason. Every time you have an opportunity for one of life's blessings, you sabotage it, as if you were not only judge and jury but executioner as well.

In many cases, the self-deprivation takes a specific form corresponding to what the person feels guilty about. If you blame yourself for mistreating someone, for example, you might go overboard to be nice to people and become a doormat or a wimp. If you did something unethical in a business deal, you might give yourself the short end of every new transaction. If you committed a sexual transgression, you might deny yourself sex. I've known people who stayed celibate for years because every time they were attracted to someone the parole officer in their brain made them take a cold shower.

Those who inherit a rigid standard of duty and responsibility find it especially hard to escape the jaws of guilt, often becoming workaholics as a result. Did your parents teach you that grown-ups take life very seriously and those who treat it lightly end up losers? Were you told to keep your nose to the grindstone at all times or you'll lose your edge and everything will fall apart? Whenever you start to have a little too much fun, does a voice in your head growl, "Get back to work, you lazy bum"? Some guilt-prone people always feel that they're not doing enough for those who depend on them. Taken to an extreme, that tendency produces martyrdom, in which the person is emotionally dying so that others can be happy.

People who are prone to guilt may also judge themselves harshly for having certain thoughts and feelings. Guilty thoughts are usually sexual, aggressive, or mean-spirited in nature. You fantasize going to bed with that foxy stranger and immediately feel as though you'd actually betrayed your spouse. You imagine beating someone up, then punish yourself as if you'd actually committed assault. You have a resentful thought about your parents and punish yourself for being ungrateful or, worse, a horrible person.

Many people feel guilty for simply having certain emotions. In some households, for instance, it is considered wrong to be sad; in others, even feeling happy is unacceptable. Have you ever told yourself that you should not feel rage, jealousy, despair, or other feelings that were unacceptable to your caregivers? You may be using guilt to camouflage those forbidden emotions. It's absolutely vital to remember that we all have thoughts and feelings that we think we're not supposed to have; venal, malicious notions flicker across the screen of everyone's mind. Rarely do they have actual consequences. Punishing yourself, or imagining that you're going to rot in hell, is to attribute magical power to your thoughts or to view God as cruel and unforgiving—and yourself as a hopeless sinner.

IRRATIONAL GUILT

Sometimes we do something patently wrong, perhaps even reprehensible, with consequences so horrible that mere remorse seems inadequate. At such times the self-imprisonment of perpetual guilt seems to be the only appropriate justice. One day a client of mine named Alfred got behind the wheel of his car while drunk and smashed into a concrete barrier. He survived, but he wishes he hadn't. His two-year-old son was killed. Every minute of Alfred's life is hell. Forgiveness is out of the question; he can't even hear the word without losing his temper. He feels he does not deserve to live. If he didn't have a wife and daughter to care for, he would have committed suicide by now. Alfred the judge has convicted Alfred the criminal to eternal guilt. It will be a very long time before he sees fit to reduce the sentence to remorse.

In most cases, however, the torment of constant guilt amounts to life without parole for a misdemeanor—cruel and unusual punishment by any reasonable standard. Let's look at another example. Justin and Carolyn Hart live in Los Angeles. Six years ago, their daughter was brutally murdered in Boston by a psychopath who had stalked her for weeks. To lose your only child in such a nightmarish way is more painful than anything one can imagine. But Carolyn compounded her grief with irrational guilt. The murder occurred between Christmas and the New Year. The Harts had urged their daughter to come home for the holidays, but she had decided to stay in Boston to move into her new apartment. "We should have mailed her a plane ticket," lamented Carolyn as she wept uncontrollably. "We should have *insisted* that she come home." Their daughter was 35 when she was killed. She had no intention of spending the holiday in California, ticket or no ticket. Yet Carolyn has tortured herself for six years now, with no let-up in sight. Every time she lets her guard down and begins to laugh or enjoy herself, the demon of guilt pounces: "You could have saved your child. You have no right to feel good!"

Alfred lost a child and the Harts lost a child. Their grief can't be measured. But the guilt in Alfred's case has a sense of logic and justice to it. Carolyn's guilt is unreasonable and unfair. Why do people subject themselves to such irrational torment? One factor is a propensity for guilt that was internalized in early childhood. Another is distorted thinking. The most common guilt-inducing thought patterns are:

- *Self-blaming:* You see problems and crises as your fault, whether the facts support that conclusion or not.
- *Catastrophizing:* You anticipate disasters and assume the worst.
- *Discounting the positive:* You ignore the positive influence you have on events and focus on the negative, even in the absence of evidence.
- *Exaggeration:* You believe your impact is greater than it actually is.
- *Either/or thinking:* You see everything you do as either terrific or awful.
- *Emotional reasoning:* You assume that if you feel something, it must be true in actuality.
- *Shoulding:* Your self-talk is overrun with words like *should, shouldn't, must,* and *mustn't,* signaling rigid rules and directives.

Do any of those patterns help explain your irrational guilt? Are you sure, for example, that the harm you think you caused actually occurred? Are you certain that the problems you see were actually created by your actions? By recognizing distorted thought patterns, you can reduce the guilt associated with past events and stop future guilt in its tracks.

THE USES OF GUILT

Are you willing to relieve yourself of the burden of guilt? Before you answer, "Yes, yes, of course I am!" take a moment to consider what you'll be giving up. There are reasons we guilt ourselves. Consider some of the hidden payoffs:

- *Guilt bolsters your self-image.* It may sound paradoxical, but the discomfort of guilt can allow you to demonstrate that you are a genuinely caring, responsible person. The more anguish you inflict on yourself, the more superior you believe yourself to be.
- *Guilt reduces your risks.* When you find yourself in conflict with the values of your upbringing or the larger society, feeling guilty can spare you the discomfort of declaring your own uniqueness and standing up for your own beliefs. It's often easier to punish yourself for breaking the rules than to challenge their validity.
- *Guilt earns you sympathy.* If you tell others how guilty you feel, you can bask in their comforting words. You might even be praised for your virtue. In most cases displays of guilt only make you an object of pity, but it's easy to mistake that for sympathy.
- *Guilt gives you an excuse.* By filling your time with ruminations about the past, guilt can be a highly effective way to avoid present challenges. It also gives you a way to rationalize failure: You don't deserve success because you're guilty of horrible offenses.
- *Guilt gives you the illusion of exoneration.* Unconsciously, you think that if you make yourself miserable enough, you'll somehow be absolved of past misdeeds. This is especially common with religious people who feel that God will hear their self-punishing thoughts and forgive them. But it occurs with non-religious people as well; on some level, everyone suspects that the universe operates under an omniscient code of justice.

Is your guilt providing you with any of these hidden payoffs? Are you are willing to trade them for peace of mind?

BREAKING THE GRIP OF GUILT

To a large extent, freeing yourself from the prison of guilt means developing a more realistic and compassionate view of yourself and your past actions. It's time to get beyond self-blame and accept life as it has unfolded. You did what you did. It can't be undone. But it can be better understood, and it can be forgiven—if not yet completely, then at least enough for you to emerge from the prison you've placed yourself in and start life afresh.

It might help to remember that the mere fact that you feel guilty is a sign of a healthy conscience. It shows that there is love and goodness in you, and that you care about the consequences of your actions. Your guilt may be excessive or irrational, but that is a far better state of affairs than being incapable of guilt. Complete absence of guilt is the primary characteristic of the sociopath, who proceeds through life cheating, stealing, and swindling without any regard for others.

"A man should never be afraid to own he has been in the wrong," wrote Alexander Pope, "which is but saying, in other words, that he is wiser today than he was yesterday." Owning up to your past actions is mature and healthy when placed in the proper context: with the realization that you were less wise than you are now.

Another important step is to look at the actions you feel guilty about and identify what you did that was right and good in the same context or a similar one. This will help you get over the feeling that you're all bad. Also, examine the rules and values that lay behind your guilt feelings. Are they yours or someone else's? Do they represent the standards by which you choose to measure your actions? If your guilt is tied to other people's ideas about the right way to live, give yourself permission to be a unique individual with standards of your own.

APPEALING YOUR VERDICT

You have prosecuted yourself and sentenced yourself to feeling guilty. Are you ready to appeal the verdict? Let's take it to the supreme court—the court of higher awareness.

As with the earlier visualizations, I recommend that you make a tape recording of the following instructions. Once again, begin by sitting comfortably. Take five deep breaths and relax completely, as described on page 27. Once you're completely relaxed, begin the visualization.

Imagine yourself in a courtroom. See yourself sitting in the defendant's chair, with handcuffs on your wrists. Next to you is the calm, dignified figure of your defense attorney. Behind the judge's desk sits an embodiment of wisdom, compassion, and truth. Perhaps it's a religious or spiritual figure you revere, or some respected person from your own life, or a man or woman from history, or perhaps your higher self. Choose an appropriate image for you.

The judge calls the proceedings to order. Your attorney rises and speaks to the court on your behalf, acknowledging your responsibility for what happened and explaining all the mitigating circumstances that contributed to the event. If there were misunderstandings involved, those are described. If the consequences of your action were not as catastrophic as previously believed, those corrections are placed in the record. If you were less culpable than the prosecution portrayed you to be, that is made clear. Have your attorney make as strong a case as possible for exonerating you or reducing your sentence. If appropriate, bring in character witnesses to testify about the good things you've done in your life and of your value to your family and community.

Now it's your turn to address the court. Rise and speak from the heart. Explain how badly you feel for what happened in the past. Describe the lessons you've learned because of what happened. Show remorse. Express your willingness to make amends. If appropriate, ask for mercy.

Sit for a moment in silence as the judge contemplates the testimony.

Now the judge is ready to speak. Allow him or her to render a new verdict. Are you absolved of all wrongdoing? Is your sentence commuted to time already served? Are you placed on probation? Are you given a creative alternative to the imprisonment of guilt, such as community service? Are you told to make amends to the injured party? If so, what must you do?

When your judge is finished speaking, you rise and express gratitude to the court for its mercy and compassion. You promise to abide by the verdict. Your handcuffs are removed.

Now you see a door with an EXIT sign. You open it, and immediately you're surrounded by white light. Let the light fill your body with healing warmth, dissolving all remaining guilt and regret. The torment of needless self-recrimination is washed away, just as the darkness in a room is dispersed when you turn on the light. As you walk into the world a free person, you're at peace with yourself.

When you feel ready, slowly open your eyes.

You can practice this visualization for every issue that has caused you to feel guilty. Feel free to repeat it every day for as long as the guilt remains. You might also practice a healing light imagery. Light is the source of all life, warmth, and healing energy. Healing light visualizations have been used as an effective adjunct to conventional medical treatment, with everything from minor wounds to cancer. Using it as a daily practice can lighten your load and enhance your inner peace. Simply take a few deep breaths and feel the radiant light embrace you and penetrate each part of you. Relax with this inner light for 5 or 10 minutes, then slowly open your eyes. If you experience any lingering pressure in your head or any irritability, be sure to take some additional time to rest.

EXPRESSING YOUR GUILT

We resist making our guilt feelings known for a number of reasons: We fear embarrassment, humiliation, or retaliation; we fear that others will lose respect for us or renounce us entirely; we fear that the information will be used against us. If you can overcome these fears, confession may be good for your soul. But only if it's appropriate, if the benefits outweigh the risks, and if it can be done in a safe environment.

The first question that must be answered is whether to confess to the person you have injured, assuming he or she does not already know what you did. In some cases, confession is vital and healing for everyone concerned; in others, it may be a relief to the confessor but a crushing blow to someone else. Laura had been riddled with guilt for nearly a year because, in a moment of careless lust, she'd had (protected) sex with her friend's fiancé. Haunted by guilt, she thought she ought to own up to both her friend and her own husband. She thought the truth might help her friend see what a jerk she was about to marry. She thought it might even make her own marriage better, since it would bring her discontent to the surface. But she could not bring herself to confess. While she tried to summon the courage, her friend's engagement ended of its own accord. Still, Laura agonized over whether she should come clean. Didn't she owe it to her husband to tell him everything? Wouldn't her friend learn a valuable lesson? In the end, though, she realized that her urge to tell all was selfish; she wanted relief from the terrible burden she was carrying. But her friend was now rebuilding her life, and she and her husband were seeing a counselor. Confession would only cause pain to people she loved—and probably damage her children as well. It might even mark the end of her friendship and her marriage. By remaining silent and being the best wife and friend she could be, Laura was able to make amends in her own way and preserve both relationships.

As a therapist I have had countless guilt-ridden people tell me about their extramarital affairs and ask if they should tell their spouses. It is always a wrenching decision, and there is no clearcut formula for making it, with one exception: when the sex was not safe and a serious health risk is involved. Research indicates that coming clean more often than not leads to the destruction of the marriage. That does not mean it should never be done. In some cases, the couple's love is strong enough to endure the turbulence that such a revelation always unleashes, whereas it might *not* withstand the slow erosion of intimacy that can take place if the guilty partner were to hold onto the secret forever. In other instances, discretion is indeed the better part of valor, particularly if the adulterer can strengthen the relationship by channeling his or her guilt into a deeper commitment and more generous love. (The same reasoning applies to other guilty actions, from an ethical lapse in business to betraying a friend's confidence.)

It is very important to determine whether confession will do more harm than good. Ask yourself how the other person is likely to react. Usually there is no precedent for knowing this; you might have to infer what will happen on the basis of related experiences and your knowledge of the person's character. In some cases, the opinion of a therapist or trusted friend can be very helpful. Ask yourself if your relationship can withstand the anger that might erupt. How will you hold up to hostility, bitterness, mistrust, or revenge? Above all, look clearly and rationally at the impact your confession might have on the other person. Honesty is an important virtue, but love and compassion are even more important. Will the other person be better off if he or she knows what you did? Is your urge to confess an act of generosity and contrition, or a selfish attempt to expiate your guilt and soothe your conscience? Whom will it really serve?

These are extremely difficult judgments to make, and good people will disagree on the right course of action in any given situation. Ultimately, it comes down to knowing yourself and the person you've wronged.

If you do decide to get it off your chest, do it in as safe a setting as possible. Especially with something as devastating as an affair, the when, where, and how should be thought through carefully, perhaps with the help of a therapist. In some cases, you may want to write to the other person, to give him or her more time to reflect, and follow up with an in-person conversation when the time is right. You should also go into this with your eyes wide open. Accept the fact that no matter how contrite you are, no matter how sincerely you promise never to do it again, the injured party may not believe you. You might have to batten down the hatches, for you could be in for a storm. You may be accused, cursed, and blamed for everything under the sun. It's very important to give the person room to be as furious and outraged as necessary. Be prepared to listen and absorb. In fact, it's best to encourage the person to get it all out. Just don't resist the onslaught. Don't defend yourself. Don't nitpick about the details. Don't show any sign of impatience, no matter how many times the same statements are repeated. Resist the temptation to explain yourself, unless you are asked to do so. Save the discussion for after the storm passes.

Also, be prepared to stay in the doghouse for a while. Whether you've cheated on a spouse, deceived a business colleague, or gossiped about a friend, you'll have to earn back their trust, and that may take a lot longer than you think. You might be on probation for quite a while. And be prepared for revenge.

If, after careful consideration, you decide it would best for all concerned if you do not confess, you may need to find another way to relieve your burden. One way is to write it out. As we saw in chapter 3, expressing your feelings in writing can be profoundly healing. It can also help you clarify the incidents you feel guilty about so you can make sensible choices about future behavior.

Write down all the things you feel guilty about (consulting your list of regrets might help). Tell each story in as much detail as you can. Exactly what happened? What did you do? Why do you feel guilty about it? Explain the consequences of your actions. Was someone hurt? Did people suffer as a result of your actions? Express exactly how you feel about what happened. Allow yourself to feel all the emotions that arise—pain, embarrassment, anguish, compassion, despair, and anything else that may come up. If you feel like crying, go ahead and cry. If you feel like shouting, shout. If you feel like cursing yourself, or fate, or God, go ahead. Get it all out verbally, and express those feelings on the page.

You might also want to express your guilt verbally to someone who has no personal stake in the incident—a therapist, perhaps, or a clergyperson or close friend—and whose good sense and understanding you value. You must feel absolutely sure that your relationship with that person will not be jeopardized by your confession and that you can count on him or her to honor your confidentiality. Choose a safe, comfortable setting, and let the person know whether you just want an opportunity to be heard or would like their advice or opinion.

MAKING AMENDS

One reason 12-step programs are so effective is the power of steps 8 and 9. They require that you make a list of everyone you've harmed and make amends to all of them "wherever possible, except when to do so would injure them or others."

Making amends is not always easy. You may not know what to do. You may be too embarrassed to admit that you've done wrong or to accept blame for what happened. You may be afraid to face the person you've hurt. It requires courage to take this step, and it's easy to find reasons not to: "It's too late," "Nothing I can do will make a difference," "It's beyond repair," and so forth. Try not to rationalize your way out of it. It may be true that nothing you can do will mend the situation or restore the relationship to its previous status. But, if done with generosity, compassion, and genuine remorse, making amends is always worthwhile and always healing.

Exactly *how* to make amends is a crucial consideration and should not be taken lightly. It's very important to understand that spilling your guts is usually not enough. You may have to *show* you're sorry, not just say it. And you may have to use your imagination to win back the trust and respect of the person you've hurt—and be redeemed in your own eyes. For minor offenses, a simple gesture like sending flowers may suffice. But for serious hurts, restitution is usually required.

One way to determine a proper form of restitution is to simply ask, "Is there something I can do to make this up to you?" or, "What would it take for me to regain your trust?" You might add, "I hope we can figure out something that is reasonable by way of making amends." Be prepared, however, for the person to demand something you are unwilling or unable to give, and to use the demand as a basis for a counteroffer.

Ask yourself, "If I were in the other person's shoes, what would it take for me to be able to forgive and trust again?" Think about what he or she values most and try to find something that appeals to those values. If the injured party is your spouse or lover, you're essentially going to have to win him or her anew. Do everything you can to show your appreciation. Try to rekindle the sense of romance. Be as attentive as possible. But do it from the heart. At a time like this, any sign of insincerity will be pounced upon as phony and self-serving. You might also encounter rejection, ambivalence, sarcasm, hostility, and skepticism. It's only natural that your efforts will be met with suspicion at first, especially if you're trying to win back your partner's trust after an affair. He or she might think you're on your best behavior temporarily, like a kid who behaves like an angel after he's punished but can't wait to misbehave again. It's vital to take it one day at a time; be patient and try to find tangible ways to demonstrate that your contrition is real and you deserve to be forgiven.

Perhaps the most important thing to do when looking for forgiveness is to work on forgiving yourself. If you expect the wounded person to forgive you before you can forgive yourself, you're essentially making him or her responsible for your peace of mind. That amounts to piling an additional burden onto someone who is already under strain. It's fine to say that you would like to be forgiven, but don't have your own self-forgiveness depend on it. That can be found only in the privacy of your own heart, or perhaps through your religion. Every tradition has a system for atonement and expiation.

Once you achieve a certain level of self-forgiveness, you will probably bring a new level of dignity and sincerity to the table when you ask the other person to forgive you. The request may well be refused anyway. It's only natural for the wounded party to not make it easy for you—and to test your sincerity a bit longer. Go back another time and try again. You might want to do what the Jewish tradition recommends: Ask three times for forgiveness. If at that point you are still refused, it is said, you have done all you can and the burden shifts to the other party. God will let you off the hook—as long as your atonement and your efforts to make amends are sincere.

Every situation demands a different form of restitution. Your job is to find one that is just and proper while satisfying the needs of your conscience. Take the case of Billy Roy Pitts. In 1966, Pitts was one of a gang of Ku Klux Klansmen who burned down the home of black civil rights leader Vernon Dahmer, killing Dahmer and causing his family unimaginable grief. The ringleader of that atrocity, Sam Bowers, was tried four times in Mississippi courts and was acquitted each time by an all-white jury. Thirty-two years later, he was finally convicted. The key witness was Billy Roy Pitts. "I owed Vernon Dahmer's family that much," he told ABC's *Nightline.* "This thing had haunted me over the years and I felt . . . that I had to do what was right."

But not even Bowers's conviction was enough. Pitts felt he needed to do something more: to ask Vernon Dahmer's family for forgiveness. When he received it, he called it "the greatest thing that could happen to anybody." "I've publicly confessed my sin," he said, "and I feel like now . . . I can go on with life."

Sometimes making amends directly to the injured party is impossible or inappropriate, and sometimes anything you can think of seems hopelessly inadequate. But even making amends indirectly can help ease the burden of guilt. One powerful way is to be of service to people in need, especially if their situation is in some way associated with the kind of action you feel guilty about. Remember Alfred, the drunk driver whose carelessness cost the life of his son? Obviously, his guilt transcends the concept of making amends. But he found a way to redeem himself. Alfred, who hasn't touched a drop of alcohol since the day of the accident, devotes a good deal of time to counseling parents whose children have died. He is also a tireless fundraiser for Mothers Against Drunk Driving. And he had his vasectomy reversed so he and his wife could bring another child into the world. That child will have an exceptionally loving father.

There are countless ways to make amends. Look deep within your own heart and find your way.

5

Resolving the Grief That Will Not End

YOUR HEART'S PATH OF LOVING, LOSING, AND LEARNING

And through all the tears and sadness and pain,
comes the one thought that can make me smile again.

I have loved.

—PETER MCWILLIAMS

When Ellen was 19, her father died of cancer. Because it had been a prolonged illness with no hope of recovery, Ellen had anticipated her father's passing and accepted the news with a sense of relief. She attended to the needs of her bereft mother and her frightened younger brothers, helped with the funeral arrangements and sundry practical details, and returned to college four days later. She felt that getting on with her life was the strong thing to do—and exactly what her father would want. She immersed herself in her studies to such an extent that she earned straight A's that semester for the first and last time. Then followed a period of confusion about her future. After graduation, she drifted from job to job and place to place, at one point living with a spiritual cult for several years. Eventually, she settled in San Diego and became an artist, but she never quite realized her creative potential and was forced to take a variety of odd jobs to pay her bills. Her love affairs were all short-lived until she married a businessman who left her after nine years.

That's when Ellen came to me for therapy. At age 41, she had been suffering from a low-grade chronic depression for years. Once upon a time, she told me wistfully, she had been an ebullient, life-loving free spirit. When did she lose those qualities? It was hard to pinpoint, she said, but sometime toward the end of her college days. When I pointed out that her father died around that time, she dismissed the possibility that the two events were connected. "I loved my father, and I missed him," she said, "but he was in awful pain, so I was okay with his death."

She hadn't *really* been okay with it, and she still wasn't. For Ellen had never properly grieved the loss. That became abundantly clear when I asked her to describe what had taken place at the time.

Her father had taught her to be strong, she told me. You didn't cry in front of others. You faced tragedies with a stiff upper lip. You did what had to be done, put the past behind you, and moved on. He also told Ellen that religious rituals were for the weak. "Don't waste your time visiting my grave," he said, "just remember me in your heart." Ellen followed those injunctions to the letter. When I asked her if she'd ever had a good cry over her loss, she described a scene in the funeral parlor, when she was alone with her father's body: "I had a window of opportunity, and I went to say good-bye. I bent over to kiss his forehead, and I started to weep. I tried to fight it, but I couldn't. Then I heard a voice behind me cry out, 'It's so sad!' It was one of my aunts. She was watching me. I was so self-conscious, I just shut down my tears and walked out of the room."

Those sobs never had a chance to come out. They settled into Ellen's psyche and turned to mud, gumming up all aspects of her Quintessential Self. In the sessions that followed, she came to realize that for 22 years she'd been carrying a heavy weight of sorrow that had robbed her of her *joie de vivre* and optimism. What also emerged was a huge stockpile of anger. She was mad at her father for leaving. He'd been the one who believed in her, the one she could turn to, the one whose guidance she could trust, and he wasn't there for her when she went through the turmoil of early adulthood. She was furious at her mother, too, for not taking her father's place in her life and for turning to mush when he died. She was angry at her father's doctors for not doing more, angry at her brothers for needing her so much, angry at the aunt who interrupted her mourning, and angry at God for creating a world in which fathers die too young.

Ellen's buried emotions poured from her heart like a mighty river. It was the start of a long-overdue grieving process—and the beginning of the end of her chronic depression.

Ellen was one of dozens of clients I've seen whose problems stemmed from unresolved losses and who did not make the connection until it was explained to them. In most cases the losses were major, such as the death of a loved one or the breakup of a marriage. But you would be surprised how many lesser losses have long-term impact, partly because we don't think of them as needing to be mourned—the death of a schoolteacher, for instance, or a neighbor who moved away, or a mentor who left the company, even an investment gone sour.

It also applies to events we don't think of as losses. Examples include graduating from school, moving away from home, an illness or injury (the loss of health), the realization that a cherished belief was wrong, discovering that a long-term goal is unattainable, the end of a special time in your life, and retirement. These are, in fact, losses. Some losses are even more disguised because they're accompanied by gains: success, for example, can result in the loss of striving; the birth of a child brings the loss of certain freedoms; a great new job may signal the loss of independence or free time. Then there are losses associated with aging, from the loss of innocence to the loss of beauty and athleticism, from the loss of hair and slim hips to the decline of vision, hearing, and sex drive. They may be inevitable, but they are losses just the same.

If your life was impacted by losses and you were not allowed to grieve, did not feel safe to grieve, or did not know *how* to grieve, you may never have fully recovered. You may still be carrying the pain and sorrow of those losses, paying a heavy price you are not even aware of.

THE STAGES OF RECOVERY

Every loss is different. The death of a child is different from the death of a parent: One feels like an abomination, while the other is in the natural order of things. A sudden loss is different from an anticipated loss. The death of a spouse is different from a divorce, and a divorce is different from the end of a romantic fling. Leaving someone is different from being left. Every loss has a character of its own, and its impact varies depending on your age, the way you found out about it, whether or not there was a perpetrator, and a variety of other circumstances.

But every loss is the same in one crucial respect: Healing from its impact always entails three distinct phases, and if that process is not completed, the effects of the loss will linger, like an injury that never quite heals. The emotional wounds that result from loss are just as real as a contusion or a cut or a broken bone. They require just as much care and attention, and in most cases more time and patience. Unfortunately, few of us know how to treat the wounds of loss, and society as a whole, with the decline of community, the scattering of extended families, and the breakdown of traditional rituals, does not offer much assistance. As a result, many of us do not heal properly. We limp along emotionally just as we would limp on a broken ankle that hasn't fully mended.

Let's look at the three stages of recovery from loss:

STAGE 1: SHOCK AND DENIAL

Shock is a coping mechanism. It's what allows us to run out of a burning building on a broken leg or lift a car to save a child. To help us cope with an emotional blow, shock numbs us to the pain. It can last anywhere from a few seconds to several weeks, depending on the magnitude of the loss and the circumstances under which it occurs.

Shock is usually accompanied by denial, which is the mind's way of protecting us from the unimaginable: "I can't believe this happened." "It can't be!" "It's impossible!" That is the voice of denial, and sometimes the mind takes it literally, actually refusing to accept the reality of what has taken place. You know you're still in this stage when you find yourself stunned if something reminds you of the loss. Most of the time we quickly face up to reality, but the subconscious mind might still deny its *impact*—the pain and devastation we just can't bear to feel. Just as we might tell our friends, "I'm fine. Really, I'm okay," we try to convince ourselves as well. Religious people often aid and abet that denial by telling themselves, "It was God's will," or, "It was meant to be," or, "It was my karma." People like Ellen, who believe that strength lies in stoicism, reinforce the denial mechanism with sheer willpower. In many instances, emotional numbness takes over as a way to keep difficult feelings at bay—often compounded by pain-numbing alcohol or drugs.

How long the numbness and denial last depends on a variety of factors. One is whether there are other people to take care of and details to attend to. In that case, denial serves a practical purpose: You could not do what needs to be done if you were to stop and feel the pain. Nowadays, the pressures of modern life and the demands of employers work to reinforce denial. Most people have to be back at their jobs a week after the death of a loved one, and in many cases sooner. Numbing their feelings may help them get back to work quickly, but often at a terrible emotional price.

STAGE 2: ANGER, FEAR, AND SADNESS

After the shock and denial, when the numbness wears off and reality sets in, you move into the mourning phase. Now it's time to deal with the grief. Aside from raw pain, the most common emotions that arise at that stage are anger, fear, and depression—or all of the above in varying degrees and for different lengths of time. The anger may be totally irrational—directed at the loved one who died, for instance, or at a relative for somehow not preventing the death. I have counseled many people who were furious at their ex-spouses for the breakup of a marriage—which would make perfect sense except for one thing: They, the angry clients, were the ones who did the leaving. Sometimes the anger is justified but exaggerated out of proportion to reality: rage at someone who said the wrong thing at the funeral, for example, or at a friend for not warning you about the lover who dumped you. After a loss, irrational or exaggerated rage feels just as real as anger toward a father who left his family or a careless smoker who burned down a house. It's just as automatic and just as natural, and it must be acknowledged and expressed.

Loss not only makes you angry, it can also make you afraid: afraid of being alone, afraid of uncertainty, afraid that things will get even worse, afraid the pain will never go away. And it can make you depressed as well. Despair, hopelessness, fatigue, and deep, seemingly impenetrable sadness are all symptoms of depression and natural companions of loss. Depending on the circumstances, you might also be tormented by guilt and regret. It's natural for the mind to erupt with "if only" scenarios of how you could have prevented the loss. In the case of death, all the things you wish you'd said while the person was alive often flood the mind.

Perhaps the most poignant source of guilt is the thought that springs from the dark side of the psyche: "I'm glad he/she is dead." Very few thoughts are more unacceptable to us. A young client named Louis, for instance, lost his older brother when he was 15. Missing his brother desperately, he plunged into deep despair and loneliness. But once or twice he found himself thinking, "Maybe I'll finally get some attention from my parents now that their superstar is gone." He felt so guilty for having the thought that he contemplated suicide.

Exactly how Stage 2's cauldron of emotions is expressed varies widely, as does the length of time it lasts. Grief has as many legitimate patterns as there are grievers. What's important is for every emotion that arises to be experienced fully.

STAGE 3: UNDERSTANDING AND ACCEPTANCE

The pain has been felt, the anger has been vented, the depression has lifted, and you have survived. Your energy and strength have returned. You have accepted that life will never be the same, but that it still can be lived with satisfaction, and you can face the future with a measure of optimism and hope. In short, you can now move on.

When this phase is completed successfully, the result is resolution. But if you try to get to understanding and acceptance without completely going through the previous stages, the loss will remain unresolved and its effects will linger indefinitely.

HOW LOSS REMAINS UNRESOLVED AND PAINFUL

Essentially, there are two possible roadblocks to achieving resolution. You can get stuck in Stage 1, remaining in denial and numbness; or you can pass through that stage successfully only to bog down in depression, anger, and fear.

GETTING STUCK IN DENIAL

Like Ellen, whom we met earlier, Leonard stalled in the first stage. When his wife left him, he was stunned. Once the initial shock wore off, however, he felt liberated. The struggle to make the marriage work had ended in defeat, but at least it was over. Finally, the squabbles and tantrums were gone. "It wasn't meant to be," Leonard would tell his friends. "We had some good years, but it didn't work out, and it's time to move on." His only regret, he said, was that he hadn't ended it five years earlier. Gradually, he adjusted to being alone and claimed to be doing just fine. But he drank a bottle of wine with dinner each night and refused to get involved with women beyond a couple of dates. Then, three years after his divorce, he met someone he liked and let himself take the plunge. Two months later, the woman broke off the relationship, saying that Leonard was "not in touch with his feelings." Shocked by the rejection, Leonard came to see me, he said, because he wanted a prescription for an antidepressant. He needed more than that.

It quickly became apparent that the breakup of the short-lived affair was not the issue. That had merely brought to the surface all the feelings he'd suppressed three years earlier when his marriage broke up. This is a common phenomenon: Unresolved losses from the past get reactivated with each subsequent loss—especially those that resemble the original. In psychotherapy, Leonard got deeply in touch with the pain of his divorce and all the horrible emotions he could not face at the time: fury toward his ex-wife for betraying him; self-contempt for not being able to make the marriage work; the awful fear that he was unlovable and would live a life of lonely desperation. Long-buried tears streamed from his eyes in buckets. They were as necessary as April rain: Leonard gradually came alive again, like a parched field after a long drought.

On the heels of a loss, many people are terrified to let themselves fully feel the pain. They're afraid it will never stop. They think the sadness will be so overwhelming that they'll lose control and crack up. But what you resist, persists. By resisting the grief, you ensure that the grief will end up sticking to you like a glue that hardens over time. What happened with Ellen and Leonard is extremely common: They tried to skip the second stage of healing and go straight to moving on. But the denial they used to sedate the pain also numbed their capacity for love and joy.

GETTING STUCK IN GRIEF

Christine was getting dressed to celebrate her first wedding anniversary when she received a phone call that changed her life irrevocably. Her husband, Dean, had been on a business trip. When his meetings ran late and he missed his flight, he chartered a private plane to get home. Nothing was going to stop him from being with his beloved on their anniversary. Tragically, something did. The plane crashed.

The only thing that kept her from ending her own life, Christine said, was her determination to see the airplane company brought to justice for criminal negligence. Other than cooperate with the investigation, she did little but pore over photographs of Dean and stare out the window at an ocean view as vast as the hole in her heart. She would weep uncontrollably at every reminder of Dean, whom she depicted as a virtual saint, the perfect combination of sensitivity and strength.

Eighteen months later, nothing much had changed except that Christine had lost some of her friends because they could not stand the constant repetition of her woes. She had difficulty sleeping, was lethargic most of the time, and went through the paces of living without enthusiasm. Despite the urging of loved ones, she refused to return to her job or take on volunteer work.

She turned down almost all social invitations: She felt that it would disgrace her husband's memory if she had a laugh or enjoyed an evening out.

When she came to me for therapy, Christine looked much older than her 28 years. Depression was written on her face as if in neon lights. In one of our first sessions, I had her relax deeply, close her eyes, and imagine Dean sitting opposite her. This was her chance to tell him everything she'd been feeling since his death. She began with a heart-rending expression of pain and declarations of her abiding love. Then came the fear of being alone and childless forever. Then she let loose the rage—not just toward fate and the charter company, but toward Dean himself: for not leaving that conference sooner, for leaving their finances in a mess, and for various hurts that he caused while still alive.

Christine had suppressed those angry feelings toward Dean because they made her feel that she was a horrible person. But the venting was a crucial step in her recovery. Her need to idealize the departed—a very common phenomenon after a death—had helped keep her unacceptable anger at bay, but it also kept her tied to the past and stuck in loss. Only when she was able to recognize this and accept her late husband for who he was, with all his shortcomings, was she able to truly accept his death. Now she could see that clinging to the role of grieving widow was neither a tribute to Dean nor proof of how much she loved him.

It took a good deal of time and work, but Christine eventually realized that achieving acceptance and resolution—even with so grievous a loss as hers—is not dishonorable. She had been afraid that moving on would be tantamount to forgetting her husband. She had to be assured that sometimes resolution means accepting the fact that you can still have a rewarding life even though you'll walk the rest of your days with a measure of sadness in your heart. "Only nature has a right to grieve perpetually," said Henry David Thoreau, "for she only is innocent." That is something everyone who gets stuck in the second stage of recovery needs gently to be reminded of.

Making peace does not mean forgetting what you lost, acting as though the loss never occurred, or pretending that you are unscathed. Ken Druck is a dear friend and colleague whose daughter was killed in a bus accident while she was studying abroad. In Jenna's memory, Ken established a foundation called Families Helping Families, which provides workshops and other services for grieving parents. I asked him what "making peace" means in the context of such a devastating loss. "When you lose a child, something in you truly dies," he said. "To somehow find a way to justify your life—every joy, every pleasure, every moment of triumph, every breath—when your child is no longer drawing breath is a lifelong sentence of agony. Part of successful adjustment is accepting that it's always going to be this way. You may come to a point where you feel it's okay to laugh and enjoy the good things, but there's a hole and it will always be there."

The depression that follows a major loss can make life seem utterly useless and hopeless. Many people get stuck in the feeling, "Life will never be the same now, so why bother?" Moving on does not mean replacing what can't be replaced; it means rebuilding your life from the ashes of loss and turning the agony into an opportunity for service and growth.

SIGNS AND SYMPTOMS OF UNRESOLVED LOSS

People cling to the grief stage for a variety of reasons. Some, such as the need to idealize the one who was lost and the belief that living happily would dishonor the departed, we've already mentioned. Another is that the person's identity is so dependent on what was lost—the spouse, the home, the job, and so forth—that he or she does not know quite how to function without it. Constructing a new identity takes courage and time. Yet another reason for holding onto grief is the fear that moving on will mark you as unfeeling or immoral and people will accuse you of not grieving enough. It is extremely important to understand that there is no right way to grieve and no official timetable for mourning. Grief is a messy and highly individualized process: Everyone has to do it in his or her own way.

If you did not navigate successfully through the three stages of loss, you probably resumed life's journey dragging a heavy weight behind you. The possible consequences are many and varied. See if any of these applies to you:

DEPRESSION

With the thousands of people I've treated for chronic depression, unresolved grief is a frequent cause. After a major loss, deep pockets of vulnerability and venom are deposited beneath the surface of consciousness. They seep out like toxic gas in the form of emptiness, helplessness, and hopelessness. Persistent feelings such as "I'll never get over it," "It's not worth the effort," or "I'm miserable and nothing's going to change that," can be surface signals of deep unresolved loss.

PHYSICAL ILLNESS

When combined with a biological predisposition and a life crisis, the sorrow of unresolved loss can trigger or exacerbate almost any disease. Chronic problems such as difficulty sleeping, lack of energy, and various aches and pains are common symptoms. And when a serious illness strikes, the underlying hopelessness can compromise your will to live and diminish your healing capacity.

LONELINESS

Many people won't let anyone get close to them because they're terrified of going through the loss of another love. They keep people at arm's length, sabotage promising relationships, or walk away from love affairs before the other person can leave them.

CYNICISM AND BITTERNESS

If your attitude toward life is summed up in phrases like, "It's a cruel world," "Life's a bitch," "You can't trust anyone," or "People are basically out for themselves," you may have acquired that cynicism through unresolved losses. This edgy sense of mistrust is rooted in self-protection. The problem is, it can easily turn into self-suffocation.

EXTREME REACTION TO PRESENT LOSSES

Because they trigger the pain of unresolved losses, you may respond to each new loss, even minor ones, with excessive and unnecessary anguish. One patient of mine was rendered helpless with grief over the death of a co-worker. The death had unleashed a torrent of unexpressed pain over the disappearance of his brother two years earlier.

INORDINATE FEAR OF LOSS

A fear of abandonment, triggered by the painful memory of losing someone in the past, can cause you to overreact to any perceived threat of loss. The fear can cause you to stay too long in inappropriate relationships or become so compliant and needy as to drive people away.

BELLIGERENCE

If you tend to be argumentative, defensive, or testy, unexpressed anger over a past loss may be festering close to the surface. This pugnacious posture can cause you to lose even more.

GUILT AND REGRET

As mentioned earlier, many people with unresolved grief replay the circumstances of their losses over and over again, torturing themselves with "If only . . ." and "I should've . . ." Most common is the agony of having a parent die before you are able to reconcile your differences or say the things that should have been said. As a psychotherapist, I've often wished there was a magic formula that would make it totally unnecessary for anyone to ever again utter the words, "I never had a chance to say 'I love you.'"

FEAR-BASED BEHAVIOR

People who were powerfully affected by the premature death of a loved one often internalize a fear of the same thing happening to them. This can lead to extreme risk-avoidance—or worse.

OVERROMANTICIZING

Unresolved losses can keep you mired in a romanticized version of the past at the expense of a boring present and a bleak future. This can manifest as continual yearning for a long-lost love, the constant rehashing of the same old stories, or a perpetual longing for the good old days. The good old days may have been high school, when you were the most beautiful, the most popular, the sharpest dresser, the brightest student, the star athlete—or just simply happy and carefree. I see it a lot in my fellow middle-aged children of the 1960s, who long for the Woodstock era, when they—like their hair—ran high and wild, love was not only free but safe and uncomplicated, and the drugs they took were not prescribed.

ADDICTION

Addiction is one of the most serious health problems in America, and unresolved loss is a major cause. Almost always the addict is running away from suffering and is compulsively racing for pleasure—in all the wrong places—hoping to experience something wonderful to take away the pain of the past.

Naturally, many of these patterns can be caused by something other than a major loss. If any of them are familiar to you, try to trace their origins and see if they may have started in response to a significant loss.

NAMING THE PAIN

The first step in resolving losses that were incompletely grieved is to name them. Let's begin with the times that death has intruded in your life. If you lost a parent, spouse, sibling, or child, those are no doubt the most painful losses. But don't limit yourself to those. You may have lost a cousin or friend, or perhaps a mentor or colleague. Pay particular attention to the deaths you may have experienced as a child. You may have been affected more deeply than you realize by the loss of a grandparent or an elderly uncle or aunt. Adults tend to shield children from unpleasant truths, not realizing how much they actually know and how frightened they get when their safe world is shaken by death. Grownups seldom recognize that children need to grieve in their own way and to express their feelings. I have had numerous clients sob in my office remembering the death of their grandparents. Many are still angry because they were not permitted to view the body or attend the funeral.

Write down the losses you've endured through death, beginning with those whose impact on you was the greatest. Describe the circumstances surrounding each event. These questions will help you capture the details:

- How old were you at the time?
- How did you first get the news that the person had died?
- Was it sudden or expected?
- How did you feel at the time? Were you enraged? Frightened? Distraught? Disbelieving?
- Were you able to—or allowed to—express your feelings fully?
- What were the ancillary losses? The death may have altered the nature of your friendships, for example, or severed your connection to an entire side of your family. You may have lost a source of income or a home. You may have lost an activity that you shared only with the departed. Think through the chain of short- and long-term losses that resulted from each death.
- Did any of the deaths have a permanent effect on your emotions or behavior? Did they leave you feeling like a victim of fate, for instance, or make you bitter and cynical?
- Now that you know about the stages of recovery, do you think you adequately grieved each loss? Which ones still need healing? What was left undone, unfelt, or unsaid at the time?

It may be hard to remember the details, especially if your loss occurred when you were very young. Do your best and keep in mind that the emotional truth is more important than the historical truth. And be prepared for unexpected feelings to arise: anger, fear, sorrow, and any number of painful emotions that were buried at the time of the loss. Feeling these emotions now may be uncomfortable, and it may seem crazy after so long a time, but it may be necessary to complete the grieving process and cleanse yourself of the residue of unresolved loss. Let yourself be with the pain and let yourself cry if that's what comes up. As the Jewish proverb says, "What soap is for the body, tears are for the soul."

At the same time, bear in mind that it's perfectly normal *not* to cry and *not* to feel pain. Simply writing about your experience may be enough to facilitate completion. As I said earlier, everyone grieves in his or her own manner, and everyone has to resolve unfinished grief in his or her unique way. The question "Am I doing this wrong?" should never be entertained. It is quite possible that the fear of not grieving "right" stopped the process the first time around.

After you finish describing the times you were visited by death, move on to other major losses, once again noting the details. Adapt the questions listed above to the circumstances. This list will help you identify additional losses:

- Marriages and love affairs that ended painfully
- Loss of a home or a job
- Loss of money or possessions
- Rape or other violent crime
- Moving to a new home or city
- Major illness or injury
- Permanent handicap or disfigurement
- Serious car accident

NOT-SO-OBVIOUS LOSSES

- Loss of a cherished ideal or belief
- Broken dreams (of love or glory)
- Unfulfilled goals
- Loss of romance
- Loss of youth, beauty, or vitality
- Loss of freedom and independence
- Loss of community
- Disappointments and unfulfilled expectations
- Menopause
- Retirement
- Loss of sex drive or performance
- Loss of a friend to marriage or relocation
- Loss of a colleague or teammate
- Business failure or financial setback

Don't censor yourself because a particular loss seems trivial now. You may not have given it the time and attention it deserved, and the wound may never have healed. You would be surprised at the number of patients who have wept in my office over the pet that was taken away from them at age 5 or 6, or the best friend who moved to another city when they were 10. Reflect on these smaller losses as you did the major losses, and give them the care they need to heal. "Nothing that grieves us can be called little," Mark Twain once said. "By the eternal laws of proportion a child's loss of a doll and a king's loss of a crown are events of the same size."

MOVING FROM GRIEF TO GAIN

To every thing there is a season,
and a time to every purpose under the heaven:
A time to be born, and a time to die; a time to plant,
and a time to pluck up that which is planted;
A time to kill, and a time to heal; a time to break down,
and a time to build up;
A time to weep, and a time to laugh; a time to mourn,
and a time to dance . . .
—ECCLESIASTES 3:1–4

The following sections contain suggestions and exercises that have proven to be extremely powerful in helping people achieve a more complete and heartfelt resolution after a loss. Be gentle with yourself, and try to have no set expectations as to what the results should look like. Everyone experiences the exercises differently; some of us are, by nature, more emotionally expressive than others. No matter what your personal response is, the processes have great value, and they are effective regardless of how much time has passed. You may want to repeat some of the exercises. But you don't want to use them as an excuse not to move on or become obsessed with them at the expense of achieving resolution.

GAINING PERSPECTIVE ON YOUR LOSSES

Loss is part of the fabric of life. Without it, growth and change would be impossible. Leaves fall and buds bloom. Caterpillars disappear and butterflies emerge. Elders die and babies are born—and even in that miracle of birth there is loss: Gone is the bliss and unity of the womb. With our first breath begins the parade of losses, each one a small death, and each one accompanied by gain. We lose childhood and gain maturity. We lose friends and gain new ones. We lose dreams and gain wisdom. Even in the most senseless tragedies, where the torment seems unbearable and finding anything positive seems unthinkable and even grotesque, gains can be found if you are willing to look for them—not at the moment, perhaps, but eventually, in the due course of time. The wise have always known the redemptive power of grief and pain. There is an ancient Eskimo maxim, for example, cited by Joseph Campbell in *Primitive Mythology: The Masks of God*: "The only true wisdom lies far from Mankind, out in the great loneliness, and it can be reached only through suffering. Privation and suffering alone can open the mind of a man to all that is hidden to others."

Go through your list of losses and write down what you gained from each one. To help you identify the gains, here are some examples of statements made by people who have done this exercise.

"I saw how precious life is and vowed to live every day fully."

"I discovered strength and courage I never knew I had."

"I reconnected with the Church and formed a new relationship with God."

"I learned who my true friends are."

"I gained an understanding of grief. Now I have more to give to others who suffer losses."

"After the funeral I reconciled with my sister after twelve years of not speaking to each other."

"I learned I was capable of deeper feelings than I ever thought possible."

"I'm no longer afraid of death."

"I discovered that I could be self-sufficient."

"I joined AA and got sober."

"I was forced to find new ways to make life meaningful, and I did."

"I learned that I can survive anything."

If you can't locate a positive gain in the ashes of your loss, ask yourself what *can* be gained. If you think it's impossible to gain *anything*, think of my friend Ken Druck, who found a way to channel the grief of his daughter's death into a force for helping others. Think of Christopher Reeve, whose paralyzing accident has brought hope to millions of people and boosted funding for research on spinal injuries. And think of a German-born American named Kurt Klein. In the late 1930s, as Hitler's intentions became clear, Klein's parents sent him and his siblings to America. He grew up yearning to be reunited with his mother and father, but their efforts to get to America were thwarted at every turn. Klein eventually joined the U.S. Army. He was sent to Germany, where he was among the troops who liberated the Nazi death camps and witnessed the horrors that had been perpetrated. He never saw his parents again. They had been killed in one of those camps. But out of that unspeakable tragedy came a blessing, like a flower blossoming in the midst of ruins. At a concentration camp vacated by the fleeing Nazis, he met an emaciated young woman struggling to bring water to inmates who were too weak to walk. That woman became his lifelong mate.

The alchemy of loss and gain is a great and wondrous mystery. From the tragedy of crushing loss can come a triumph of courage, resilience, and generosity of spirit. Without even realizing it, you may already have gained a great blessing from your loss. If you haven't, it's never too late; try to find a way to create those gains now.

HELPING OTHERS

If you feel stuck in sadness and self-pity over a past loss, one of the best remedies is to reach out to others who need help. This is much more than a great way of taking your mind off your troubles for a while. It gives you something to feel good about, something to restore your sense of purpose and make you feel like a worthwhile human being.

Altruism and service are not only healing, they make life more satisfying—and possibly healthier and longer as well. Studies have shown that people who do volunteer work have a higher life expectancy than those who do not, and that self-centered people are more likely to develop coronary artery disease, depression, and anxiety.

It doesn't take much time to gain the benefits of helping others. Here are some tips to make your efforts most beneficial to you and those you help:

- Choose an activity that appeals to your interests and skills.
- Don't be attached to the outcome of your efforts. The payoff is in the process itself.
- Favor one-to-one activities that foster strong personal connections.
- Do the activity on a regular basis. Establish a set schedule if you can.
- Choose work that empowers others rather than making them more dependent.
- Don't expect anything in return.
- Don't limit yourself to formal volunteer work. As the saying goes, practice random acts of kindness.

As former Congresswoman Pat Schroeder put it, "You can't wring your hands and roll up your sleeves at the same time." Rolling them up in the service of others will help wring self-pity out of your heart.

CLEARING SPACE FOR MOVING ON

Keeping mementos of a loved one can be a beautiful way to keep memories alive and hold the person close to your heart. But if it goes too far, it can keep you tied to the past and prevent you from moving on to a healthy acceptance of the loss.

Removing unhealthy reminders is especially important in the case of a divorce or a love affair that ended in a broken heart. It's hard to be open to new love if you're surrounded by artifacts that exert a subtle pull toward the past. After going through a painful marital breakup, Joanna would come home to her husband-empty house after work each night and go through a barrage of troublesome feelings—anger, fear, regret, longing, and the nagging suspicion that she had made a huge mistake. Eventually, though, she regained her footing and put that chapter of her life behind her. Or so she thought. She said she wasn't ready to date, but was content with her busy social life. She spent every evening dining with friends or going to classes, concerts, and plays. When I asked if she spent any time at home alone, she admitted that she seldom did because she would sometimes break down and cry for no apparent reason.

It turned out that Joanna's ex-husband still had keys to the house and continued to receive faxes and packages there. She said it was merely a convenience, since her ex was living in a temporary apartment. The arrangement had no bearing whatsoever on her state of mind, she claimed. Upon reflection, she realized that the constant reminder of her ex's presence kept triggering the sadness of her divorce and the fear of being alone. She changed the locks on her door and told her husband to remove the fax machine and get a post office box for his packages. It was an essential rite of closure and a vital assertion of acceptance in Joanna's passage to a fresh start.

You might want to take inventory of your belongings. Discard superfluous items that are keeping you stuck in the past, and keep cherishing those that provide loving memories.

THE FAREWELL HEART LETTER

Expressing the feelings associated with major losses is a vital step in making peace. An excellent way to do this is to write letters of farewell to the important people you have lost. As with previous letter-writing exercises, this one does not have to be seen by anyone but you. It is your chance to say everything you feel about the loss.

Before beginning, you may want to spend some time evoking the memory of the person you'll be writing to. Now is the time to bring out the photographs, letters, and other mementos you decided to keep. Listen to songs the person was fond of. Read a poem or a passage from a book he or she loved. Watch his or her favorite movie. You may also want to listen to music or watch a film that you associate with the time of the loss. In addition, movies whose themes are similar to your loss may trigger memories and help you access your feelings.

Anything you can do to stimulate your memory or elicit feelings about the person you lost can be useful preparation.

When you're ready to begin, choose a quiet place to write and give yourself at least half an hour of uninterrupted time. Be completely honest, and don't stop to analyze or edit what you're writing. Ask your intellect to take a nap; this is not about accuracy or logic, it is about emotions, and it doesn't matter if you find yourself becoming irrational. Reason is the intellect's tool for blocking feelings. Give yourself permission to express everything that needs to be let out—the rage, the terror, the pain, the love, the longing, and the gratitude.

While allowing for the spontaneous expression of feeling, it's a good idea to have the content of your letter follow the three stages of recovery. Begin with the shock and pain of loss, move on to the feelings associated with the stage of mourning, and conclude with the theme of understanding and acceptance. The following phrases will help you get in touch with buried feelings. Use whichever ones apply to your situation and move you to write:

SECTION 1: SHOCK AND DENIAL

"When I heard that you had died . . ."
"When you abandoned me . . ."
"The first thing I felt was . . ."
"The shock was so great that . . ."
"The initial pain was . . ."

SECTION 2: ANGER, FEAR, AND SADNESS

"I was angry because . . ."
"What really made me mad was . . ."
"I've always resented that . . ."
"I got scared when . . ."
"I was so sad I . . ."
"It hurt me when . . ."
"I miss you when . . ."
"I wish . . ."
"My biggest regrets are . . ."

SECTION 3: UNDERSTANDING AND ACCEPTANCE

"I realize now that . . ."
"I forgive you for . . ."
"I hope you can forgive me for . . ."
"I'll always be grateful that . . ."
"I'll always love you because . . ."

Consider writing a farewell love letter for each of the significant people you've lost. If the loss was due to death, you may want to keep the letter for future reference, and for the exercise that follows. If the person you're writing to is an ex-spouse or lover whom you lost due to a breakup, you may want to perform some kind of ceremony of closure. Unfortunately, society does not have rites and rituals to help us fully resolve the death of a marriage or a love affair. But you can invent one of your own, using one of the five elements:

1. **Fire:** Burn the letter.
2. **Water:** Flush it down the toilet, or rip it up and throw it into a body of water.
3. **Earth:** Stomp on it and bury it in the ground.
4. **Air:** Tear it up and toss it into the wind from a high place, or stuff it in a balloon and let it fly away.
5. **Spirit:** Say a prayer over it or commend it to God and let it go in a way that gives you a strong sense of completion.

A SECOND CHANCE TO SAY GOOD-BYE

Remember Ellen, the woman who lost her father as a teenager and never had the chance to fully grieve? Once she understood how deeply the loss had affected her life, she was filled with regret for never visiting her father's grave or participating in the memorial rituals that are part of her religious tradition. I recommended the following process to her. She resisted at first, calling it corny and contrived, but once she agreed to try it she plunged in whole-heartedly. Afterward, she called it one of the most powerful experiences of her life. "I feel a wonderful lightness," she said. "It's as if

I've lost fifty pounds." The emotional poundage she lost was the heavy weight of old, stale sorrow.

This exercise will help you to complete the grieving process for the death of a loved one. It is especially important if you did not attend the funeral service, if you were a child at the time, or if the experience was somehow flawed or truncated. You will also find it useful if you have not participated in memorial rituals subsequent to the funeral. This is your chance to say good-bye once again, only this time in your own way and with greater awareness. This exercise can be especially poignant when done on the anniversary of the death.

The process entails a visit to the gravesite. If for any reason you can't go to the actual grave, or if there is no grave, locate a cemetery near your home that can serve as a surrogate. If that is not possible or does not feel appropriate, choose a quiet, secluded place instead—a clearing in the woods, a deserted beach, or even your own backyard.

Bring with you five mementos of your loved one—photographs, a favorite prayer or religious artifact, a poem or book, small personal items like a scarf or a ring—anything that evokes fond memories. Bring some flowers as well, and a copy of the Farewell Heart Letter you wrote to the departed. If you like, you may also bring a tape deck to play some appropriate funeral or grief-evoking music.

If you are in a cemetery other than the actual burial place, you'll have to select a grave that symbolically represents your loved one's resting place. Wander among the headstones until you find one that draws you to it. Ideally, it should be in a peaceful location where you will have privacy. If you are someplace in nature, choose a spot where you won't be disturbed. Find something that resembles a headstone or grave marker, or create one using rocks, a tree branch, or some twigs and leaves.

Sit or kneel next to grave. Place the flowers on it as an offering to the departed. Lay the mementos on the ground before you. Look at them for a while, allowing your warmest memories and feelings of love and appreciation to naturally rise within you. Let your mind drift back to the time of the actual death. Feel the pain you felt at the time—and the pain you suppressed because you were afraid or busy taking care of others.

When you are ready, close your eyes and imagine that you're looking into an open grave at your loved one, who lies peacefully at rest. Set aside for now any lingering feelings of anger, blame, or resentment. You've expressed those feelings in writing, and you will have opportunities to revisit them later in the book. For now, in this belated memorial, focus on the love, compassion, and tenderness you feel for the departed. If you feel comfortable doing so, speak aloud directly from your heart, or read appropriate portions of your Farewell Heart Letter. If you prefer, you can speak in the privacy of your imagination. Say how much you miss your loved one and how much he or she meant to you. Describe the qualities you most admired. Express the aching sadness you feel in his or her absence, your longing to see him or her again, and your appreciation for all you shared with one another. Say what you wish you'd said while he or she was still alive. Say what you'd like him or her to know now.

If powerful emotions arise, let them come. This is your chance to grieve as you couldn't grieve before. But don't be alarmed if you feel at peace and no strong emotions come up. Don't think you're doing it wrong or that the process isn't working. As with grief itself, everyone experiences this ritual differently. It has enormous value in and of itself, regardless of what feelings arise or don't arise.

Take as much time as you need. Don't leave until you feel a sense of peace and completion.

This exercise should be reserved for departed loved ones who were very close to you. There may be several such people. I recommend not doing more than two in a single day, and only if the two are somehow connected emotionally—both parents, for example. Use a different site for each person.

If you are currently in psychotherapy, consult with your therapist before doing this exercise. If you feel particularly vulnerable, or if you are concerned about being alone—or your ability to drive—after the ritual, you might ask someone to join you. He or she doesn't have to go to the gravesite itself; he or she can wait someplace at a distance and be there for you when you're finished.

Feel free to modify this exercise to suit your individual need for resolution. For example, instead of visiting a real or surrogate grave, you may want to perform a symbolic burial or cremation.

(This is an excellent alternative if there was no actual funeral service or if you were unable to attend.) Select an object (or objects) that symbolizes your loved one—a photograph, perhaps, or an article of clothing. Place the object in an appropriate container and bury it, or cremate it, in a setting that suits the spirit of your loved one. You can create as simple or elaborate a ritual as you'd like for this occasion, perhaps consulting a spiritual advisor if you wish to have religious content. You may also want to invite others who were close to the departed to share in this experience.

THE GARDEN OF LOVE, LOSS, AND LIGHT

The following visualization can be a great aid in the grieving process. As before, I recommend reading the instructions into a tape recorder and playing them back to guide you through the practice. Begin by settling down as per the instructions on page 27. When you are deeply relaxed, begin the visualization.

Picture a majestic garden, abundant with fresh greenery and gorgeous, colorful flowers. You see a path that winds through the garden and leads to the top of a hill. You wander along the path, breathing deeply of the fragrant air. You stop before a rose bush. It is bursting with red, white, and yellow roses at different stages of life. There are bare stems, tiny buds, early blooms, mature flowers, and old roses whose petals are floating to the earth, where they will feed the soil for new life. You pause to reflect on the life cycle, knowing that with each stage of growth something is lost and something is gained. You sniff deeply of the roses and allow the sweet perfume to permeate your body.

You stroll along the path and meander up the hill. At the top there is a magnificent, sturdy tree with dozens and dozens of healthy branches and glorious leaves. Perhaps it's a mighty oak, or a stately birch, or a durable redwood. This is your tree of life. Dangling from a nearby branch is a cocoon. Inside, in the darkness, is all the heartache and anguish from all the losses you've ever endured, and all the painful consequences that resulted from unresolved grief.

But also within that cocoon something magical is taking place: the mystery and miracle of transformation, regulated by the creative intelligence that governs all of life. All the pain that was stored inside is disappearing now, just like a caterpillar as it gives way to a new form of being.

Now the cocoon opens up. A beautiful multicolored butterfly springs into the light of day. It floats and flutters, playfully celebrating its new existence. The losses of the past have been transformed.

Now the butterfly beckons to you. You follow it as it flies through the garden and comes to a clearing in a magnificent, flower-filled meadow. There before you stand your loved ones who died. They stand together now, reaching out to you with all the love you've yearned for. They want to give that love to the new you—the person who has bravely worked through grief and at long last attained resolution for all your losses. They're proud of you. They love you. And they want you to know they'll always be present for you in the sanctuary of your heart. Receive their love. Let it fill you.

Now a golden light appears above them. It surrounds and permeates your loved ones. You watch as they slowly dissolve into the light. And you reach out to that radiant ball of light and pull it toward you and hold it to your heart. It enters your body and radiates upward to your throat, to your forehead, to the crown of your head. It radiates downward, filling your belly, your genitals, your legs, and your arms. Love and light now fill every fiber of your being. You are ready to move on now, knowing that the best of the past will always remain with you. The pain of loss is gone. You can walk boldly forward to create a beautiful, meaningful future.

6

Your Story of Love

THE BLISS AND BLISTERS OF YOUR SEXUAL AND ROMANTIC HISTORY

Life without love and passion is a life not worth having lived.
— RUMI

It was the relationship they both had dreamed of. The meeting was magical. The attraction was magnetic. The sex was magnificent. They saw eye to eye on everything important. Disagreements were minor and quickly resolved. They finished each other's sentences. They made each other laugh. They couldn't stop touching. They hated being apart. "It felt like destiny," Terri recalls, "like the angels had brought us together and blessed us." Everyone who knew them agreed: No couple ever seemed so perfect. Even their names were perfect: Terri and Terry.

Terry proposed. At 38, he had had enough conquests, enough anonymous sex. What was a little independence compared to a love so thrilling and so pure? Terri accepted eagerly. Having endured a loveless marriage, which had ended five years earlier, she was ecstatic to find that her romantic dreams were not just delusional fantasies. On the day of their wedding, happily ever after seemed written in the stars.

When they came to see me, four years later, they were at each other's throats. The tension and bitterness were palpable. Terri said she was frightened by Terry's explosive screaming fits. She complained that her husband did not appreciate her and had stopped showing interest in making love. They had not had sex in months. Terry blamed that on his wife's hostility. "How can you be passionate with someone who's picking on you all the time?" he said. He felt trapped, oppressed, and "constantly hassled." What finally precipitated their coming to therapy was that Terri discovered her husband's affair. It was, Terry declared, his way of asserting his freedom and proving to himself that he could still perform sexually.

Terry and Terri were a perfect match, all right, but not just for the reasons they thought when they vowed to love, honor, and cherish. They were "perfect" because they brought out in each other the psychological patterns that had kept them from having fulfilling relationships in the past—and because deep down they loved each other so much that they were willing to look honestly at their demons and work hard to conquer them.

Terri grew up in a large, poor family in rural Virginia. Her father, a factory worker, ruled his roost with brute force. "My earliest memory is waking up in the night to screams," she said. "I came out of my room, terrified, and saw my father pounding my mother with his fists. I saw scenes like that about every other week." As soon as Terri was old enough to understand, her mother taught her in no uncertain terms that men were bastards. She had visible contempt for Terri's father but was afraid that if she stood up to him he'd either get more violent or leave. Instead, she shrank in his presence, allowed him to humiliate her in front of others, and meekly did his bidding. Her only form of retaliation was to make demeaning remarks.

Terri vowed never to live like her mother. She longed for the day when she'd be old enough to leave the house, dreaming of a Cinderella future in which she'd be swept away by a man who was totally unlike her dad. For her parents' marriage was not her only model; there were also fairy tales and movies and love songs, in which good girls found safety and love in the arms of a prince.

When she was 17 she married a man who was kind and gentle and good. But he was not Prince Charming. He was meek and unexciting and had no ambition. After seven years of financial struggle and constant bickering, Terri took her two children and left. Then came a series of failed love affairs, some with mild-mannered men who lacked passion and some with fiery, sexy men who treated her badly. When she met Terry she thought her luck had changed and all the soul-searching she had done had finally paid off.

Terry grew up the older of two children in a middle-class home in Boston. His mother was an unhappy, domineering woman who got her way through emotional manipulation. "She would say, 'You'll give me a nervous breakdown,' or 'I'm going to have a heart attack because of you,'" Terry recalled. "Sometimes she'd threaten me with, 'God will punish you!' Mostly she used in-your-face guilt: 'I gave up everything for you,' 'If I didn't have to care for you, I'd leave that miserable father of yours.'"

That "miserable father" was a decent, hard-working salesman who grew increasingly depressed and withdrawn. It was his way of coping with his wife's constant criticism and complaints. But sometimes the rage would build to a point where he could no longer hold it in. He would explode, shaking his fists in the air and screaming so loudly, the neighbors could hear. "I watched my father's spirit get sucked out of him," said Terry. "I came to see marriage as a dismal prison."

Afraid of following in his father's weary footsteps, he rebelled against his mother's influence, finding ways to defy her every chance he could. On the streets of his neighborhood, he learned a different way of being a man, one who measured his worth by his number of sexual conquests. He aspired to the lifestyle glorified in magazines like *Playboy*. Adept at using charm and deceit to seduce girls, he would get what he wanted and move on as soon as things got sticky. That pattern continued into his thirties. When he met Terri, he felt as though he had stumbled onto a treasure he didn't even know he was looking for. He had found love for the first time.

This one will be different, they both thought. And for a couple of years it was. Then the past caught up with them. As the minor annoyances and disappointments accumulated and the flames of passion diminished, Terry started to see marriage as the prison he'd always feared. He began to withdraw, like his father. Terri, feeling ignored, decided it was time to stop sheepishly enduring her frustration, as she had in her previous relationships. Instead, she would make her needs and wishes known. But the only way she knew how to do this was to whine and complain and toss out a sarcastic remark now and then—like her mother.

This only exacerbated Terry's feeling of imprisonment. His wife was now reminding him of his own mother. He responded with a page out of his father's book—sullen brooding followed by explosions of screaming, fist-shaking rage. For Terri, those tantrums triggered ugly memories of her own father. Like her mother, she would cower and comply in the face of rage.

The rebellious kid in Terry wanted out. But his father's son would never abandon his family, even if it killed him. He compromised by sticking it out and resorting to his old ways behind Terri's back. When she learned of her husband's affair, Terri was heartbroken.

Only their memory of what they once had together—and a powerful yearning to get it back—prompted them to come for therapy. At first, each blamed the other for their problems. But they soon came to see that the patterns each of them had learned in the past were intersecting like tongues of flame and turning into conflagrations. That was the first step in healing the pain they had caused one another. In time, they learned new, more loving ways to behave and communicate.

In this chapter, we'll use the same tools to help you unlock your own romantic baggage and peek inside. By becoming conscious of the forces that have shaped your love story thus far, you can begin to break their grip and learn to love more authentically. To some extent, you've already begun this process. Your work on shame, regret, guilt, and loss has no doubt put you in touch with issues surrounding love and sex. Now, because those aspects of life mean so much to all of us, we'll pay special attention to them.

WOUNDS OF THE HEART

We each have a deep yearning to love and be loved. Yet maintaining a satisfying intimate relationship can be one of life's greatest challenges. The obstacles may derive from painful childhood or adolescent experiences. They may also stem from the pain and disappointment of previous relationships and the resulting fear that we'll get hurt again.

To what extent do you need to make peace with your romantic and sexual past? The opposite of intimacy is intimidation, and sadly, most of us were raised with more of the latter. The more the following statements fit you, the more healing you have to do.

- I'm not sure I can have faith in love when love has proven so disappointing in the past.
- I'm afraid of being rejected or abandoned yet again.
- I'm not sure I can be a worthy love partner, I've been so unfaithful in the past.
- I worry that I can't perform sexually the way I once did.
- I'm scared I'll end up feeling trapped again.
- I always think, "This time it will be different," but it's always the same old story.
- I always seem to attract partners who are:
  - ❏ self-centered
  - ❏ emotionally distant
  - ❏ abusive
  - ❏ irresponsible
  - ❏ immature
  - ❏ unable to commit
  - ❏ married, in love with someone else, or otherwise unavailable
  - ❏ just like my mother/father
- I'm afraid I'll end up in an unhappy marriage, just like my parents.
- I doubt I'll ever find what I'm looking for.
- I sometimes think all men/women are bastards/bitches.
- I'm tired of being taken advantage of.
- I've never gotten over [name a long-lost love].
- I yearn for the kind of romance and sexual excitement I once had.
- I wish men/women found me as sexually attractive as they used to.
- I feel guilty whenever I have sex.
- I'm afraid I'm basically unlovable.

OUR CROWDED BEDROOMS

It's standing room only in the bedroom. Surrounding you and your spouse or lover are both sets of parents, all the friends and relatives who talked to you about love and sex, all the priests and preachers whose moral precepts affected your views about sex, and of course, all your previous lovers. Also intruding are your and your partner's personal memories—both the sweet, soft-focus reveries that make you yearn for the past and the nightmares that make you afraid to repeat it.

In addition, each of us carries with us a complex cultural legacy when it comes to sex. Our societal attitudes are profoundly ambiguous, reflecting the simultaneous attraction and fear that reside in the human psyche. The Puritan past collides with the permissive present every day of our lives. Conservative values and religious maxims clash with titillating messages from the media, where sex is used to sell cigarettes, jeans, beer, movies, and just about everything else you can think of. Romantic songs and stories fill us with dreams of love everlasting, while the divorce rate climbs and new family structures are legitimized and the single life is glorified. Sex is portrayed as an instrument of the highest purpose—and as depraved and animalistic. It's seen as a natural drive that ought to be satisfied—and as a dark force that must be controlled. It is extolled as the ultimate form of human pleasure and intimacy—and degraded as an instrument of power and a measuring rod of status and competency. Men are taught that women are sex objects to be used for their pleasure—and creatures to be cherished, protected, and sacrificed for. Women are taught that men are brutes who are out for only one thing—and that they will provide for you and keep you safe.

None of us can escape this ambiguity. But still, of all the influences that determine the success of our relationships, the single most important one is the quality of our parents' marriage.

DECIPHERING YOUR PARENTS' MESSAGES
Of all the ghosts hovering about your bedroom, the figures of Mom and Dad loom the largest. When it comes to the way men and women should—or should not—relate to one another, they

were your most significant role models. For better or worse, their marriage was your first exposure to the male-female bond, and as such it helped shape your attitudes and behavior. The messages you received from them—explicit and implicit, intentional and unintentional—have left a mark on every love affair you've ever had. In other words, the style of loving you adopted is in some ways modeled after your parents', much as you modeled their style of walking and speaking and laughing.

As you saw with Terri and Terry, some patterns come from direct, unconscious imitation of our parents, often in spite of our best intentions. Have you ever found, to your astonishment, that under certain conditions you do exactly what one of your parents did (most likely the parent of the same sex) even though you vowed to do exactly the opposite? Other negative patterns develop because we succeed in *not* adopting traits that repulsed or scared us as children; compulsive rebellion can simply substitute one troublesome set of behaviors for another.

If you were lucky, you grew up watching two adults treat each other with kindness, respect, and open affection, who appreciated one another and ironed out their differences in a civilized manner. Such an upbringing would instill a positive, optimistic attitude about love and sex.

But if you grew up watching two unhappy people shuffle through life battling with one another, the chances of you forming healthy relationships—or even believing it's possible—are lower. If your parents argued a lot, for example, you may have absorbed the message, "Love is a power struggle," and as a result either create conflicts in your own relationships or avoid them at all costs. If your father abused your mother, the message you took in may have been, "Marriage is brutal for a woman"—or, if you're a man, you may have concluded, "You have to stay on top." If your father was manipulated and dominated by your mother, the message may have been, "Women are controlling"—or "You get your way in marriage by controlling your partner."

Messages about sex can also be transmitted in subtle ways. For instance, if your mother and father were openly affectionate and sexually playful—by kissing passionately at times (not just exchanging ritual kisses), or dancing romantically, or touching openly and often—you are more likely to have developed a healthy sexual attitude. But if you saw your mother reject your father, or get embarrassed or annoyed when he tried to embrace her, you may have (if you're female) learned that sex is something to be withheld—or (if you're male) that women are not interested in sex and have to be cajoled or manipulated into giving it up.

IMPLICIT MESSAGES

What implicit messages did you receive by watching your parents interact?

Which of their behaviors did you imitate?

Which did you rebel against?

How has that imitation and rebellion negatively affected your relationships?

If you're a woman, do you tend to attract men who treat you the way your father treated your mother?

If you're a man, do you tend to attract women who treat you the way your mother treated your father?

EXPLICIT MESSAGES

Of course, many negative parental messages about love and sex are handed down deliberately. If you're a woman, did your parents tell you any of the following?

- "When you find the right man, you'll be happy."
- "It's better to be unhappily married than an old maid."
- "You'll never be happy unless you have a husband and children."
- "Sex is dirty/disgusting."
- "Sex will get you into trouble."
- "Men are only after one thing."
- "Nice girls don't."
- "Pretend you like it to please your man."
- "Marry the first good man who comes along."
- "To get him to do what you want, give him sex."
- "It's a man's job to satisfy you."
- "No one will ever love you like your father."

- "Always put your husband's needs ahead of your own."
- "No man is good enough for my daughter."

No matter what was going on at home, Roz's mother would always say, "My own mother taught me, 'Your husband can do no wrong.'" The message was hammered home every time Roz got upset with the man in her life. As a result, she's still single at 47, much to her mother's dismay. One reason is that Roz internalized the message in a way that was never intended. Each time she discovered a man's flaws or saw him make a mistake, her subconscious mind would reason, "If your husband can do no wrong, then this guy is clearly not husband material." She not only developed unrealistic expectations, but also became so critical that many a man scampered away in self-defense.

If you're a man, did your parents tell you any of the following?

- "Women! You can't live with 'em, you can't live without 'em."
- "No woman is good enough for my son."
- "No one will ever love you like your mother."
- "Women always want to control you."
- "You're not a man if you can't provide for your woman."
- "Don't turn your back or they'll cheat on you."
- "Women don't believe in sex after marriage."
- "Fooling around is okay as long as you don't get caught."
- "Real men are always ready for sex."

Make a list of the messages your parents taught you about love and sex. Which of them did you accept? Which did you reject? Which do you still struggle with today? And don't forget the message of silence: Perhaps your parents said nothing at all about love and sex, conveying the notion that those areas of life are best kept secret. What was the hidden emotional charge beneath the silence; for example, rage, frustration, fear, guilt, lust, or shame?

In many instances, we receive contradictory messages from our parents. What one parent says or does may directly contradict what the other says or does. Or, the same parent doles out a conflicting double message. For example, you may have been encouraged to be a strong, independent child and at the same time made to feel that you wouldn't be loved if you went against your parents' wishes. If you're a woman, you may have been told that you should marry for love, but also that landing a rich man—or a man of the same ethnic background—would *really* ensure your happiness.

Mixed messages put you in a double bind: by obeying one, you're disobeying the other. Look back at the explicit and implicit messages you received from your parents. Do any of them contradict each other? How have those double binds affected you romantically and sexually?

THE WAY YOU WERE LOVED

In addition to the example our parents set and the explicit messages they give us, we also learn how to love by the way they love *us*. If, for example, a boy's mother doles out love depending on how obedient he is, he may grow up to be a pleaser, always doing what his wife wants him to do in order to keep her love. If a girl's father knows no way to demonstrate love besides giving her presents, she may grow up "spoiled," with unrealistic material expectations ("If you really loved me, you'd buy it for me"), and perhaps a lack of appreciation for more genuine expressions of love.

The way your parents treated you as a child may have conditioned you to expect the same kind of interaction in your adult intimate relationships. If, for example, you were bullied by the parent of the opposite sex, you may subconsciously expect your partner to treat you that way. In fact, you may repeatedly attract lovers who do just that. If your parents rejected you when you needed love or protection, you may expect rejection from the men or women you're attracted to—and that expectation could become self-fulfilling. If you felt dominated and controlled by your parents, you may attract domineering, controlling partners—or you may overreact whenever a lover asserts his or her desires. You might accuse your partner of trying to control you, when what's really controlling you are the unresolved ghosts of childhood.

You may have heard "I love you" from your parents, but what was the real nature of their message? Was their love:

- something you had to earn ("I'll love you if you do this or that")?
- smothering?

- overprotective?
- mixed with guilt or fear?
- dependent on their mercurial moods?
- given to get something in return, such as obedience or affection?
- a replacement for the love your parents didn't get from each other?
- something that was bought with gifts?
- strained, forced, and insincere?
- sacrificial or martyred ("Everything I do I do for you")?
- doled out in small portions, like candy?

How did your parents' style of loving you affect the way you have been loved as an adult?

How did the ways they expected you to love them affect the way you loved the men/women in your life?

UNFINISHED BUSINESS WITH A DIFFICULT PARENT

Janet was raised by a dictatorial father whose style of discipline was to belittle his children (when he was not belittling his wife). As a young adult, she had a series of love affairs with men who did the same, all of which ended when she could no longer stand being criticized and ridiculed. By contrast, Janet's younger sister, Allison, vowed early on that she would not end up like her mother. She trained her radar to detect tyrannical men and avoided them like a ship's captain steering clear of icebergs. But she, too, had a series of failed relationships. The men she was drawn to were the opposite of her father, but so meek and compliant she could not respect them.

In their own ways, both sisters were doing the same thing: choosing partners who enabled them to play out unfinished business with a difficult parent. As we've seen, the repetition compulsion can recreate in the present what we did not complete in the past. Hence, we may experience with our love partners the same feelings we felt as children, whether it's hurt, rage, guilt, entrapment, or any other unresolved emotion.

The variations on this theme are endless. Here are just a few possibilities:

- Your parent was demanding and overbearing, so you get angry whenever your partner expresses a legitimate need or makes a simple request.
- Your mother criticized everything you did, so you get defensive whenever your wife corrects you.
- Your father was cold and aloof, so you're attracted to the strong, silent type—only to get enraged by his lack of demonstrable affection.
- Your parents got divorced when you were young, so you're drawn to insecure partners who would never leave you—only to feel trapped by their clingy insecurity.

What unfinished business do you have with one or both parents that may be affecting your choice of partners and the way you relate to them?

OTHER MESSENGERS

The messages you received from your parents were not the only ones you internalized. You also learned about love and sex from your older siblings (or cousins, aunts and uncles, etc.); your peers, especially in the impressionable years of puberty and adolescence; schoolteachers; religious leaders; books; and the mass media. Many of those sources reinforced what you learned from your parents, while others directly contradicted them. Most likely, the contradictions created a sense of ambivalence inside you, perhaps even an agonizing conflict.

For instance, you may have been told by your parents that nice girls don't enjoy sex, or by your religion that sex is only for procreation—only to be assaulted by books and magazine articles telling you that you deserve an orgasm every time you make love. You may have been taught at home that a man is the king of his castle—only to have the message of equal partnership hammered into you by more contemporary sources.

Many of the problematic messages we get from peers and the media have to do with sexual expectations. Messages about male prowess, for example, set unrealizable standards and put enormous pressure on men. They are summed up well in this chapter title in *Male Sexuality* by Bernie Zilbergeld: "It's Two Feet Long, Hard as Steel, and Can Go All Night." We are also affected by fantasy images of ecstatic lovemaking. Expecting fireworks every time you have intercourse is a recipe for disappointment and feelings of inadequacy for both partners. But the movies you saw and the novels you read may have promulgated such messages—and the exaggerations (perhaps even lies) of high school friends may have reinforced them.

Other problematic media messages include:

- Only gorgeous young women are sexually desirable.
- Real men never doubt their sexual ability.
- A woman's satisfaction is the man's responsibility.
- Sex is unsuccessful unless both partners have orgasms.
- Women are turned on by wealth and power.
- Sex has nothing to do with emotions.
- Sex should always be initiated by men.
- Women who initiate sex are sluts.
- A man should always be ready to have sex.
- Sex should always be easy and spontaneous.

Which messages about sex and love did you receive outside your childhood home?

Which ones reinforced the messages you received from your parents?

Which ones contradicted them?

How have the resulting conflicts affected your relationships?

THE GHOST OF LOVE PAST

Nowadays, by the time we're 25, most of us have been through the love wars. We've hurt and been hurt, we've won some and lost some, we've been lifted to the sky and sent crashing to the ground. From our first crush to our last date, from our first kiss to the last time we made love with our mates, we have gathered lessons and accumulated wounds that affect how we love today.

We bring to each new love the gift of hard-earned wisdom—and we come bearing calluses over our hearts. We bring the determination never to make the same mistakes again—and the fear that we may do exactly that. We bring the fervent hope that this promising love will be pure and good and lasting—and the nagging suspicion that it won't work out and we'll end up alone and brokenhearted once again. Even if we've been with the same partner for years, we are still influenced by previous loves, along with all the experiences we've shared with our beloved. The wounds of love can't be eliminated entirely, but they can be brought to conscious awareness and their influence reduced so we can love and be loved the way we truly want to be.

I often say there are two kinds of people who come to me for therapy: those who wish they could find a good relationship, and those who want out of the one they're in. That dichotomy reflects a deep ambivalence that lives in the hearts of a great many people today. With the memory of past pain vivid in their minds, many single people are afraid they'll end up hurt and disappointed again. At the same time, they're terrified that they'll end up alone. The twin fears lead to arm's-length relationships, in which they are not alone but also not involved enough to be vulnerable. The sad irony is that the more we resist being open and vulnerable, the less chance we have of finding the intimacy we crave—and the more our loneliness and frustration persist.

The same dual fears are frequently present in those who are *in* relationships. Every day I see married people who long for greater intimacy but can't truly open up to it because they're terrified of getting hurt again, like a hungry man who's surrounded by fish but is afraid to go near the water.

Are you afraid of getting hurt again? You probably are if any of the following statements apply to you:

- "As soon as someone gets too close, I start feeling trapped."
- "I worry that my partner will get tired of me and leave."
- "Relationships seem to bring out the worst in me."
- "I seem to attract only people who are afraid of commitment."
- "I'm giving too much and getting too little in return."
- "I don't know if I could live with someone again."

- "The thought of going through what I went through with my ex terrifies me."
- "I keep getting involved with the wrong people."
- "I sometimes feel like my partner is a stranger."
- "I could probably find someone better, but what if I don't?"
- "I bend over backward to please him/her because I'm afraid he/she will leave."
- "I get extremely jealous, often without good reason."
- "Why bother? I'll only screw up this one, too."

To the extent that you have associated love with pain, you may be keeping it at arm's length. Perhaps it's time to drop the protective stance and open your arms to love once more. Yes, love can hurt. But, as Bette Midler sang so poignantly in "The Rose," "It's the heart afraid of breaking that never learns to dance."

Don't just dwell on the pain of love past; recall the blessings as well. You may have had unhappy relationships, but you've also been deeply touched by love—not just with lovers and spouses, but with family and friends. Allow those moments into your imagination, not to feel the loss or to regret its absence, but to enjoy the sights, the sounds, the feelings of love, and to remember the possibilities. Those experiences are in the past, but the qualities of love they represent are still alive within you and can contribute to your life. Now that you're wiser, you can love more fully and perhaps avoid the pain that may have accompanied love in the past.

THE DAYS OF WINE AND ROSES

Between outbursts of tears, Sarah bemoaned the fate of many a single woman turning 40: The only good men out there are married or gay; every man I've been with the past 20 years has disappointed me; maybe I'm destined to be a lonely old hag. It was the same heart-rending litany I'd heard many times from women her age, but with Sarah there was a difference. As I listened to her story, I couldn't help thinking, This is a stunning woman who looks 10 years younger than her age, with an MBA from Stanford and a high-paid executive position at a telecommunications firm, a great sense of humor, excellent taste, and a sweet, friendly nature. So what's the problem?

The problem turned out to be the memory of her first and greatest love. She had met Miguel when she was a junior in college. He was a graduate student from Argentina, and their romance seemed like a fairy tale come true. But the ending was a tearjerker. Her family disapproved, citing their age, geography, and religious differences. When Miguel returned to Buenos Aires, Sarah dreamed he would return and marry her despite the obstacles. She has never gotten over the disappointment.

Every man she's ever met has been compared to Miguel—not just the reality of the young man himself, but the romanticized memory of their time together and the fantasy of what might have been. No one could possibly measure up to that.

Sarah exemplifies another way past love can affect our current relationships: by presenting a distorted, idealized basis of comparison. There is nothing like first love, nothing like the combustible chemistry of youthful passion or the glee of infatuation. We remember the thrill of discovery, the moonlight strolls, the time-stopping gazes into a pair of loving eyes, the marathon sex. We forget that in most cases there were good reasons the relationship didn't last. We also lose sight of the hard truth that a love built on excitement alone is doomed to either go up in smoke or remain in an infantile state. Sometimes, making peace with the past means accepting that you're no longer a 19-year-old with galloping hormones.

It is not just the thrill of highly charged romance that can keep us stuck in the past; the memory of a mature love that was lost to tragedy or breakup can also do it. That's why it's so vital to complete the grieving process and stop comparing your present relationship to the (possibly idealized) love that was lost. In therapy one day, Yvonne said she'd always felt that Daniel, her husband of 30 years, was withholding some of his love. "I've never had his complete, undivided affection," she said. "There's always been a part of him I can't reach." It took some prodding, but eventually Daniel revealed a secret that he'd kept for three decades: In his heart, a flame still burned for the sweetheart who broke off their engagement. He had met Yvonne on the rebound. He loved her deeply, but she was in some respects different from his ex-fiancée and his thoughts would often stray to what might have been.

Daniel thought his confession would destroy his wife. Instead, Yvonne felt relieved. At long last, she understood why her husband had never truly been her own, and why he could not look directly into her eyes when they made love. Her reaction set off a flood of tears in Daniel. For the first time, he truly appreciated the depth of Yvonne's love and all the qualities she had that the lover of his youth could not have matched. The door was open to a brand-new start.

Are distorted or romanticized memories of past love keeping you from getting close to potential mates?

Are those memories blocking the intimacy of your current relationship?

Are you comparing present-day lovers and sexual experiences to impossible standards based on the past?

Are you pining for something that never was but might have been?

If the answer to any of these questions is yes, it's time to take a good honest look at who you are and what you have. The treasure you long for may not be in the misty corridors of memory, but right before your eyes.

RIGID SEXUAL ROLES

Sometimes the messages we internalize get woven into rigid roles—a coping style initially learned during childhood or adolescence. In most cases the pattern has roots in the primordial need for a parent's love. As children, we will do anything for that love, including distorting our true selves. We adopt roles to gain our parents' approval or to avoid their anger so they don't abandon us. These patterns become like carved pathways that limit your ability to flow in other, more fulfilling directions. Part of the task of making peace with the past, therefore, is to free yourself from these roles so you can approach love as a self-animated being who is in touch with his or her needs and preferences, not as a puppet on a string.

Here are some negative patterns and rigid roles that people commonly adopt. See if any of them apply to you or the lovers you attract.

THE MARTYR

Martyrs yield to the needs of others, but their sacrifices are not made in the spirit of generosity. Their secret expectation is to be loved in return. They seldom get that love, however. They always seem to meet the wrong person and get taken advantage of, or marry someone who is only too happy to perpetuate their martyr-dom. Rarely do they have good sexual experiences, because they don't make a priority of getting their needs met.

In most cases martyrs are born in childhood, when they inter-nalize the message that their own needs come last and their sense of self depends upon fulfilling the wishes of others. The role is either demanded of them by a parent or modeled for them by a parent who was a martyr him- or herself.

The chief task of the martyr is to practice being more assertive. They have to take their power and learn to ask for what they need, both in and out of bed.

THE PERFORMER

By being held to excessively high parental expectations, perform-ers internalize the message that their worth depends upon achievement. When they fail at something or do not measure up to expectations, they are shamed, made to feel unworthy, or deprived of love and attention. In addition, some people become performers by observing parents who feel like failures; they take a sacred oath that they will never be so humiliated.

As adults, performers become perfectionists, constantly strain-ing to be more than they are. But, just as they feared in childhood that they wouldn't be loved unless they performed well, they live in secret fear of rejection because they're not quite good enough. When they're in a relationship, they usually feel overly responsible for their partner's sexual fulfillment. They may also strive to pile up achievements as a way of saying to their mates—as they did to their parents—"Now do you love me?" This may work in the ini-tial stages of a love affair, but inevitably they feel tremendous pressure to keep up the performance, and fear they'll be abandoned if they don't. This leads to a constant battle with feelings of inade-quacy—and eventually to resentment for having to perform in order to be loved.

The task of performers is to become a human *being* as opposed to a human *doing*. They need to accomplish what matters most without subjecting themselves to unrealistic, perfectionist, guilt-loaded pressures—and to relax, play, and live more fully in the present. It's also vital for them to understand the distinction between self-worth and self-esteem (see page 63) and learn to feel worthy of love even when they're not performing.

THE VICTIM

Victims try to get love by expressing their pain and suffering. Past tragedies are endlessly recounted in hopes of finding sympathy and perhaps special treatment. Refusing to take responsibility for their fates, they constantly complain about lovers or spouses who abandoned them or made them miserable. Victims try to control their love partners by making them feel guilty.

Most victims learned as children that the way to get love and attention was to be hurt, ill, or in pain. Another way is to model a parent who felt like a victim—perhaps even complaining about the burden of parenting and making the child feel unwanted—or who actually *was* a victim of disability, spousal abuse, or illness, and received lots of sympathy and attention because of it. Some victims are created by overprotective or overcontrolling parents who relay messages such as, "Don't play with that, you'll get germs," or "Stay away from those kids, they're a bad influence." They learn to attribute the locus of control to forces outside themselves and end up constantly feeling vulnerable. Finally, many victims adopted the role when they were teased, tormented, and provoked by peers or siblings and ran to their parents for comfort and safety.

Victims have to learn to take responsibility for their choices and agree to be held accountable for the outcomes. They need to forgive those who hurt them in the past, assume a sense of personal power, and learn to get love and attention for the right reasons.

THE PLEASER

Compliant, smiling, seemingly cheerful, pleasers are always ready to say "yes." They never display anger and never risk confrontation. In bed, pleasers are completely riveted on their partner's pleasure, not their own. Am I going to fast? Too slow? Do you like this? How about that? Desperate to please, their satisfaction comes vicariously or not at all.

Initially, their lovers are very happy with them, but the novelty usually wears off quickly—unless the partner is a narcissist, in which case they like the pleaser just fine, thank you. Eventually, though, the pleaser comes to feel cheated, manipulated, trapped, and resentful. But because they go to such great lengths to please, they tend to stay in bad relationships much longer than they should.

The pleaser usually learned as a child that love has to be earned. Compliance becomes a survival mechanism, since disobedience is an invitation to the parents' wrath. In an effort to control the chaos or avoid the rage, the child becomes vigilant about monitoring moods, learning to anticipate what the parents need and want. There are more female pleasers than male pleasers because girls are raised to be nice and boys are typically given more latitude to be aggressive and rebellious.

Pleasers need to practice saying no. They have to understand that you can be loved even when you're not always nice and agreeable. They also have to get over their need for constant reassurance and their fear of disapproval, rejection, and abandonment. Above all, they have to learn to be more assertive, more authentic, more in touch with their own needs and wishes—and to please themselves. When they do, they often find, to their surprise, that their partners are delighted.

THE OBSESSIVE

These people are so obsessed with sex, romance, or relationships as to be addictive. They are constantly on the prowl for the next sexual thrill, the next over-the-top infatuation, or the next emotional entanglement.

Sex addicts are hooked on either conquest, the glee of defying social convention, or the sheer physiological high of sexual activity. They gotta have it, and they gotta have it now. Obsessional romantics are attracted to attraction itself. They crave the giddy high of new love, and sometimes the yearning of unrequited love, often falling for a fantasy only to resent their lover for not living up to it. Relationship junkies are hooked on attachment. They get so enmeshed in each new lover that they lose sight of their own identities and boundaries. They define themselves in terms of the relationship, often regressing to infantile or adolescent states of dependency.

Like alcoholics or drug addicts, obsessives require higher and higher "doses" to satisfy their hunger. Their behavior gets progressively more frenetic, and when they can't get a fix they go through withdrawal, becoming increasingly desperate as time goes on.

For the obsessed, the link to the past is usually deprivation. A lack of love in childhood can lead to a desperate thirst for it as adults. Sexual compulsion, for example, can begin with parents who don't give their children physical stimulation. Since every child needs to be held, cuddled, and stroked, those who are deprived of touch often grow up with a compulsive need for physical attention of any kind.

Other obsessives were inappropriately sexualized as children. Many were victims of abuse who learned that the way to get love is to be an object of sexual gratification. In some cases, their early experience instilled in them a veiled hatred of the opposite sex; their compulsive sexual behavior is a way of getting back at men or women, who subconsciously represent their hated father or mother.

Other early experiences can also play a role. Women who are compulsive romantics, for instance, may have been groomed for that role by unhappy mothers who regretted marrying their husbands and taught their daughters not to settle. The "Someday your prince will come" message can create an addiction to the dizzy infatuation of new love. As soon as reality sets in, they are overcome by disappointment and run away, only to repeat the pattern again and again.

If you are obsessed in sex and love, your most important task is to fully understand that you are more than the sum of your habits, more than a conditioned stimulus-response machine, more than a pain-avoider or thrill-seeker. You can rise above your obsessive thoughts and compulsive actions to achieve a quintessential wholeness in which your emotional and physical needs are integrated with the highest aspirations of your mental, social, and spiritual selves.

You can overcome your compulsive behavior by taking two steps that are absolutely necessary in overcoming habits: 1) heighten your awareness of your pattern, recognize when it arises, and admit that it has power over you, and 2) adopt healthier habits and repeat them over and over again. The suggestions and exercises in this chapter will help you do both. (If your compulsive behavior rises to the level of a true addiction, you would be wise to seek specialized treatment and an addiction support group.)

In addition to the patterns just described, here are some other habitual roles people play in love and sex:

- **The Hero or Heroine.** Boys and girls who are treated like stars, or are raised to be the family genius or the family celebrity, often grow up seeking glory as a substitute for love. They are frequently attracted to needy people whom they can attempt to save or heal.
- **The Clown.** Those who were expected to amuse their families and not express sadness are always trying to keep things light in their relationships. They use humor to ward off conflict and defend themselves against the risks of intimacy.
- **The Loner.** Having been hurt too many times, loners have seemingly become self-sufficient. They have detached from their emotions and resent feeling obligated to satisfy a partner's needs.
- **The Critic.** They were either picked on by their parents or watched one parent constantly criticize the other. They learned that love means being critical of your loved one. The critic projects feelings of inadequacy by becoming frustrated and bitter with the world. Nothing can please them; their love partners always fall short.

Do you recognize yourself in any of those repetitive patterns? Can you understand its origins in your past? Are you committed to breaking its grip on you? What positive behaviors would you like to replace it with?

YOUR LOVE STORY

Let's try to look at your romantic history with fresh eyes. Make a list of the significant loves of your past. Take some time to reflect on each major relationship. Recall the good times and bad; the hurts and the pleasures; the beginnings, middles, and ends.

If you were reading a book about your love story as a whole or seeing it portrayed on screen, how would you feel about it? Would you call it:

- A tragedy?
- A romantic comedy?
- A thriller?
- A violin-soaked tearjerker?
- A farce?
- A combination of some of these genres?

What would you say is the moral of the story?

What are the main themes that run through it?

Did you make the same emotional errors repeatedly? How would you describe those mistakes?

If you could gather together all the love partners in your story, what would you tell them?

What are the main lessons your character has to learn?

What can you do now to make sure your story has a happy ending?

THE HEALING POWER OF LOVE

If only you could love enough you would be the happiest and most powerful being in the world.

—EMMETT FOX

A new love relationship always brings up old wounds to be felt afresh. When you start to feel safe with an intimate partner, fears emerge that were too intense and too walled off to be grappled with before. Each partner re-experiences the traumas of the past in contemporary form. The choice is to flee or to work through the upheaval and experience, perhaps for the first time, a deep, mature intimacy. You will certainly love better if you have made peace with your romantic and sexual past. But the reverse is also true: Learning to love well, here and now, will help you heal the pain of love past. There is no greater healer than love. It is the candle that dispels the darkness, regardless of how or why the darkness was created.

As apprentices in the art of love, we all started out by packaging and marketing ourselves so that someone would love us, an approach that has brought us pain and disillusionment. Now it's time to move to a higher level. Here are some valuable tips for loving better now:

1. *Check Your Assumptions.* It's only natural to make assumptions about what your partner is thinking or feeling based on your past experiences. But you can easily be wrong. Furthermore, it is unreasonable, and a breach of trust, to contradict what your lover *says* he or she feels. The solution is simple: Ask what your partner is feeling and accept the report as true. Cultivate your ability to listen well, without interrupting or leaping to conclusions.

2. *Don't Demand Perfection.* The residual pain of past loves can make you gun-shy. You might have a tendency to overreact at the first sign of upset. Try to remember that love comes with a guarantee of a certain amount of hurt, anger, and frustration. When your partner is upset, try to put yourself in his or her place and ask yourself, "Why does he/she feel this way? What made him/her behave this way? What can I do to convey more love and understanding right now?" Try to use the conflicts that arise as opportunities to grow and learn together.

3. *Curb Your Need to Be Right.* If you felt dominated in your previous relationships, you may enter a new one determined to have your way. But trying to "win" when you and your partner disagree is futile. Fierce competition usually leads to both of you losing, thanks to diminished affection and the tendency of the "loser" to want to win even more the next time. Most disagreements have to do with priorities, choices, values, and

opinions, for which there are no absolute standards of right or wrong. When you find yourself in a dispute with your partner, try to aim for a resolution in which both of you win, both of you are right, and, to the greatest extent possible, both of your needs are fulfilled. Learn to accept reasonable criticism without becoming defensive or vengeful. Don't argue, don't attempt to justify your actions, and above all, don't respond immediately with a criticism of your own. The more you resist listening, the more your partner will persist in telling you what you don't want to hear.

4. *Acknowledge and Appreciate.* If you felt unappreciated in your past relationships, you may crave it even more now. Remember, it's only natural for long-term partners to slack off in expressing appreciation—and to feel that they're taken for granted. The best way to get your partner to acknowledge your best qualities is to first acknowledge his or hers. Get into the habit of thanking your partner for the small ways he or she makes your life better, and expressing your admiration for the things he or she does well. Appreciation is contagious.

5. *Balance Passion and Peace.* As mentioned earlier, many of us learn to equate love with the intense rush of adrenaline and endorphins that comes with the early stage of lusty romance. But the body can't maintain that level of excitement; it inevitably leads to exhaustion, depletion, and boredom. Yet the memory of the high makes us crave it in the present. This is a surefire recipe for disappointment. Try to strike a healthy balance between passion and the quiet pleasures of mature love and inner peace.

6. *Steer Clear of the "Green-Eyed Monster."* One of the great ironies of love is that the more zealously we try to control it, the more likely we are to drive it away. Jealousy, as Shakespeare depicted in *Othello*, can be as destructive as a raging tornado—and the surest way to lose the person you are afraid of losing. If you've been betrayed in the past, you may tend toward excessive vigilance in the present. When you feel jealousy rising within you, try to step back and ask yourself if it's really justified. Was that conversation between your partner and the attractive stranger really flirtation, or just an interesting discussion?

7. *Don't Try to Change Your Partner.* You may have entered your relationship hoping that your lover would be everything your previous partners were not. When he or she turns out to have flaws like everyone else, you have a choice: acceptance or coercion. With the exception of certain nonnegotiables like infidelity, substance abuse, and violence, most of the qualities you might be tempted to try and change are probably minor traits you're better off learning to live with. Certainly, you can make requests, express your preferences and wishes, and offer feedback, but manipulating your lover into becoming something he or she is not—or does not care to be—is a prescription for resentment. Don't attach strings to your love. When you say, "I love you, but . . . ," you are implying, "I won't really love you unless you change." If, on the other hand, you say, "I love you and I prefer . . . ," you're communicating acceptance, and your feedback is more likely to be heard.

8. *Take Responsibility for Your Own Happiness.* Many of us enter love relationships with the unconscious expectation that our partner will rescue us and make us happy. But no matter how committed your relationship is, you will always be single in one important sense: Your happiness is your own responsibility. Not even the most devoted and caring partner can solve all your problems, erase all the pain of your past, or magically bestow happiness upon you. Therefore, while giving appropriately to your lover, make every effort to care for yourself. Treat yourself kindly, attend to your physical and emotional health, engage your interests, develop your talents and skills, allow yourself pleasure, and let yourself play.

9. *Give Each Other Space.* If you've been ignored or abandoned by lovers in the past, you may have a tendency to be clingy. The thought of being apart might make you feel insecure. Remember, in mature love, individuality must be respected and autonomy must be honored. Time apart can be extremely valuable, as absence does make the heart grow fonder and romance can be rekindled by the excitement of returning to each other's arms. By giving you new stories to share, periods of separation also make you more interesting to one another. Don't smother your love with possessiveness.

SEXUAL HEALING

"For some, sex leads to sainthood," declared Henry Miller. "For others, it is the road to hell." Most of us have encountered both ends of that spectrum in our sexual past. Like other powerful forms of energy, sexuality can be harnessed for pleasure, passion, and progress, or for destruction, depravity, and despair. It can trigger the most sacred feelings of the human heart and generate the miracle of life, or it can trigger the harshest pain and generate disease and death.

Virtually all of us carry some hardened scars and open wounds from our sexual past. When you look back at the sex scenes in your love story, which of the following do you see?

- Excitement
- Intimacy
- Joy
- Confidence
- Release
- Openness
- Ecstasy
- Disappointment
- Despair
- Disgust
- Frustration
- Resistance
- Shame
- Guilt
- Embarrassment
- Humiliation
- Rage

Chances are that you've experienced most of those feelings at one time or another. Our sexual histories tend to be a complex mix of bliss and blisters, and each swing of the pendulum leaves its mark: The bliss becomes a standard we try to duplicate or exceed; the blisters become burning memories we try to erase, negate, and avoid repeating.

Regardless of the specifics, one element is usually present in anyone who has to make peace with his or her sexual past: fear. Which of the following apply to you when you think of sex?

- I'm afraid I'll be hurt emotionally.
- I'm afraid I won't perform well.
- I'm afraid I'll let my partner down.
- I'm afraid I'll be physically hurt.
- I'm afraid he/she will find my body repulsive.
- I'm afraid I'll get too emotionally attached.
- I'm afraid to be humiliated.
- I'm afraid I'll end up frustrated.
- I'm afraid of being used and discarded.
- I'm afraid of being trapped.
- I'm afraid no one will want me.
- I'm afraid I'll never have fulfilling sex.

The roots of those fears are imbedded somewhere in your past—in the way you were touched or not touched as an infant; in the subtle messages you received from your parents; in the explicit lessons your elders tried to teach you; in your religious upbringing; in the banter of your peers in puberty and adolescence; in your early flirtations and your first sexual experiments; and in all the sexual encounters of your adult life.

To the extent that shame, guilt, regret, and loss contribute to your present fears, I recommend returning to the previous chapters and giving special attention to sexual issues. If you are currently dealing with a persistent sexual dysfunction, I strongly urge you to see a licensed sex therapist or psychotherapist—and, if the problem could possibly have a physical component, a urologist or gynecologist. Such conditions are beyond the scope of this book. Here, we'll focus on how to give your sexuality a fresh beginning.

As a society, we've gone from compliance with Puritan morality to defiance. We've all done damage by suppressing our sexual energy and by expressing it in ways we've come to regret. Now it's time for *alliance*—to join together heart and libido, soul and flesh, heaven and earth. The aim is to slay your sexual demons by creating a deep, meaningful, mature erotic love—one that is not merely a means of physical gratification but also a sacred act that becomes, in Kierkegaard's phrase, "spirit in action." That kind of sex is not just more satisfying, it is also healing. Here are some simple tips for exorcising the demons of your sexual past and freeing up your sexual energy for maximum pleasure and passion.

1. *Put Love First.* "Joy in sex is experienced only when physical intimacy is at the same time the intimacy of loving," said the renowned psychiatrist Erich Fromm. Love is the foundation for great sex, not the other way around. At its deepest and most profound level, the sexual drive has the primal force of universal love behind it. It seeks not just gratification but union with a sacred "other." When you and your partner can bring patience, commitment, trust, and emotional openness to your passion, you will generate a limitless flow of sexual energy and greater pleasure than you've imagined.

2. *Love Your Body.* Many of us feel contempt for our bodies. Very few can measure themselves against the standards of models and movie stars and not find themselves wanting. How do you feel about your body? How do you feel when you notice signs of aging or weight gain? How confident are you about being seen undressing or wearing a bathing suit? The following exercise is very helpful in learning to accept and appreciate every inch of your body.

   Stand nude in front of a full-length mirror. What parts of your body do you like best? Which arouse a sense of shame or inadequacy? Look at the image in the mirror and say, "I love you." You may feel foolish doing this. You may think it's the height of silliness. Try it anyway. Say, "I love you" several times. Keep saying it until all the awkward feelings disappear and you find that you truly mean it.

   Now pay attention to your genitals. Most of us fail to appreciate the beauty and wonder of our own sexual organs; we feel much more self-conscious looking at them than we do our legs or bellies. Gaze at them. Touch them lovingly. (If you're a woman, you might want to lie on your back and use a hand mirror to take a good long look at your vulva.) Whisper words of appreciation and gratitude to your genitals. Apologize for any blame or shame you projected onto them in the past. They are divine gifts for pleasure and procreation.

3. *Presence, Not Performance.* One of the chief causes of sexual dissatisfaction is the tendency to think of sex solely as a means to an end, the "end" being orgasm. That orientation diminishes everything else about lovemaking, detracting from the inherent beauty of kissing, fondling, and other aspects of what we disparagingly call foreplay. It also puts tremendous pressure on both partners and turns what should be spontaneous, intuitive, harmonious sharing into a performance. Think about the implications of that word: acting for an audience, putting your skills on the line, being evaluated, rising to the occasion. Is that what intimacy should be?

Good sex is whatever is good for both of you at the time. Give yourself and your partner permission to simply enjoy each other's presence without measuring how much, how many, or how often. And take your time! An orchestra doesn't open with a crescendo. Slow down and give yourselves the time to tune into your bodies and feelings.

4. *Make Sex a Touching Experience.* Many couples touch each other only when they're trying to make something happen— like get aroused. This deprives them of a delightful form of sensory pleasure, an exquisite form of intimacy, and a powerful healing tool. Ever since psychiatrist Rene Spitz discovered that babies who are deprived of touch can fail to thrive and grow, researchers have learned that the need to be cuddled, caressed, and stroked is as basic as the need for food and water. It has even been shown that children who are not lovingly touched will go to great lengths to get it—even acting in ways that precipitate receiving a blow rather than have no touch at all.

I highly recommend that you and your partner create a safe space where you can just touch, cuddle, hug, caress, and stroke each other. Use music, candles, and lighting to create a warm, soothing environment, and agree beforehand that this session is not about arousal, orgasm, or any other goal besides sensual pleasure. Take turns giving each other the kind of touch each of you likes best for as long as you wish. Doing this is especially important if either of you was deprived of touch in child-hood, or has suffered substantial pain associated with sexuality. (If you're not currently in a relationship, provide yourself with touch by gently stroking and massaging your entire body.)

5. *Be Creative.* In the early stages of a relationship, it doesn't take much to turn each other on. As it progresses, merely touching each other or seeing each other undress is often not enough. In addition, a certain monotony can set in, with both partners doing the same things they've always done. But the boredom and sexual malaise many couples complain of is not—repeat, *not*—an inevitable part of long-term bonding. The solution is simple: Use your imagination. By all means, keep doing what works, but add to it and enhance it. Don't be a prisoner of routine. You don't give each other the same birthday presents every year, so why give each other the same gifts each time you make love?

You can aid the creative process—and spice up your evening—by doing this exercise: Separately, you and your partner complete the following statements in writing. Then sit together and exchange your answers.

- "A sexual delight I'd love to share with you is . . ."
- "I feel most turned on when you . . ."
- "I would love to turn you on by . . ."
- "The way I like to be touched is . . ."
- "A sexual fantasy I'd like to act out with you is . . ."

6. *Speak Intimately with Your Partner.* The more willing you are to share your deepest fears and feelings about sex, the greater your chances of putting the past behind you and achieving a higher level of intimacy. Intimate talks create a bond of trust that alleviates the pressure to perform and reduces the fear of judgment and rejection. The more open, honest, and specific you are, the better. Here are some discussion openers that will help create a window of sexual discovery:

- "The best thing about our sex life is . . ."
- "We could improve our lovemaking by . . ."
- "I get frustrated when . . ."
- "What I need you to know about my sexual needs is . . ."
- "What I'd like to know about you sexually is . . ."

- "I would feel less pressured if . . ."
- "My biggest sexual fear is . . ."
- "A sexual secret I would like to share is . . ."
- "I find myself withdrawing when . . ."
- "I would love it if you . . ."

7. *Breathe Together.* A terrific way to enhance harmony and intimacy between you and your partner is to lie together and coordinate your breathing. Choose a calm, comfortable setting. Dressed, partly dressed, or undressed, lie in either a face-to-face embrace or in the front-to-back spoon position. Begin by closing your eyes and putting your attention on the rhythms of your own breath. After a minute or two, each of you shifts the focus to your partner's breath. Now, begin to breathe, calmly and deeply, in unison. Don't strain. Adjust to each other's patterns by lengthening or shortening your breaths.

Ten or 15 minutes of coordinated breathing will bring you closer and help you become better attuned to each other's bodies. Feel free to do it longer if you are moved to do so. For all its simplicity, the exercise is a powerful healing tool.

8. *Releasing Past Trauma.* I recommend the following exercise to all couples, but especially those in which one or both partners have had traumatic sexual experiences in the past. Our bodies store the effects of abuse, humiliation, and frustration as somatic memories that can lead to illness or sexual dysfunction. One way to heal those wounds is through touch. Set aside an hour during which you can create a soothing, intimate, utterly undisturbed bedroom environment. During this time, one of you will be the giver and the other the recipient. Don't switch roles during this session; set aside another time for that.

With the room warm and the lighting soft, the recipient lies down nude on his or her back (keep a sheet and blanket handy in case you get chilly). The giver gently massages the receiver's body as he or she relaxes completely. Use scented body oil if you wish. Begin with the feet and work lovingly and slowly up each leg, one at a time. Don't touch the genitals.

The purpose of the exercise is not to arouse but to heal. In the same manner, massage the hands, arms, face, chest, belly, and abdomen, again moving slowly toward the pelvic region without touching the genitals.

Throughout the session, the receiver should relax completely, breathing deeply and smoothly and focusing on the area being massaged. If your partner is touching you too lightly or too firmly, let him or her know in gentle words or gestures.

When it feels right to do so, the giver should focus attention on the pelvic area, where we tend to store a great deal of tension from past sexual experiences. Taking your time, massage the inner thighs, the groin, the perineum (between the anus and the genitals), and just above and below the pubic bone. Press firmly, but take care not to cause pain. Again, the idea is not to arouse but to physically undo the bodily memories of past trauma and free the energy in that region for full sexual expression.

If at any time strong emotions arise, understand that they are the result of releasing pent-up feelings from the past. Allow them to come out. The giver should stop what he or she is doing and listen reassuringly without attempting to stop the process or negate the partner's feelings. When the emotions subside, resume the process. Give the session 30 to 60 minutes, but be prepared to end it any time the recipient wishes to stop. When you're finished, lie together in a relaxed embrace until the receiver is ready to get up. This is a tremendously healing exercise. Treat it with tender loving care.

THE FINAL WORD ON LOVE

Whether your love story so far has been a travesty or a tragedy, the final chapters can be turned into a sacred text. For the last word on the subject, I turn gratefully to the woman who taught me how to love: my wife, Dr. Sirah Vettese. This passage is from her book *What Happened to the Prince I Married: Spiritual Healing for a Wounded Relationship:*

Love is based, first of all, on caring for your own emotional well-being. At the same time, it requires that you care for your mate as you care for yourself. If you can come to better understand what love is and refuse to suffocate it or take it for granted, then love becomes an invigorating force that reaches into the future and sets a foundation for trust and excitement, for wholehearted sharing, for impassioned, meaningful living. Loving relationships are built, not found. They depend on a foundation of safety and trust and have little if anything to do with luck. And, contrary to popular opinion, they have absolutely nothing to do with "being made for each other."

7

Beyond the Bitterness of Blame

FROM RESENTMENT TO FORGIVENESS

Hate never yet dispelled hate. Only love dispels hate. This is the law, ancient and inexhaustible.

— BUDDHA

Are you bitter about the past? Do you blame family or significant others for what went wrong in your life? Are you harboring resentment for old hurts? If you're holding a major grudge against someone, you probably think about it often. You may be reminded of your hurt even if you never see the person—when his or her name comes up, or a new situation triggers memories of what occurred in the past. But you may also cling to resentments that you're not completely aware of, or that you haven't been willing to admit to yourself. It's much more comfortable to pretend that the emotional chasm between you and another person doesn't really exist, or to tell yourself, "It's a thing of the past." But suppressing your resentments can be costly. Here are some signs that the bitterness of blame may be lurking beneath the surface:

- You explode over minor matters and later regret what you said.
- You feel unappreciated or taken for granted at home or at work.

- You keep telling someone off in the privacy of your mind.
- You're holding an emotional "weapon" to use when it's time for payback.
- You find ways to remind people of how they hurt you in the past.
- You use alcohol, drugs, food, or sex to keep your bitterness at bay.
- You feel that life has dealt you a rotten hand.
- You feel that others (e.g., siblings or co-workers) were given special treatment or were favored over you.
- You like telling sob stories to get sympathy from others.
- You don't trust people.
- You feel that you never got the love and support you deserved from those closest to you.
- You think about how great life would have been if only so-and-so hadn't done such-and-such.
- You find yourself plotting revenge.

If any of these signs apply to you, it is time to identify and heal your resentment before bitterness and mistrust consume you.

THE BLIGHT OF BLAME

The tendency to blame begins in childhood as a method of survival. Because they need the consistent help of others to meet their needs for food, shelter, and comfort, children learn to behave in ways that will get their caregivers to provide what they can't provide for themselves. They discover the value of crying when they're hungry, pouting when they're upset, or throwing a temper tantrum when they don't get their way. Children also need to make sense of the big, strange, mysterious world they find themselves in. When they feel pain or discomfort, they need to understand why. In the simplicity of a child's mind, it's either my fault or his/her/their fault.

As we mature, our physical survival may not be threatened by the things people do, but our emotional survival—our self-esteem, our reputation, our sense of stability, our faith, our feelings—can certainly be placed in jeopardy, and our minds insist on knowing why. Most of us learn that life is complicated and blame is not always easy to assign. But some retain the childhood assumption that responsibility for their needs rests with forces outside themselves. When things don't work out, they allocate fault to others, sparing themselves the shame and self-contempt that might arise if they were to accept responsibility themselves.

In many families, children learn to blame by modeling parents who constantly accuse each other—or outside forces—when things go wrong. In some cases, the object of parental blame is actually the child. If you grew up hearing statements like, "Look what you've done, you've made me very upset!" you are more likely to have become a blamer yourself, since blame begets blame.

A patient of mine named George, for instance, grew up with a mother who blamed every problem that came up on the husband who left her. George absorbed that message. He remained bitter toward his father well into adulthood, blaming him for his own lack of focus, insecurity, and other negative traits that interfered with his happiness and success. Each new blow that life dealt him resonated unconsciously with the pain of abandonment, and once again he was the hurt little child whose father ruined everything. Of course, George could not blame everything on his father. Responsibility for some current difficulties were ascribed to his boss, his girlfriend, his neighbor, his friend, or just plain *them*. Anyone but himself.

It was only when I urged George to have a heart-to-heart talk with his father that he began to see through his tendency to blame. In that long-delayed conversation, he discovered that his parents' divorce was not entirely the old man's fault. He saw for the first time that his parents were poorly matched, and that his mother's caustic, critical nature was not born with the divorce. In fact, it may have contributed to it. His father had left with a heavy heart, not knowing any other way to end the misery. Seeing before him a flawed but decent man who had suffered deep regret not only made reconciliation possible, it forced George to look more honestly at himself. He came to realize that blame was his way of avoiding responsibility and that the one it hurt the most was the blamer himself.

Not all blame is habitual, of course, and not all blame is unjustified. Some acts are clearly indefensible, and some situations are unequivocally someone else's fault. You can accept full responsibility for your life and still not excuse the actions of someone who brought devastation to you or others. Whether your bitterness carries the strength of a low-voltage grudge or high-intensity vindictiveness usually depends on how you perceive the impact of the wound. If you see it as powerful and enduring, so will be your resentment.

Blame can be a complex matter, but two simple truths are vital to understand:

1. While you may bear no actual responsibility for what happened, you *are* responsible for how long you carry the grudge and how tightly you cling to it. As Viktor Frankl, a survivor of Hitler's concentration camps, wrote in *Man's Search for Meaning*, the one freedom that cannot be taken away from a human being is the freedom to "choose one's attitude in any given set of circumstances."

2. Getting over resentment is not an act of charity or mercy, it is an act of self-preservation. No matter how justified your anger, no matter how blameworthy the perpetrator, the longer you remain bitter, the more damage you do to yourself. When you give up a grudge, you pluck from your soul a huge emotional splinter.

EXAMINING THE BENEFITS OF BLAME

While blame is ultimately debilitating, we often find it hard to give it up because it serves our emotional needs. Might you be holding onto anger and resentment for any of the following reasons?

JUSTICE MUST BE SERVED
You might feel that giving up blame would be tantamount to letting the guilty go free with a slap on the wrist. It's as if you've put the person who hurt you behind bars and you don't feel that he or she deserves to be paroled.

We're all heirs to an ambivalent Judeo-Christian tradition. On the one hand, we believe in an eye for an eye. On the other hand, we're exhorted to show mercy and compassion to those who "trespass against us." But regardless of how you balance the scales of justice, it is ultimately *you* who are imprisoned by your resentment and *you* who deserve to be released. You can free yourself without absolving the culprit.

IT GIVES YOU A FEELING OF CONTROL

Like guilt trips, blame can be a way of manipulating others to satisfy your needs. But you can't always control the people you resent. More important, you can't control the anger that underlies the blame. You will display it through pouting, thinly veiled accusations, acerbic comments, moralizing, complaining, or therapizing—telling them what's wrong with them and trying to fix them—or arguments over minor slights. When rage is left to fester, it can erupt at any time, whether in misguided revenge or small, barely perceptible acts of destruction.

IT MAKES YOU FEEL POWERFUL

Blame mobilizes the body to defend itself, and with that may come a feeling of strength. It makes you feel safer, better able to avoid the kind of incidents that hurt you in the past. But it's not genuine safety you feel, just a hypervigilance that can make you overly suspicious and guarded. When expressed outwardly, blame can also serve as a demonstration of power, sending a message to others that you are not to be messed with. But that apparent power is dwarfed by its *disempowering* effect: Blame shifts the locus of control to forces outside yourself, making your happiness and peace of mind dependent on others.

IT PROTECTS YOU FROM DIFFICULT FEELINGS

Blaming others shields you from self-doubt, fear of inadequacy, and painful emotions such as sadness, disappointment, and fear. But your subconscious mind knows the truth and will find a way to express it. Furthermore, blame can be like a black hole, swallowing up positive emotions along with the negative.

IT BRINGS YOU SYMPATHY

Blame can bring you the comfort and reassurance of others. But the longer you rely on it, the more your identity becomes defined by bitterness and the harder it is to give it up. You become Angry Man or Angry Woman. Eventually, people will pull away from you; no one wants to hear sob stories forever.

IT SHIELDS YOU FROM ACCOUNTABILITY

One of the chief functions of blame is to deflect responsibility for the conditions of your life and keep your flaws and weaknesses safely hidden from view. But abdicating responsibility makes it harder to make positive changes in your life. You may even stop looking for sources of happiness or ways to remedy your problems.

IT MAKES LIFE COMPREHENSIBLE

By assigning liability for conditions that are too complex to fathom, blame can help you make sense of the universe. It lends a certain amount of order to what might otherwise seem random and chaotic. But you're trading veracity for a fragile sense of certainty. Life is not only more interesting when you accept its mysteries, it's far more honest, and in the long run more manageable.

"Nothing on earth consumes a man more quickly than the passion of resentment," wrote Friedrich Nietzsche. In my experience as a family counselor and psychotherapist, it is just as likely to consume a man or woman slowly. The benefits of blame are dwarfed by the damage it does to your Quintessential Self. It poisons the emotional self, bringing bitterness where there could be sweet love, and depression where there could be joy. It corrupts the mind with cynicism and negativity. With enough resentment, you come to see the world as a nasty place where no one can be counted on and dreams get wrenched from your grasp, like flower petals in a storm. Blame poisons the body, filling it with toxicity that can cause or exacerbate disease. It wreaks havoc with the relational self. The repetition compulsion virtually guarantees that you will project your nemeses from the past onto people in the present. If you're bitter about a dictatorial father, you might be drawn to dictatorial bosses. If you're angry at peers who humiliated you as a teenager, you might be overly competitive with friends in the present. If you're carrying a grudge against a former spouse, you might leak hostility toward members of the opposite sex and perhaps get attracted to someone just like your ex.

Above all, blame stifles the spirit. It turns the universe into a dark, unfriendly place. It severs your connection to all that is sacred and holy and cuts you off from the purest part of yourself—the soul that is capable of profound, blissful appreciation for the gifts of life.

CHOOSING NOT TO BLAME

Blame is not something you heal, it's something you stop doing. It's a choice. At some point, you have to decide that it's time to take back your power and assert that you and you alone are responsible for your life. What was done to you may have been heinous. You may have been a completely innocent victim. The wounds might have been devastating. But whatever happened was part of your soul's curriculum. You may not have realized that you'd signed up for that particular course, but now that you're in the classroom, why not ace the final exam? You can keep on blaming. Or you can stand tall and declare that blame has outlived its usefulness and it's time to put it behind you. The best revenge is to live a free and happy life.

Be assured that electing to end blame in no way minimizes your suffering. It does not diminish the pain you feel or reduce by one ounce the compassion you deserve. It in no way absolves the person or persons who hurt you. It does not require that you forget what happened. If you need inspiration in that regard, look at two shining examples on the world stage.

When he was asked to name the most important teacher in his life, the Dalai Lama of Tibet replied, "Mao Zedong." Needless to say, he was not excusing the Chinese invasion of his homeland that forced him into exile, nor minimizing the brutal oppression, torture, and murder of millions of Tibetans. He will not cease his tireless efforts to free his people. No, Mao was a teacher because he and his totalitarian successors presented a great challenge to the qualities that the Dalai Lama, as a spiritual leader, held dear. "If you know how to develop a just attitude," he said, "your enemies become your spiritual masters, because their presence gives you an opportunity to grow in tolerance, patience, and understanding."

When the apartheid regime that had for so long oppressed the black majority of South Africa was finally toppled, a bloodbath might have ensued. But leaders like Nelson Mandela and Bishop Desmond Tutu knew that the power of understanding was stronger and far more healing than vengeance. During his 27 years as a political prisoner, Mandela had learned that "the oppressor must be liberated just as surely as the oppressed . . . . [Both] are robbed of their freedom." For the sake of their nation's survival, the new authorities calmed the instinct for revenge and created the Truth and Reconciliation Commission, in which victims were given the opportunity to tell their stories and mercy was extended to guilty parties who showed genuine remorse. "Without forgiveness, resentment builds in us," said Bishop Tutu, "a resentment which turns into hostility and anger. Hatred eats away at our well-being."

Putting an end to blame is not just a matter of morality or ethics; it's first and foremost for your own health, happiness, and peace of mind. You owe it to yourself and those you love to make that choice.

HEALING YOUR RESENTMENTS

While giving up blame is a choice, healing the resentment and anger that form its foundation takes effort. Without that healing, the choice to stop blaming has less chance to pass the test of time. But if you work effectively on your wounds you can resume your life's journey stronger than ever, like an athlete who returns to the playing field faster and more agile after healing an injury that had slowed him down.

You can begin the process by making a Most Wanted list. Name the culprits who hurt you in the past. Write out exactly what they did to earn your resentment. Don't limit yourself to your adult experience. Go back to childhood and adolescence and identify all the sources of unresolved pain, shame, and blame. (Refer back to the work you did in earlier chapters.)

Don't be surprised if the people you name are those you love most. One of Freud's most enduring contributions to psychology was the insight that love always contains the seeds of hatred. We all have ambivalent feelings toward our loved ones. Give yourself permission to list everyone for whom you hold resentment, without feeling guilty or blaming yourself for being unfair. You can love them deeply and still acknowledge what their dark sides have done.

Don't limit yourself to individuals. You may feel bitter toward a group of people, like your in-laws or former colleagues. You may harbor hostility toward a category of humanity or an institution. I have counseled a number of men and women, for example, who were corrosively bitter toward the giant corporation that downsized them. Their resentment was just as tangible as if they'd been wronged by a brother, but they could not focus their blame on anyone whose name or face they knew. Similarly, I have treated Vietnam veterans who wore their bitterness on their sleeves like sergeant's stripes. One man used the war to justify being a lonely, cantankerous substance abuser for more than 20 years, directing his anger at "society," "gutless politicians," and "hippie protesters." Most heart-rending was the moment he realized that underneath it all he blamed himself.

Another client, an African-American social worker, came to me for help in overcoming her hatred and mistrust of white people. Steeped in the racial history of the nation, Irma's animosity was informed and understandable. As a little girl in Arkansas, she had seen her father beaten so badly at a civil rights demonstration that he had to stop farming his land and limped the rest of his life. As an adult she experienced first-hand the ravages of subtle racism. She knew that across-the-board prejudice was wrong, but she couldn't drive the hatred from her system. What moved her to get help was a gift of the heart: Her daughter had fallen in love with a white man. By working with the exercises in this chapter, Irma was able to make peace with her personal and ancestral past—just in time to bond with her future in-laws.

It's good to examine the prejudices you may have internalized as a child. You may have heard bitter remarks or stereotypical put-downs aimed at all men or all women, for instance, or at the poor or the rich, or at liberals or conservatives. Who was the "them" to your family? Which group was identified as the enemy or the threat? Grudges toward an institution or group are often hard to deal with because the target is so abstract, but they are important to identify.

To help you recognize the less-than-obvious resentments you may be harboring, here is a list of offenses that can give rise to blame. Did anyone:

- Tell lies about you?
- Reveal a secret about you?
- Break an important promise?
- Cheat you out of money?
- Lie to you?
- Commit a violent act against you?
- Humiliate you publicly?
- Betray you in love, business, or friendship?
- Steal something of value from you?
- Abandon you?
- Let you down in time of need?
- Do any of the above to someone you care about?

WRITING THE WRONG

Finding safe ways to release built-up resentment is a crucial step in making peace with your past. The following exercises have helped thousands of clients and workshop participants to stop playing the blame game. Remember, they are for your own emotional housecleaning; the people for whom you harbor resentment are nonparticipants.

MAKING THE LIST
Begin by writing down what you resent about every person for whom you harbor blame, whether they're alive or dead. Make a

separate list for each person. Beginning with the words "I resent," use specific language to describe every hurt. Here are some examples, drawn from lists that my patients have made.

Toward a father:
"I resent that you always compared me to Susanne and never accepted me for who I was."
"I resent that you didn't save enough money to pay for my college education."

Toward a mother:
"I resent that you tried to talk me out of marrying Bob."
"I resent that you badgered Dad so much he had to leave us to save his sanity."

Toward an ex-spouse:
"I resent that you constantly criticized me and made me feel like I wasn't good enough."
"I resent that you refused to see a counselor and didn't try harder to save our marriage."

Toward a sibling:
"I resent that you didn't lift a finger to help when Mom was sick."
"I resent that you were a goody two-shoes and told Mom and Dad everything I did wrong."

When you think you've recorded enough for each person on your list, take a break, then come back to it later to see if you've left out anything important. When you're done, take a few deep breaths and relax. If feelings of anger, sadness, or grief come up, don't be afraid to let them out. You've been holding these resentments for a long time; it is only natural that expressing them might bring up old emotions.

COMPOSING THE LETTER

As with previous writing exercises, this is your chance to let it all out. Allow your thoughts and feelings to pour forth in a letter to each person for whom you hold major resentment. No one but you will see the letter, of course, so don't hold back or censor yourself in any way. The purpose is to release pent-up feelings, not to articulate a coherent argument. Remember, you are writing this letter to one part of the person only—the part that hurt you. Don't let your love stop you from telling his or her dark side how you feel.

This exercise should take you deeper into your feelings than simply making a list. Wherever there is anger, there is hurt. Dig beneath the bitterness and blame and tap into your innermost pain. Get it out of your system.

By way of illustration, here is an excerpt from a long letter one of my clients, a surgeon named Elliot, wrote to his late father:

DAD:

I can't tell you how much I look forward to expressing what I feel. I could never do that growing up—you never let me show any emotion. You and Mom were Mr. and Mrs. Stoic, bottling up your emotions till they killed you and left her a tired, bitter, old widow hooked on tranquilizers.

Every time I got upset or scared, you taunted me. If I got mad at you or Mom, you punished me. You said I had no right to feel that way. You made me feel like a horrible, despicable, worthless kid. Whenever I got exuberant or joyful, you'd yell, "Knock it off!" It's a wonder I survived without becoming a total zombie.

I was never good enough for you. If I got a B+ you wanted to know why I didn't get an A. And when I went straight A, you said the teachers must have been overly generous and I'd better do it again next semester. You never gave me any credit or said you were proud of me. You just threw out challenges and threats. When I came to you for help, you looked at me with disdain. You once called me stupid for not knowing how to fix my bicycle! Did you think it would make me want to do better? It made me want to get on the bike and ride away so I'd never have to see you again.

You were a bully. You humiliated Mom every chance you could get. You never listened to her. You never comforted her. Maybe you kissed her on the cheek when you left on a trip or hugged her on her birthday, but most of the time you just bossed her around and put her in her place—under your thumb. You had a heart of stone. It's no wonder it cracked and killed you at age 52.

I was so mad at you by then that part of me was glad you died. Do you know what it's like to be glad your own father is dead? I thought I was a monster! But I was also sad. I wanted just once in my life to hear you say "I love you" or "I'm proud of you, son." I worked my ass off. I became pretty damn successful. But even when I won awards you never once said you were proud. Always criticizing, always diminishing.

No kid should have to go through life feeling unworthy of his father's love. All my relationships were messed up by that feeling inside that I'm basically unworthy. That's why I've been divorced twice. I wish I'd realized that I'm not unlovable but you were just incapable of showing love—to me or anyone else. Mom once flat out asked if you loved her. You know what you said? "I work hard to make sure you have food on the table and a roof over your head, don't I?" I feel sorry for you, Dad. I may have felt unloved, but you had it worse. You couldn't love! You were a cold, miserable, unfeeling, pathetic shell of a man.

I wish you were here so I could tell you all this to your face. I always wanted to tell you off. I fantasized going into your office and humiliating you in front of your boss and your coworkers— just like you humiliated me in front of my friends. Remember the one time you bothered to show up at a Little League game? I was so nervous with you there I struck out without even swinging the bat. I just froze. Remember what you did? You yelled, "Swing the damn bat, you chickenshit!" Do you have any idea how that made me feel? I couldn't bear the thought of going through that again, so I faked an injury and I went to the bathroom to throw up. I have to stop now, Dad, because I'm about to cry. And you can't stop me this time.

When he got to that point, Elliot broke down and wept. To his surprise, however, he wasn't finished. He resumed writing and didn't stop until he had filled another nine pages.

Many people are amazed to discover how deep their wells of resentment run. Keep writing until you feel spent, whether that's after 1 page or 30. If you need to rest, take a break and come back to the letter when you're ready, even if it's not until the next day. Don't be surprised if you can't bring yourself to stop even if you're repeating yourself. That simply means that the feelings need to come out.

EXORCISING RAGE

Stream-of-consciousness writing is a great way to let out anger and resentment. But rage may need a more physical release. Whereas anger is a natural response to hurt, rage is an automatic emotional response to severe rejection, betrayal, abuse, or a threat to your survival. It is characterized by the intention to destroy. For most of us, this destructive impulse is frightening, so we bury it inside. It is essential to acknowledge the presence of rage and to find a safe way to release it.

As mentioned earlier, there are many ways to appropriately vent anger: pounding pillows or a punching bag with your fists; tearing up a phone book; smashing furniture with a rolled-up newspaper; stomping on a cardboard box; throwing old dishes or empty cans against a wall; playing sports like tennis or racquetball, where you get to hit something. Feel free to use any or all of these techniques.

The method I recommend most often is to use a bat made of plastic or foam. Place a large pillow on the floor in front of you, or kneel before a bed or sofa. Imagine the face of the person you're enraged at, then pound away. As you bash the person, use your voice. Scream as loud as you can (if you're concerned about the neighbors, turn up the stereo). When Elliot bashed the negative aspects of his father, he found himself yelling things like, "You bastard! You mean, miserable son of a bitch! I hate you! I despise you!" He also found himself wailing like a hurt little boy at one point— and at another point laughing hysterically, from the sheer exhilaration of release.

Take this opportunity to purge the rage from your system once and for all. Be careful not to injure yourself, but give yourself permission to pound, smash, wail, scream, kick, and punch until you feel totally spent.

When you are exhausted, lie down and rest until you are ready to resume activity.

THE POWER OF FORGIVENESS

Without forgiveness life is governed by an endless cycle of resentment and retaliation.
— ROBERTO ASSAGLIOLI

Trying to forgive before you fully acknowledge your hurt and give voice to pent-up resentment can lead to internal conflict and incomplete healing. Now that you've had a chance to express your feelings, you may be ready to contemplate truly forgiving those who harmed you.

We are exhorted by every major religion to forgive. The traditions of Judaism and Islam direct their followers to emulate a merciful God and, in the words of the Koran, "pardon and forbear." And Jesus instructed his disciples, "If thy brother trespass against thee, rebuke him; and if he repent, forgive him. And if he trespass against thee seven times in a day, and seven times in a day turn again to thee, saying, I repent; thou shalt forgive him." No doubt the great sages of antiquity knew that forgiveness is not just a moral imperative or a way to score points in heaven. It is, quite literally, *for giving*. Giving to whom? Possibly to the person you're forgiving, who stands to gain relief from guilt and the restoration of your trust and affection. But that is secondary; when you forgive, the one to whom you give the most is you. You are giving back to yourself the vital life energy that had been consumed by bitterness.

What spiritual leaders have told us for centuries about forgiveness is now being verified by modern scientists. One study, by Charlotte van Oyen Witvliet of Hope College, found significant physiological differences between subjects who forgave and those who did not. Stress levels were considerably higher when the person thought of revenge as opposed to forgiveness. According to *Time* magazine, interviews revealed that the subjects "felt in even greater control when they tried to empathize with their offenders and enjoyed the greatest sense of power, well-being, and resolution when they managed to grant forgiveness."[1]

You have every reason to make the effort to forgive. But you may also have very good reasons *not* to. Let me ease the pressure you might already be feeling by declaring right now that *you can make peace with your past without forgiving everyone who hurt you.*

To be truly effective, forgiveness has to be an examined choice, not just lip service or a contrived attempt to feel something you don't really feel. If, after examining all the ramifications, you conclude that you just can't bring yourself to forgive, the choice can be a healthy one—if you find inner peace and resolution without forgiving. But the potential benefits of forgiveness are so great that you owe it to yourself to consider the option carefully. The first step is to examine your resistance.

OVERCOMING YOUR RESISTANCE

There are many reasons why we find it hard to forgive. You might feel that doing so would imply that you condone what was done to you. You might feel that saying "I forgive you" would allow the offender to feel exonerated. Forgiveness might seem cowardly, as if you were surrendering or caving in. It might seem to mock your sense of justice. Those are all understandable objections. But there is no reason you can't find forgiveness in your heart and still take a firm, unwavering stand about the wrong that was done and the pain it caused. You can declare the offender guilty as charged and hold him or her fully accountable. And you can reserve the right *not* to actually say, "I forgive you." Once you forgive in your heart, you get to choose whether or not to express your forgiveness outwardly.

Another reason we resist forgiveness is that we think it entails forgetting. "Forgive and forget" is a nice expression, but it's hard to live up to without suppressing the memory of your pain. You may feel you need that memory to protect you from further injury, just as recollecting a painful sunburn reminds you to put on sunblock. "The stupid neither forgive nor forget; the naïve forgive and forget; the wise forgive but do not forget," said psychiatrist Thomas Szasz. The trick is to remember without setting yourself up to be an everlasting martyr to a painful past.

Perhaps the biggest source of resistance is fear. If you forgive the person who hurt you, are you not setting yourself up for another blow? Does it not make you more vulnerable to the same offense? A client of mine named Amanda is a prime example of why this is a legitimate concern. A 32-year-old real estate broker, Amanda was a devout Christian who believed strongly in mercy and forgiveness. She tried very hard to extend those virtues to her husband. Bart was a gentleman when sober, but when he drank he became verbally and physically violent—sometimes toward his children as well as his wife. With her generous spirit, Amanda tried to understand the torment that drove Bart to such nightmarish acts. Her heart ached when she thought of him as a child with an alcoholic, physically abusive mother and a sullen father who eventually walked out, never to be heard from again. Amanda kept on forgiving her husband. The problem was, what she thought was compassion was more like pity; what she thought was spiritual resolve was actually resignation; and what she thought was forgiveness was really enabling. She suppressed her pain and kept on taking abuse instead of taking her power.

Amanda's counseling enabled her to finally establish boundaries and appropriately protect herself and her children. When her husband next became physically abusive, she took the kids and left. Only then did Bart join AA and seek professional help himself.

Forgiveness is never meant to embolden an abusive or manipulative person to take further advantage of you. It does not mean you have to make excuses for the offender or reconcile with him, or have anything further to do with him. If necessary, it can entail letting go of the person who hurt you so you won't get hurt again. With adequate preparation and strength of conviction, forgiveness should make you *less* vulnerable, not more so. "The weak can never forgive," observed Mahatma Gandhi. "Forgiveness is the attribute of the strong."

Why are you resisting forgiveness? Here is a quick and easy way to identify the attitudes and emotions that are blocking your wish to forgive.

Draw a vertical line down a sheet of paper, making two columns (use a computer if you're comfortable with word processing). In the left column, write, "I forgive you,_____," filling in the name of a person against whom you're holding a grudge. Then close your eyes and notice what thoughts and feelings come up. Look for signs of resistance—a feeling of tension, perhaps, or an urge to cross out the sentence. Listen for nasty remarks, sarcastic comments, or statements that contradict "I forgive you" and challenge your intention to forgive. In the right-hand column, write down whatever comes to mind.

Continue to write "I forgive you (the same person's name)" on the left and your gut reactions on the right. After a while, you should start to feel the resistance easing off. When you have written "I forgive you" three times without any negating statements, consider the exercise complete for now. To illustrate the kind of responses that may come up, here is an example of one person's list:

I forgive you, Mother.	Yeah, right!
I forgive you, Mother.	You don't deserve it.
I forgive you, Mother.	Not after the way you shamed me.
I forgive you, Mother.	I can't let you off that easy.
I forgive you, Mother.	You'll just keep on humiliating me.
I forgive you, Mother.	It would help if you'd admit you were wrong.
I forgive you, Mother.	I'm tired of fighting it.
I forgive you, Mother.	Maybe.
I forgive you, Mother.	I really want to.
I forgive you, Mother.	I wish I could let go of my anger and show you how much I love you.
I forgive you, Mother.	I have compassion for your suffering.
I forgive you, Mother.	_____.
I forgive you, Mother.	_____.
I forgive you, Mother.	_____.

The exercise is simple, but often powerful enough to work out all the resistance to forgiving. It might take only a few statements to run through your resistance, or it might take several pages and several sittings. If, later on, you find that you're still unable to make the commitment, do the exercise again. Naturally, it would be good to do it for every important person for whom you harbor resentment and blame. If there are several, begin with those you find easiest to forgive and work up to the more difficult cases.

CULTIVATING COMPASSION

If we could read the secret history of our enemies, we should find in each man's life sorrow and suffering enough to disarm all hostility.

—HENRY WADSWORTH LONGFELLOW

When Carlos entered my office he had the lithe, muscular physique and catlike grace of a professional dancer. He was having anxiety attacks, he said, precipitated by a decision he was struggling with. He was thinking about leaving San Diego and moving to New York to pursue his dream of dancing on Broadway. But that was an expensive and uncertain proposition, and his lover did not want to go. When I asked where his family was located, a dissonant mix of sorrow and rage swept over him. "My family is here," he said, "but they may as well be back in El Salvador." Two years earlier, when Carlos came out of the closet, his father denounced him, disowned him, and threatened the rest of the family with banishment and disinheritance if they ever saw him again. When he left my office after telling that story, Carlos had the stiff, stooped look of a troubled old man.

In our therapy sessions, Carlos made great progress in resolving his grief over the loss of his family. He held firm in his wrath toward his father, though, vowing he would never forgive the man even if he were to beg on hands and knees. He left for New York with hope in his eyes.

The next time I saw him he had death in his eyes. It was four years later and Carlos was gaunt and frail with AIDS and terminal cancer. "If I'm going to die," he said, "I want to die in the town of my birth, with my mother and sisters at my side."

"Then you've reunited with your family?" I said.

"That's why I came to see you," he replied. "About a year ago, my father had a change of heart. He sent my sister to find me and tell me it's okay to come back. Seeing my mother and sisters again has been a wonderful blessing, but I refuse to see my father. He never apologized, and he never accepted who I am, and I can't forgive him for what he did."

Carlos did not want to die bitter. He wanted more than anything to reconcile with his father before it was too late, but he could not find it in his heart to forgive.

Instead of focusing directly on the issues he presented, I had Carlos explore who his father was. With the help of his mother and a box of old photographs, he began to see the roots of his father's attitudes. He saw a little boy in an El Salvadoran village, living in a house the size of an average American living room with eight kids and no indoor plumbing. He began to understand his father's strict Catholic upbringing and the culture of machismo that rigidly defined what a man should be. He could appreciate the deeply ingrained survival instinct that said a man must work with his hands, side by side with his father, and sire children of his own. He could feel the pain his father must have felt when his own parents died at the hands of guerrillas, and the terror he endured when he wrenched himself from his roots and traveled overland to America to start a new life. He comprehended for the first time the anguish his father must have felt when he learned he had a homosexual son—and the courage it took to extend his hand in reconciliation.

One of the most moving moments of my career was when I saw Carlos and his father embrace a month before Carlos died.

LETTING GO OF THE UNFORGIVABLE

If you can see those who hurt you with fresh eyes, you will take a giant step toward forgiveness. Try to look past the acts themselves and see the pain, fear, and emotional wounds behind them. Consider the origins of their behavior—not to find excuses, but to comprehend what drove them to do what they did. If you look far enough into a person's past, you are likely to find that he or she also has people to blame, and they too have people to blame, and so on back to the Garden of Eden. Those who hurt others have often been hurt themselves. Parents who shame their children were likely raised by parents who shamed them. This does not absolve anyone of wrongdoing, of course, but it may foster forgiving why it happened: not the *what*, but the *why*.

If possible, try to find out what life was like for the person you resent when he or she was a child. What were his or her parents like? How were they influenced by their religious and cultural heritage? Was the family intact, or was there a divorce or early death? Was it a loving, supportive home or a tense, troubled home? Was there a history of alcoholism, abuse, or violence? Can you see inside the person you know and perceive the hurt child who aches for love and is still trying to get his or her needs met? What about his or her adolescence? Were there humiliations, rejections, abandonments, and betrayals? In early adulthood, were there failures, heartbreaks, and traumatic losses? Any information about the forces that shaped the personality that hurt you can help you understand more fully what took place.

Another important way to achieve empathy is to put yourself in the offender's shoes at the time he or she hurt you. What was going on in his life? What unusual circumstances might explain her state of mind?

Also, ask yourself if there are other ways of perceiving what happened. Is there another side to the story? Is it possible you did something to precipitate the offender's behavior? Could he or she have misunderstood something you said or did? (These last questions should not result in blaming *yourself.* They are intended only to expand your perspective in case they apply. If they feel inappropriate, it's okay to skip them.)

TO FORGIVE OR NOT FORGIVE

If you are sincere in your desire to overcome blame, you owe it to yourself to reach into your heart and see if you come up with a handful of forgiveness. But don't be surprised if you can forgive only partially, or if you are willing to forgive but still feel resentment. Rest assured that ambivalence and continued resistance are perfectly normal. Forgiveness is an ongoing process. It may take some time before it solidifies and becomes a fixed part of you.

It is also important to remember that forgiveness is not an absolute requirement for healing. Two reasonable people can suffer virtually identical hurts and come to opposite decisions on the question of forgiveness. For a prime example of that, consider what happened to a pair of close friends, Robin and Michelle, when their seemingly perfect lives were shattered by the discovery that their husbands had had a series of affairs with women they'd met through their work.

Michelle and Robin let loose their rage in therapy and screamed at their spouses in the privacy of their homes. Their husbands expressed deep, apparently genuine remorse and vowed never to do it again. They begged to be forgiven. The women agonized. Each one had a profound desire to keep her family intact. In private therapy and couples counseling, they probed their husbands' pasts to find out what drove them to infidelity. All things considered, the women achieved a remarkable degree of compassion for the men who betrayed them. They also worked through a cauldron of difficult emotions and learned a great deal about themselves, not all of which was easy to face.

In the end, despite their parallel paths, the two women arrived at different places. Robin chose to forgive. "I can see the kind, loving man he really is, and I want to grow old with that man," she said. "It will take a while before I can trust him completely, but I feel that this experience can make us closer and stronger."

This is what Michelle said: "It's not that I can't forgive, it's that I *won't* forgive. I'm satisfied that I made my best effort. I'm not a vengeful person. I'm simply taking a stand. What he did offends everything I hold sacred. I consider it unforgivable."

Why did these two women reach such vastly different conclusions? The answer lies in a complex web of upbringing, personality differences, history, and values. For whatever reasons, each did what she had to do. Now, three years later, Robin is still with her husband and Michelle lives alone with her children. Both women report that they are at peace with their decisions.

Forgive or not forgive? The decision rests on your assessment of the crime that has been committed and the personal values that determine what, to you, is forgivable and what is not. If you forgive, make sure it is genuine and heartfelt. If you don't forgive, make sure you resolve your resentment and find peace within yourself.

FORGIVING FROM THE HEART

The following visualization will help you complete the process of forgiveness. As before, find a quiet, comfortable place where you will not be disturbed for 20 or 30 minutes, and follow the relaxation instructions on page 27.

When you're ready, visualize the person you wish to forgive. See the two of you together in a safe, peaceful setting. (If for some reason you find it difficult to visualize the person, keep a photograph of him or her in front of you and glance at it as needed.) With that image in mind, see yourself saying the following in your own words: "Out of the love I have for you, and the love you have for me, there are some things I need to clear up." Now, speak your heart. As you express the resentments you hold, he or she listens attentively, giving you the respect and trust you deserve, making it completely okay to say what you feel.

When you finish airing your resentments, reveal the hurt that lay beneath your anger. Go on to express the fear you may have felt, such as, "I was afraid everything would fall apart without you." Then, if appropriate, tap into the love that was there before you were hurt ("I loved you so much, it saddens me that this happened between us").

Now the person before you looks into your eyes with an understanding and empathy you never received before. You reach out and take his or her hands. With all the warmth, compassion, and love you can muster, you say the words that will set you free: "I forgive you." Say it again, decisively and sincerely: "I forgive you, (name)."

If there is more to be said, speak it now, from the heart. Imagine that he or she feels deeply grateful for your forgiveness. You both experience a tremendous sense of relief. All the long-buried positive feelings you have for each other can now flow freely. You embrace. What a beautiful feeling it is to hold closely to your chest the one you had been pushing away.

When you're ready, he or she stands up, and, with your blessing, walks away. You are alone in this peaceful place. You feel lighter. You have made room in your heart for love and peace. A warm, healing light appears before you and enters your chest. It spreads from your heart upward to fill your upper body. You no longer have to shoulder the burden of resentment. The light rises up to your throat, which can now speak the gentle truth, and higher still to your face, which beams with courage and love. And the loving light radiates downward, filling your belly, your abdomen, your genitals, your arms and legs. Soon you are fully aglow with the light of wisdom and peace. You are free of resentment and blame.

Relax for 5 or 10 minutes with this inner light filling you from head to toe. If you feel any lingering pressure in your head, or some irritability, be sure to take additional time to rest before opening your eyes. If, later on, you experience some remaining bitterness toward the person you forgave, repeat the exercise until your forgiveness feels complete.

THE POSSIBILITY OF RECONCILIATION

Resolution is an internal process in which past issues come to be accepted, intellectually and emotionally. Absolutely essential for overcoming blame, resolution is always possible to attain. By contrast, reconciliation is *not* a prerequisite for making peace with the past, and it is *not* always possible.

By its very nature, reconciliation is not something you can control. At the very minimum, the other person has to be willing to reconcile.

But willingness alone is seldom sufficient. Especially if there has been a major betrayal, one of you—maybe both—must say or do something to put the matter to rest. Contrition may be enough, but it must be genuine. If the offender refuses to admit wrongdoing, or his apologies sound hollow and insincere, the best course of action may be to cut your losses and find resolution within.

But even genuine contrition may not be enough. For reconciliation to work, the injured party must feel safe enough to drop his or her defenses. Ask yourself what you need to be able to trust this person not to hurt you again. Do you need to hear a sincere apology? Does he or she have to make a commitment of some sort? Do you need to see signs of a bona fide change in behavior or attitude? If so, exactly what changes do you need to see, and are they reasonable to expect?

In addition, ask yourself what you have to do, internally and externally, to protect yourself against a recurrence. How can you make yourself less vulnerable in the future without becoming overly protective? Are there ways to prevent certain situations from happening again? Can you strengthen yourself so that you can handle potentially harmful situations more effectively? The stronger you feel, the easier it is to give yourself the gift of forgiving and to reconcile without fear.

TRANSFORMING
THE ENERGY OF BLAME

When you forgive your past, you can turn fully toward the future. As he was being led out of the Robben Island prison where he had spent 27 years of his life, Nelson Mandela had a profound insight. If he were to go on feeling hatred for those who had imprisoned him, he would carry his prison with him. His inner path to freedom, Mandela realized, was to forgive. But that did not extinguish his fierce will to end injustice and free his people from oppression.

As you heal your anger and resentment, you can transform the energy of blame into a healthy fierceness. You can use that ferocity to prevent a recurrence of past hurts and create something new and different for your life. In fact, you can use it to stand firm against *all* indignities and injustices, and help make the world a better place for all of us.

8

Creating a Joyful, Radiant Future

REDISCOVERING THE PASSION TO LIVE YOUR HIGHEST DESTINY

The future creates the present against the backdrop of the past.
— LAZARIS

Right now, imagine it's the end of your life. You've aged like fine wine and lived long and well. You lay on your deathbed, without pain or great discomfort, knowing that the time to leave your body is at hand. Around you are your dearest loved ones. You can feel the depth and purity of their love. They tell you they are proud of how you've lived and are eternally grateful for all you've meant to them and done for them. You search their eyes and you search your heart, and you find no words that have not been said, no feelings that have not been expressed, no unfinished business that needs to be completed. You are at peace with each of them.

Alone now, you hear voices in the next room. Your loved ones are laughing as they recall the good times with you. Their stories are filled with admiration, respect, and appreciation. They praise your courageous commitment to seeing yourself with honesty and candor, your eagerness to learn and grow, your willingness to change. They revere your compassion and concern for others, your kindness, your capacity for giving and forgiving. They adore your sense of humor, your optimism, your humility, your ability to see and nurture the best in them. They admire your achievements and your contributions to your community. They know you had flaws, but they're proud that you worked hard to overcome them. They admire you for making peace with your past and becoming the best human being you could be. When they reach the end of their lives, they want to be as content and as beloved as you are.

As you review the key moments of your life, both painful and precious, you also reflect upon your Quintessential Self. Your physical self is grateful that you have taken such good care of it, that you protected it well while allowing it the full range of sensory pleasure and enthusiastic play. Your mental self is content; you have used your intellect to full advantage in the service of a productive life, and you have honored its innate curiosity and sense of truth. Your emotional self is thrilled that you allowed it to experience the full spectrum of feelings, and that you learned to express your emotions effectively and constructively. Your relational self is proud that you have treated others with dignity, generosity, and kindness, while at the same time setting appropriate boundaries and standing up for your own needs and values. Your spiritual self is blissfully content: You have given voice to the yearning of your soul, and you have consciously explored the cosmos within.

Your Quintessential Self is at peace. If there is a voice of God, it speaks: "One such as you has never passed this way before and never will again. You are my beloved, with whom I am deeply pleased."

A GOOD DAY TO DIE

When, on his deathbed, Plato was asked to summarize the meaning of his life's work, he propped himself up on one elbow and said, "Practice dying." Many of us shy away from thoughts of our own death, and when we are forced to contemplate it, we do so with dread. But there is powerful evidence, from research scientists as well as theologians and philosophers, that acknowledging and accepting our mortality can profoundly enrich our lives. It helps us to appreciate the beauty of existence and to fully experience our own capacity for love, joy, and wonder. "One can experience an unconditional affirmation of life only when one has accepted death, not as contrary to life, but as part of life," said Joseph Campbell.

The deathbed description that opens this chapter is written in general terms. Take a few minutes now to visualize in detail your own ideal passing. After following the relaxation steps for visualization on page 27, imagine yourself at the end of your life. How do you wish to feel as you reflect upon your days? Be as specific as possible. Visualize your family and your closest friends as they come to see you, one by one, for the last time. What do they say about the role you played in their lives? How do they praise you? What do you fondly remember? As you imagine the dialogue with each person, evoke specific incidents that have occurred—or that you *want* to occur between now and then.

Imagine your funeral. How are you eulogized? What is said about the way you lived? What lessons and inspiration do the speakers derive from your example?

When you're finished, ask yourself this question: What if the end were to come today? Would you be able to go in peace? What would you regret not having made time for? What would you wish you had said to those closest to you? How different would your deathbed scene and funeral be, as compared to the ideal scenarios you just visualized? Would anyone feel sorry for you? Would people say it's a shame you never lived up to your potential? Would anyone be glad you're gone?

Ernie was in his early forties when he was diagnosed with metastatic kidney cancer and given six months to live. In one of our sessions I had him imagine his own funeral. He saw that he was about to leave behind a legacy of misery and animosity. He had three ex-wives who hated him, a bunch of kids who either didn't know him or couldn't stand him, business partners who felt so betrayed they were suing him. He couldn't bear it.

Consumed by regret, Ernie wrote a letter to every significant person from his past expressing remorse. He named all the specific ways he'd wronged them and asked their forgiveness. Then he picked up the tab for all of them to fly to California for one last face-to-face encounter. He succeeded in achieving closure with everyone who was willing.

Ernie was lucky. Not everyone is. If you wait until death is staring you in the face, it may be too late.

Take a few minutes right now to write an obituary of yourself as you would like it to read at the end of your long, happy life. Then write one as it would appear if you were to die today. You can use the gap between today's reality and your ideal as a spur to growth and a yardstick for change. I recommend that from time to time you review and update your obituary. This will help you calibrate your progress and make sure you keep on contemplating crucial questions such as, "What does it mean to be me?" "What is truly important?" and "Would I rather be stubborn and 'right' or loving and kind?"

A VISION OF THINGS TO COME

At any moment I could start being more of the person I dream to be—but which moment should I choose?
— ASHLEY BRILLIANT

Just as the child and adolescent are alive in you now, you are alive in your future self. In a sense, you are determined by your future: Your image of where you want to go and where you expect to be dictates most of your actions. Up until now, your view of the future may have been distorted by beliefs and attitudes imposed upon you by others and by the subconscious imprint of previous pain. Now it's time to design your reality according to a visionary blueprint instead of habituation to the past. As you make peace with your past, your authentic self is free to emerge, and that authentic self is vastly more powerful than the adaptive self that's been running the show until now.

As my then 16-year-old daughter, Shazara, once enlightened me, "The only way to make peace with your past is to make peace with your present." When you feel fulfilled, you are at peace with the past because you know that everything that ever happened to you has brought you to this splendid moment. A worthy goal, therefore, is to create a future so fulfilling that when, in the natural course of events, it becomes your past, you will already be at peace with it. You are not a pawn in some cosmic chess game. You are not an inert cog in the great wheel of destiny. You are the author, the inventor, the mapmaker. You can conceive your highest destiny and give birth to it.

"The future is not some place we are going, but one we are creating," said sociologist John Schaar. "The paths to it are not found but made." The key to creating a glorious future is to form a clear, specific vision—one that is bold and optimistic but grounded in the possible—and then to flexibly adapt to changing conditions as you work to realize your dreams.

You have created a vision of the ideal conclusion to your life. What about the near future? What do you want for your life in the next few years? In exploring your past, you may have uncovered some old dreams that you buried because they were "unrealistic," or because other people talked you out of them, or because "real life" intruded. Perhaps those dreams need to be revived; it's never too late, and fulfilling even one may turn your life around. Angelica had always dreamed of seeing the ancient ruins of Egypt. But, as a single mother working as a legal secretary, she had never been able to save enough money for the trip. I encouraged her to look into alternatives to commercial travel. She discovered that for a modest cost she could work as a volunteer on an archaeological expedition with a local museum. It was not only the most rewarding vacation of her life, it broke her habit of thinking that it's no use dreaming. And that was just the beginning: At age 36, she is back in school studying to become an archaeologist.

On the other hand, your heightened self-awareness may have illuminated primitive dreams or dark desires that are outmoded and no longer serve you. Perhaps it's time to slay those dreams and replace them with new ones. A client named Ken, for instance, had an adolescent dream to be a Lover Boy who would score with every beautiful woman he met. He succeeded in that quest for a good number of years, until he got married. The dream was never put to rest, however, and when he found himself in the doldrums at age 43, Lover Boy emerged from hiding and tempted him to cheat on his wife. To save his marriage, Ken had to replace Lover Boy with Loving Man. Similarly, Lindsay formed a dream of being Superwoman. She wanted to have it all: high-powered career, loving marriage, children, healthy recreation, spirituality—everything there is, and all to the max. On the brink of burnout, she realized that Superwoman was killing her. She slayed that dream and replaced it with Realwoman.

How did you view your future in the past? What did you expect? What did you hope for? You may come to realize that your vision was incomplete, inadequate, insufficient, or ill-informed. Did you set your sights too low? Did you set yourself up for disappointment with unrealistic, grandiose, or insatiable dreams? Now you can make peace with your old view and create a shining new vision for your life ahead.

Set aside 15 or 20 minutes to visualize the next chapter of your life. Follow the relaxation instructions, and when you come to your place of peace, allow yourself to form a vision of life as you wish it to be. Create a richly detailed image in which you are not just getting along, not just doing okay, but truly feeling fulfilled.

Take yourself through a day encompassing every area of your life. There you are doing work that is challenging, rewarding, and perfectly suited to who you are. What does your workplace look like? What are you doing, and how do you feel doing it? How much are you paid?

Where do you live? What kind of dwelling is it? Who else is there? A spouse? Children? Grandchildren? How do you relate to the significant people in your life? How do you handle differences? How do you play? How do you love?

How do you relate to your community? Are you involved in important causes or charities? How do your neighbors and fellow citizens perceive you?

What does your body look like? How do you maintain good health? Do you eat well? Do you get enough rest?

What excites you? What are your hobbies and pastimes? How are you doing emotionally? Are you free of the inhibitions and bottled-up feelings of the past? Do you laugh easily? Are you open and responsive, capable of feeling deeply the joys and sorrows of life? How do you tend to the needs of your spirit?

As your vision takes shape in your mind, let your soul direct the action. What does your highest self want for your life on earth? When your vision is clear, embrace it with all your heart and make a solid commitment to realize it.

When you are ready, slowly open your eyes. Now, before it slips away, record your vision in writing. Without censoring, write down in as much detail as possible what you want for yourself.

After you've finished writing out your vision, take a moment to honestly compare where you are now to where you want to be. Let the two images exist simultaneously, as if on a split screen. While it may feel uncomfortable, acknowledging the gap between here and there can create a "structural tension" that draws you naturally toward the positive future you envision.

Now that you have envisioned the life you want, put your description aside for at least a day, then take it out and evaluate it with a practical eye. Make a list of realistic step-by-step goals that you can accomplish in the next five years. Be bold; genius has daring to it. But be grounded and systematic as well; that's how visions become a manifest reality.

Once you have your list, decide what you need to accomplish or learn in the next year to start achieving those goals. What specific skills, information, and experiences do you need to obtain? Where and from whom can you find assistance, support, and advice? Next, write down what you need to do in the next month. Then describe in detail what you will do next week. Finally, what will you do in the next 24 hours? Now that the fire has been lit, the sooner you begin acting on your vision, the better.

CAST OFF YOUR MISBELIEFS

Often, people rewrite their goals and dreams only to go on acting just as they did before; old attitudes, assumptions, and beliefs keep them spinning in the same old grooves. A crucial aspect of realizing your vision of the future, therefore, is to remain on the lookout for outworn attitudes and be willing to shed them.

Gretchen was raised to believe it was "unseemly" to call attention to herself. She was taught not to make other children feel bad by standing out. Ambition and material aspirations were considered crude. At age 32, she was enormously well liked. She was considerate, kind, generous, and compassionate. But she was profoundly unfulfilled. Teaching piano was satisfying, but inside her burned a powerful desire to perform and a talent to match. Only when she identified the beliefs that were holding her back and gave herself permission to defy her upbringing was she able to let the performer within step forward and shine.

Which assumptions about life and the way things work have held you back? Which self-limiting beliefs have sabotaged your dreams? Take a minute to identify them from this list:

- The universe is an unfriendly place.
- Life is a struggle.
- No one ever changes.
- I'll only be disappointed again.
- I don't have what it takes.
- I'm not in control of my destiny.
- Something will go wrong.
- People can't be trusted.
- Things don't work out for people like me.
- Don't think too big.

Dissolving sclerotic values and erroneous assumptions is as important to your emotional health as dissolving cholesterol deposits is to your cardiac health. Your Quintessential Self is much bigger than your beliefs and attitudes. Why let them hold you back? Let your vision of the future guide you instead. Remain vigilant, so that when outmoded thought patterns interfere with your dreams you can send them on their way and replace them with positive, optimistic alternatives.

A SELF CHECK-UP

Let's assess the work you've done so far. Which areas of your past have you successfully made peace with? Which still need work?

Take a few minutes and check in with each aspect of your Quintessential Self.

Begin by taking a deep breath. Hold it for a couple of seconds, then slowly let it out. Now, gently close your eyes. Contemplate for a moment your physical self. Zero in exclusively on your physiology. On a scale of one to five, five being the most peaceful possible and one meaning the maximum stress, tension, and agitation, rate the degree to which you have made peace on the physical level. When you are ready, open your eyes and write down the score.

Again, take a deep breath, hold it, and slowly exhale. Close your eyes and this time get in touch with your intellect. On a scale of one to five, five being perfectly centered and at ease and one being the most restless, disturbed, or obsessed, where does your mental self stand with respect to past issues? Write down the score.

Repeat the procedure for your emotional self. With five being perfect contentment and equanimity and one being the most turbulent and troubled, how much peace has the emotional aspect of your Quintessential Self achieved with respect to the past?

Now turn to your relational self. With five being completely at peace and one standing for maximum conflict and strain, where do you stand with regard to your relationships, both with those closest to you and the larger human community?

Once again, inhale and exhale deeply, then close your eyes. This time tune in to your spiritual self. To what extent is that highest part of you at peace? To what degree has your soul been nurtured and honored by the work you've done so far? With five being fully at peace and one being totally disconnected and forsaken, rate your level of spiritual peace.

When you have finished this assessment, spend some time considering what it would take to raise your score to a five for each aspect of your Quintessential Self. Growth in one area need not come at the expense of others. On the contrary, they are all interrelated; the well-being of each enhances all the rest.

Why not set some specific goals for each aspect of your Quintessential Self? What do you want for your body? Your mind? Your emotions? Your relationships? Your spirit? Goals are specific, definable, action-oriented targets. The best ones are those that are just beyond your current reach but not out of sight. Set yourself up to win by being both expansive and realistic. Spell out your goals in detail, put them in writing, and update them from time to time.

CULTIVATING DESIRED QUALITIES

As you looked back on your past, did you discover traits you once had and would like to resurrect? Are there qualities you always wish you had but had been blocked from developing? Now is your chance. From the list below, identify the qualities you feel will be helpful in creating a brighter future and forging a new life purpose:

Appreciation	Balance	Calmness
Compassion	Confidence	Creativity
Dynamism	Enthusiasm	Efficiency
Faith	Friendliness	Generosity
Gratitude	Honesty	Humor
Joyfulness	Kindness	Love
Orderliness	Patience	Positivity
Power	Realism	Trust
Understanding	Vitality	Wisdom

Choose the most important of the qualities you wish to cultivate. Follow the relaxation procedure for guided imagery, and when you are completely at ease, begin to imagine yourself already having that trait. See yourself in everyday situations embodying that quality at its highest level. What would it be like at home? At work? See the look in your eyes. Observe your posture and your facial expression. How would you speak if you owned that quality? How would you act in challenging situations?

When you feel complete, repeat the procedure with another quality, or open your eyes slowly and wait for another occasion.

Fixing these images in your mind can have a powerful influence on your subconscious, replacing the negative models that were planted in the past. As a way to water their roots for maximum growth, return to the qualities you most wish to cultivate whenever you have a few undisturbed minutes to hold the images in your mind.

GO FOR IT AND LET GO

You have learned that you don't have to be a slave to the past. Take care that you don't become a slave to the future instead. Strive to realize the splendid vision you've created for the rest of your life, but don't fall into the trap of thinking, "I can't be happy until . . ." or "I won't be satisfied unless . . ." Don't set yourself up for a fall by expecting an unrealistic or overly romanticized future. Expectations hold us tightly; preferences caress us lightly. If you find that your vision is not materializing as quickly as you'd hoped, or if you think you're not contributing as much as you want to, please don't judge yourself harshly. Your desire to achieve specific goals should not keep you from living the fullness of the present. There will always be something more to want, achieve, and plan for. Enjoy the process of becoming.

The past is gone, the future has not yet arrived; you live here, now, in the eternal present, where quintessential peace can be yours at any time.

YOUR "STUFF" WILL STILL COME UP

You should never consider yourself a weak or fallen creature. Whatever may have happened up to now may be because you didn't know, but now be careful.
—SWAMI BRAHMANANDA SARASWATI

The repetition compulsion virtually assures that the more tenacious aspects of the past will cling like stubborn stains; they fade with every scrubbing, but they don't disappear completely. Traumatic memories and old behavioral patterns are most likely to resurface at times of stress, when we have a tendency to regress and revert to our old ways. They may snap at your heels when you start a new relationship, when you get into an argument with your lover, or when your parents come to town or your boss gets on your case. You'll think, "Oh, no, I thought I've dealt with this already," or "Here I go again. Will this ever end?"

You may also find that previously unexamined issues rise up long after you thought you had exhausted everything of significance from the long-ago past. A client named Millie, for instance, was about to turn 70 when she started having panic attacks whenever she was asked to baby-sit for her infant grandchild. It turned out that more than 60 years earlier, her little cousin had come to live with her family. Suddenly she had to share her room, her prized possessions, and her parents—and baby-sit. All these years later, Millie's long-buried resentment was being triggered when she was asked to take care of her grandson. She was able to overcome the phobia when, in therapy, the hurt little girl inside of her finally got to express her feelings.

Your "stuff" will continue to come up. This is to be expected. It does not mean that all your hard work has been for naught. On the contrary, it can be seen as an opportunity to complete one more piece of unfinished business and deepen your peace. The tools you've learned will make it much easier to handle old issues when they arise. Armed with the knowledge and emotional freedom you've gained, you won't give in as easily to destructive patterns that once were automatic. You're more likely to catch yourself, reframe the situation, and respond appropriately.

ENLIGHTENING THE EMOTIONS

Even more than our bodies and minds, our emotions contain our personal histories. Whenever we can slice through the mad whirl of sensory bombardment we face daily and tap into our feelings, we find a tremendous source of intelligence and understanding. Emotions are inherently neither good nor bad. It's what we do with the energy and information they contain that makes the difference. To some extent, emotions are automatic responses, but we need to take responsibility for reading, understanding, and responding appropriately to them.

Anger, disappointment, rejection, hurt, sadness—these and other emotions will occur as long as you live. With the work you've done in this book, you will now be able to respond to upheavals with greater skill and emotional intelligence. This will keep you from once again accumulating the kind of heavy baggage that had piled up in the past. Here are some additional tips for when you are emotionally upset:[1]

EMOTIONAL LITERACY

Learn to identify your feelings. When a strong emotion arises, try to name it. This may not always be possible when you're caught up in turmoil, but do the best you can. This list of common emotions will help you identify what you're feeling:

Apprehensive	Betrayed	Burdened
Diminished	Distraught	Envious
Foolish	Helpless	Inadequate
Insignificant	Intimidated	Isolated
Oppressed	Overwhelmed	Pressured
Self-pity	Shocked	Spiteful
Unlovable	Violated	Vulnerable

With practice, you will be able to distinguish among the vast array of emotions and shades of feeling.

WHAT YOU FEEL YOU CAN HEAL

Like every other human being, as long as you're alive you will be driven by the pleasure principle—always looking for greater pleasure and trying to avoid pain. But, as we've seen, avoiding painful emotions can lead to trouble, as what we resist persists and breeds further suffering. Let your attention rest fully on the physical sensations that accompany strong feelings—the constricted muscles, the pounding heart, the change in breathing, and so on—and allow the feeling to run its course. Feeling your emotions as bodily sensations makes them less threatening and more manageable, enabling you to work with your feelings and guide their inherent energy.

TAKE TIME TO PROCESS YOUR EMOTIONS

Instead of reacting in the heat of the moment and possibly doing something you'll later regret, pause. If possible, get away from the situation so you can regain your composure, think clearly, and process your emotions more fully. This is a good time to use some of the practices you've learned in this book: Write out your feelings, bash or pound to release pent-up anger, or use the many techniques described in chapter 2 for gaining a peaceful presence.

ASSESS ACCURATELY

Try to avoid leaping to conclusions or making assumptions without sufficient evidence. Especially in conflict situations, an incorrect assessment can lead to a downward spiral of misunderstanding and negativity. Take the time to figure out what's really going on and what role you played in creating the problem. Ask clarifying questions such as, "I sense that things are tense for you right now, is that right?" Or, "Are you upset with me about something, or is it the pressure of work?"

DEVELOP EMPATHY

Empathy means listening in such a way that you can understand the feelings beneath the words. It means striving to see the other person's frame of reference, including how you and your actions are being perceived. Instead of trying to convince others that they should feel different, empathy helps you understand why they feel the way they do. One of the greatest gifts you can give someone is to hear his or her anger, hurt, and criticism without becoming defensive. At any given moment, each of us is "right" from his or her own perspective. When it comes to feelings, no one is wrong.

EXPRESS EFFECTIVELY

An important part of emotional fitness is the ability to communicate your feelings appropriately and turn conflicts into opportunities to strengthen your bond with the other person. Rather than having to be "right" and make him or her "wrong," commit your energy to being effective. Instead of just venting, ask yourself why you feel the way you do and what specifically you want to change. Then find an effective way to explain what you feel and foster the results you wish to see. And be sure to acknowledge the other person for being willing to receive your feedback and listen to your needs and wants.

EMOTIONAL DEPTH

After an emotional incident, when you can look back at it with some clarity, try to reflect deeply upon what happened. What behavior patterns from your past were activated? What important lesson can you derive from this experience? What skills do you need to work on? How can you bring the incident into alignment with your future self—the person you want to be? Plumb your emotional depths.

FEEL THE MAGIC

Jean-Paul Sartre wrote that emotions are the source of "magical transformations in the world." There is alchemy in allowing yourself to experience the full range of feeling. Don't let the natural tendency to avoid discomfort deprive you of the drama and power of emotion. As you become more skilled at enhancing positive emotions and processing negative ones, rejoice in everything you feel. Emotions are catalysts for change and growth, and they're all part of the beauty and delight of being human.

SOUL SUPPORT

Your ongoing work does not have to be a do-it-yourself project. With certain issues, you may need help. What follows are suggestions and guidelines for finding the support you need.

WHEN PSYCHOTHERAPY IS NECESSARY

Most of life's difficulties and emotional crises do not require long-term therapy. Nevertheless, professional assistance may be just what you need in the following instances:

- If you repeatedly find yourself in the same predicaments.
- If you can't stop obsessing or ruminating about the past.
- If you're in an emotional crisis and the support of wise friends, family, and clergy is not enough.
- If you don't feel good about yourself most of the time.
- If you and your spouse or lover can't resolve conflicts.

- If you can't change a destructive behavior pattern despite frequent attempts.
- If you are increasingly isolated emotionally and withdrawn socially.
- If you take refuge in alcohol, drugs, overeating, or other potentially harmful behavior.
- If you feel out of control or under great strain much of the time.
- If you fear you might do harm to yourself or others.
- If you think you may be suffering from a serious mental or physical illness.

There is nothing particularly mysterious about therapy, and no therapist, no matter how brilliant, can solve your problems for you. The right one, however, can help you discover and implement your own solutions. But it is extremely important to find a good match—someone who can truly understand who you are, where you have been, and where you want to go. If you decide to pursue psychotherapy, shop around. You owe it to yourself to spend at least as much time finding a therapist as you would shopping for a car. Seek referrals from trusted friends, your physician, or local mental health agencies, then call the therapist and request an initial consultation. This is an opportunity for you to ask questions, learn about the therapist's philosophy and approach, and most of all get a sense of what it would be like working with him or her. Visit two or three therapists to determine which, if any, is most suitable.

Bear in mind that research shows that the therapist's personal style, including qualities such as empathy, is at least as important in determining therapeutic success as the therapist's theoretical persuasion or choice of techniques. Before making your final decision, consider the following questions:

- Is she a licensed mental health professional with a good reputation in the community?
- Does he have a pleasant disposition and a sense of humor?
- Do you feel safe and at ease with her?
- Do you feel comfortable telling him anything about your life?

- Is she sincere about trying to understand and help you?
- Does he treat you with dignity and respect?
- Do you like her enough to choose her as a friend?
- Is he honest, nondefensive, and kind?
- Is she empathetic and compassionate?
- Is he willing to explain his approach, including strategies, goals, and length of treatment?
- Is she rigid in her approach or flexible and open to your input?
- Does he make you feel accepted?
- Can she understand your particular background and cultural heritage, if those are relevant to your concerns?
- Does he treat you like an equal, or as though you were flawed or defective?
- Do you leave the session feeling more hopeful and empowered?

At its best, psychotherapy is an opportunity to face the challenges of life and convert them into opportunities for emotional growth and spiritual renewal. At all times, your self-respect, dignity, and privacy must be protected, and you should feel safe to disclose your innermost thoughts and feelings.

MAKING DEPRESSION A THING OF THE PAST

The traumas and struggles of your past may have led to chronic depression. Depression is the result of a biochemical imbalance in the brain and a corresponding psychological imbalance—what is sometimes called "faulty thinking." Certain people may have a genetic predisposition to clinical depression, just as some are predisposed to diabetes or heart disease. But any number of factors can trigger the condition: a painful childhood, major loss, unresolved grief, excessive stress, serious illness, troublesome relationships, substance abuse, and many more. Depression may be the ultimate sign of being stuck in the past. Every issue we've dealt with in this book—shame, loss, blame, regret, guilt, and so forth—can either precipitate or exacerbate a depression. Those feelings don't just cause you to be depressed, they can result *from* depression as well. For example, you can become depressed due to toxic shame, or you can feel ashamed because you're depressed.

The symptoms of depression include the following, according to a checklist developed by the National Institutes of Mental Health:

- Persistent sad or "empty" mood.
- Loss of interest or pleasure in ordinary activities, including sex.
- Fatigue and decreased energy.
- Sleep disturbances (insomnia, early-morning waking, or over-sleeping).
- Eating disturbances (loss of appetite and weight, or weight gain).
- Difficulty concentrating, remembering, making decisions.
- Feelings of guilt, worthlessness, helplessness.
- Thoughts of death or suicide, suicide attempts.
- Irritability.
- Excessive crying.
- Chronic aches and pains that don't respond to treatment.
- Decreased productivity.
- Being tired all the time.
- Alcohol or drug abuse.

For some people, the symptoms erupt like a flu and eventually go away. For others, they come and go like any recurring illness (people who have been depressed in the past are more likely to be depressed in the future). And in some cases they persist, month after month, year after year—the condition known as *dysthymia*, chronic low-grade depression. When depression descends upon you, despair and hopelessness shade your vision of the future. Thoughts like, "Who cares?" "Why bother?" "What's the use?" run through the mind, robbing life of meaning, purpose, and motivation.

If four or more of the symptoms on that checklist persist for more than two weeks, or are interfering with work or family life, the National Institutes of Health recommends a thorough diagnosis. See a health professional who is qualified to diagnose depression. Remember, seeking treatment does not imply a lack of character, discipline, strength, or faith in God any more than seeking help for headaches or back pain would. It is nothing to be ashamed of. Nor is it anyone's fault—not your parents', not your spouse's or lover's, not society's, not yours. Depression is simply a debilitating illness that severely diminishes the quality of life and contributes to chronic disease by suppressing the immune system.

The good news is that depression is a highly treatable disorder. You may not think so when you're in the grip of it. It may seem as though nothing can help. That's because depression interferes biologically with the brain's ability to maintain positive thoughts for any length of time. Positive thinking can no more turn the tide of negativity than planting seeds on a rock can yield flowers. But despite the illusion of hopelessness, depression can be treated. With medication—natural or synthetic—and psychotherapy, most people respond to treatment in a matter of weeks.

The specialist best qualified to diagnose and treat mental illness is the psychiatrist. Family doctors are not always well informed on the subject and are prone to misdiagnosis (a 1993 RAND survey found that less than half the general practitioners treating depression had spent more than three minutes discussing their patients' symptoms). Licensed psychotherapists are well qualified to provide therapy, but they cannot prescribe medication should that option be appropriate.

OBSESSING ABOUT THE PAST

Do you constantly ruminate about the past, examining and re-examining the same events over and over again? Do you ceaselessly beat yourself up for old mistakes? Do you play and replay the same "if-only" scenarios in your mind or imagine a different outcome for regrettable events? Such repetitive thought patterns may be a sign of Obsessive-Compulsive Disorder (OCD).

Affecting about six million people annually, OCD is as common an illness as asthma or diabetes. In addition to persistent, intrusive thoughts and images, the classic symptoms include repetitive behaviors such as ritualized hand-washing, cleaning, or list-making;

repeated checking of door locks and appliances; or extreme concern for exactness, symmetry, or repetitive counting. When such activities cause marked anxiety and consume more than an hour a day, the diagnosis is usually OCD. However, even in the absence of compulsive behavior, obsessing about the past long after the actual incidents occurred can be cause for concern.

Some research suggests that OCD is a biological illness. A portion of the brain's emotional center, the *caudate nucleus*, has been shown to be overactive, much like a phonograph record with a needle stuck in a groove. The condition is usually managed with cognitive therapy and/or anti-OCD medications. OCD patients given brain scans before and after one cognitive therapy session show a significant reduction in the over-activity of the caudate nucleus. If you think you may have OCD, make an appointment to see a psychiatrist for a professional evaluation.

NATURAL AND SYNTHETIC ANTIDEPRESSANTS

The current generation of antidepressant medicines has revolutionized the treatment of clinical depression and OCD. While they work in different ways, all medicines for depression and OCD are designed to correct chemical imbalances in the brain that can give rise to these illnesses. None of them are addictive or habit-forming, and the side effects, if any, are generally mild and disappear on their own within two or three weeks. It is important to note, however, that the best results are obtained when medication is used in conjunction with psychotherapy.

Two promising alternatives to prescription medicine have recently gained favor in the treatment of depression. Medical research suggests that the herb St. John's wort (*Hypericum perforatum*) can be an effective treatment for mild to moderate depression, with the added advantages of being less costly and available over-the-counter. SAMe (pronounced "Sammy") is a molecule that is produced by all living cells and is essential to a biological process called *methylation*, by which the brain synthesizes neurotransmitters associated with mood and emotional well-being. Research in

Europe suggests that SAMe, formally known as S-adenosylme-thionine, has promise in the treatment of depression. Speak to your health practitioner to see if St. John's wort and/or SAMe is an appropriate option for you.[2]

If you have been suffering from depression for any length of time, be aware that it may take several weeks before you start noticing significant improvement. The longer you've been depressed, the longer it is likely to take for the chemistry of the brain to be restored. Be patient. You are healing from the ravages of a life-time. In the meantime, be kind to yourself.

HERBS AS MEDICINALS OF PEACE

Joy is more than the absence of depression. It is the natural product of a peaceful, vibrant physiology. Knowing this, some of the world's great healing traditions have developed sophisticated plant-based formulas to gently reverse and repair the damage of the past and restore balance to the system.

In this context, the Ayurvedic tradition of India stands out because its core purpose is to cultivate quintessential peace and higher consciousness. The Ayurvedic products I am most familiar with were developed by Maharishi Ayur-Ved Products International (MAPI). Numerous published scientific studies indicate that MAPI's herbal formulas produce a broad range of health benefits, including some with implications for cancer and heart disease. I have gotten excellent results with the formula Amrit Kalash (Sanskrit for "golden cup of immortality"), especially with clients who have accumulated chronic stress due to a painful past. A precise combination of 44 herbs for enhancing overall health, happiness, and longevity, Amrit Kalash has been shown in several research studies to have up to a thousand times more antioxidant power than vitamins C and E.[3] Antioxidants help to reduce the damage caused by free radicals, the highly reactive molecular fragments that are a primary cause of cancer, heart disease, and other life-threatening illnesses. I also recommend two other products, Worry Free and Blissful Joy, which can further develop the nervous system's natural capacity for harmony, balance, and peace.

(For information about MAPI products call 800-255-8332 or check their website at www.mapi.com.)

EMDR FOR POST-TRAUMATIC STRESS DISORDER

A relatively new, effective technique for resolving old emotional issues is eye movement desensitization and reprocessing (EMDR). While it is not yet clear exactly how EMDR works, it has demonstrated an exceptional ability to help victims of post-traumatic stress disorder (PTSD). Combat veterans, rape victims, survivors of natural disasters, and other individuals who experienced severe trauma have found quick and lasting relief from nightmares, flashbacks, eating disorders, terror, chronic fatigue, and other PTSD symptoms.

During EMDR, the client focuses on images, thoughts, and feelings associated with the traumatic event while following the therapist's hand movement from side to side (sometimes tones in alternate ears or taps on each side of the body are used instead). The lateral movements somehow facilitate the desensitization and reprocessing of painful memories, probably by bringing into play both hemispheres of the brain. Francine Shapiro, Ph.D., who developed the technique, suggests that the "neurological loop" created at the time of the trauma stands in the way of complete emotional processing. EMDR seems to dissipate that loop and render the painful memory less capable of causing distress in the present.

EMDR is not limited to life-shattering upheavals; it has proven valuable for making peace with more commonplace traumas as well. Consult a therapist trained in its use to see if it is appropriate for you.

THE HOFFMAN QUADRINITY PROCESS

One of the most important things I did to make peace with my own past was to take the Hoffman Quadrinity Process (HQP). It led to such a profound breakthrough in my own healing that I subsequently recommended the process to friends, family, and hundreds of patients.

For more than 30 years, the Hoffman process has been quietly transforming people's lives by putting them in touch with the childhood roots of their negative attitudes and behavior patterns and helping them change those habits. I have found the promise in the HQP brochure to be accurate: "You'll learn how to reduce and resolve pain, anger and grief. You will achieve new levels of inner peace and understanding. You will find heart-felt acceptance, forgiveness and unconditional love for yourself, your parents, family members, and others in your life."

One of the unique features of the Hoffman process is total immersion. The workshop takes place over eight days in a peaceful setting. With regular psychotherapy you usually have only 50 minutes a week, with perhaps some homework in between, to focus on healing. With immersion, making peace with your past is your sole and complete purpose. This enables you to go deeper and take full advantage of some of the best therapeutic technologies modern psychology has to offer—including many of the exercises in this book—in a structured, supervised setting. Rest assured, the process is conducted in a safe, supportive manner and honors the dignity of every participant.

The Hoffman process is not a panacea, of course. But if you're looking for a breakthrough in making peace with your past, I highly recommend it. For information, call 800-506-5253, or check the website at www.hoffmaninstitute.org.

SUPPORT GROUPS

Every day, in hospitals, community centers, churches, malls, and living rooms, individuals who share a common concern get together for mutual support. Self-help groups share nurture, insight, information, and a sense of community that is virtually impossible to find elsewhere. Isolation intensifies suffering. If you are dealing with issues from your past that you keep to yourself because you fear being stigmatized, or if you have no one to talk to who truly understands what you've been through, please consider joining a support group. In many cases, the only people who can convincingly say "I understand" are those who have been through similar experiences. That is why you can find a quality of support in a self-help group that is unavailable anywhere else.

A psychotherapist, a local mental health association, or a medical clinic are good places to start tracking down a support group. The yellow pages may direct you to the kind of group you're looking for as well. There are also many national organizations for specific concerns that may be able to help you find an appropriate group in your area (see Appendix B).

Another excellent source of support is the Internet, where self-help networks have bloomed like wildflowers after a rainy spring. Online chat groups and bulletin boards have the advantages of being free, convenient, and, most of all, totally anonymous should that be a priority. Writes Tom Ferguson, M.D., in his book *Health Online*, "We can log on when we need advice with a specific problem; when we are struggling and want sympathy, comfort, and support; or when we have come through a hard time." For example, www.SurvivingLoss.com is an excellent site for those who have suffered a loss.

You might also consider starting your own *Making Peace with Your Past* support group. All it takes is a few people who want to mutually support one another. You may want to seek out people who are dealing with the same or similar issues, or you may look for insight and inspiration from those whose pasts are different from your own. Whatever their origins may be, everyone faces similar struggles in making peace with the past, and everyone deals with similar emotional content: pain, shame, loss, regret, and so forth. Sharing one another's stories can be tremendously healing.

If you do start a support group, be sure to create a safe atmosphere in which members are free to be completely open. Everyone should know that privacy will be protected and that other members will listen with empathy and an absence of judgment. I recommend that you set aside one and a half to two hours for each meeting. Begin by going around the room to give each person a chance to describe which issues from the past they are currently dealing with. You can set aside time to do the exercises in this book, or select a specific topic for each meeting (for example, How Does the Repetition Compulsion Show up in Your Life?), or simply allow each session to assume its own character. Members should all agree to avoid proselytizing, promoting unrelated agendas, and trying to "fix" one another. Try to find ways to be helpful without "therapizing." No one should take on the role of psychotherapist—except, of course, if you arrange to have a qualified therapist facilitate the group on a regular basis.

However you find it, the give and take of a support group can be an invaluable aid in your quest to make peace with your past.

FINDING YOUR SPIRITUAL FAMILY

Friends and family who care about you, who are familiar with your history and know how to listen well, can be a great source of support as you resolve your past and create a fresh new way of life. But some of the people you feel closest to may resist the changes you are trying to make because they are invested in keeping you tied to the past. In some cases, their own identities may be linked to the tragedies and triumphs they shared with you. Some may like hearing your litany of regret because it makes them feel superior or fortunate by comparison. Others may enjoy feeling noble when they offer you their sympathy. Some may simply relish the excuse to complain about their own unhappy pasts.

Whatever the reason, some people will try, deliberately or unconsciously, to keep you from letting go of the past. Even though you may start to feel uncomfortable with such people, the fear of losing or offending them may keep you from making necessary changes in your life.

After working with the exercises in this book, Joanna finally came to accept her divorce. Having resolved the anger and grief that had haunted her for over a year, she was ready to move on. Her friends were not. Divorced themselves, the women were accustomed to gathering for drinks or dinner after a day's work and sharing their stories. Much of their conversations revolved around their ex-husbands and the "jerks" who wanted to date them. Joanna was tired of hearing the same old complaints. Even worse, she was tired of hearing *herself* complain. The conversations felt out of line with the optimism and contentment she now felt. But, afraid to upset the applecart, she continued to play the role expected of her even though it was dragging her backward.

Then she met Matt. Feeling excited and liberated by the potential new romance, she couldn't wait to share the news with her friends. They immediately deflated her. "Don't get involved," they said. "You can't trust men. You're still vulnerable. You'll only get hurt again." Envious, they injected fear and cynicism when Joanna needed support and encouragement. I advised her to enlarge her friendship circle to reflect the strong, confident person she had become, not the fearful, mistrustful person she had been.

If you find that you're bored with or alienated from certain people; if you feel they have a stake in keeping you stuck in the past; if you feel that they don't understand the changes you've been undergoing, it may very well be time to drop some affiliations and create new ones in their place.

Finding your true spiritual family can be just as important as finding a life partner. Look for people with whom you are free to talk about anything and everything, who let you be your authentic self, and in whose presence your spirit can soar. In your spiritual family, you can feel truly at home; each aspect of your Quintessential Self feels safe and nourished.

A LIFE OF MEANING
AND PURPOSE

I don't know what your destiny will be, but one thing I do know: the only ones among you who will be happy are those who have sought and found how to serve.

—ALBERT SCHWEITZER

Within each of us is a fundamental urge to be the brightest light we can possibly be before our candle goes out—to be illumined and to illuminate others to the highest degree possible. This instinct calls us to a higher purpose. A purpose is more than a terrific idea. It's a passionately charged path born of a powerful urge to create and a deep commitment to serve.

German philosopher Frederick Buechner defined purpose as "the place where your deep gladness and the world's deep hunger meet." This doesn't mean you have to be Mother Teresa or Martin Luther King Jr. Your contribution can be modest or grand, anonymous or highly public. It can be expressed in your art, your science, your tenderness to those whose lives you touch, or your efforts to better the lot of those less fortunate. What matters is engaging your talents and strengths in a deeply satisfying way—as opposed to activity that makes you feel like a shell, a has-been, or a martyr—while contributing to something that is greater than yourself.

Abandoned before her birth by her father, Maggie was raised by a drug-addicted mother who passed out one night and collapsed on top of her, crushing her fibula. As a result of that incident, Maggie had a permanent limp. During an adolescence spent shuffling from one foster home to another, she was humiliated, taunted, and then isolated by her peers. Despite all this, she managed to shine academically. Study was her only salvation. After graduating with honors from Harvard Law School, she joined a prestigious law firm. Her personal life did not go as smoothly as her career, however. Men did not seem attracted to her, and the few relationships she had did not last very long. Then, at age 37, she fell in love with a man who adored her—only to lose him three years later to pancreatic cancer.

When she began therapy, Maggie resisted exploring the suppressed feelings she knew she had to deal with. Like many, she was afraid of revisiting the dark side of human nature—this time her own. Courageously, she fought through her fears to successfully process her grief, shame, and regret.

Six months after she had made peace with the excruciating elements of her past, Maggie came to see me again. She found herself in the throes of an existential crisis and desired my feedback. Becoming more comfortable at her emotional depths had freed her to more deeply examine the direction of her life—and she did not like what she saw. At home, she was lonely and yearned for someone to love. At work, she was troubled. She had earned a stellar reputation for skillfully defending multinational corporations in huge lawsuits, but in some of her most celebrated cases she came away feeling guilty, not satisfied, because she did not feel that her clients deserved the victory. The last straw came when she defended a company that had dumped toxic chemicals near a housing development, endangering the health of thousands. Getting the polluters off with a slap on the wrist left a bitter taste in her mouth.

When she was using 16-hour workdays to distract her from her pain, Maggie did not have the luxury of comparing what she did professionally with the values she held dear. Now she had gained the freedom to reappraise her life. Clearly, it was no longer enough to just make a lot of money, do her job with excellence, and win the respect of her colleagues. Maggie was at a crossroads, consumed by a crisis of meaning and purpose. "I have to find a better reason to get up every morning," she said.

Using techniques such as those in this chapter, she pondered some fundamental questions: What did she truly believe in? What was the purpose of her life? Which actions would represent the best and highest aspect of herself? How would she want to look back on her life in 40 years? Maggie made some life-changing decisions. At considerable loss of income, she quit her job and went to work for a firm that specialized in environmental law. Remembering her own troubled childhood, she devoted time pro bono to represent the interests of parentless children in court. It didn't matter that she could no longer afford some of the luxuries she'd become accustomed to, for as she proclaimed, "I've never felt better about my life."

The last time I saw Maggie she was grinning from ear to ear as she introduced me to the little girl she'd adopted. I feel confident predicting that on her 80th birthday she will look back on the second half of her life with no regrets, no guilt, and no nagging thoughts of what might have been.

As your peace with the past solidifies and the radiance of your presence grows, you are likely to notice something akin to Maggie's dilemma. Deep questions about the meaning and purpose of existence will naturally arise. You will probably feel a yearning to do more and be more. This urge may find expression within your current way of life, as you address family and career concerns. But as you begin to see more clearly, free of the blinders of the past, and love more deeply, free of the pain of the past, your perception of yourself and the world is likely to expand. You may find that your long-suppressed beauty and bounty—your wellspring of peace, maturity, wisdom, and compassion—cry out for greater expression.

Because the "heavies" of the past have lightened, you are free to look around to see if anyone else needs help with their load. Earlier, you may not have felt capable of helping. You may have believed you were too flawed to be of use to others. You may have thought, "I'll perform some service when I get my own act together." Now, because your life energy is less caught up in mending your own wounds, your innate generosity of spirit and sensitivity to suffering can reach beyond previous boundaries and borders. You no longer say, "Something should be done," but "What can I do to help?"

As the turmoil of the past dissolves into peace, the voice of quintessential conscience starts to assert itself loud and clear. Conscience has been given a bad name in recent times. Most of us were raised to believe it was synonymous with twinges of shame or "guilt trips" because the word was used when we were not being good enough or had done something wrong. Conscience is much more than that. It is the sound of our inner voice when it aligns with the compass of our highest self and calls upon us to be the best we can be. Making peace with the past allows us to notice the gut feelings and internal nudges that goad us to do better.

In urging you to heed the call to a higher purpose, I am not losing sight of your primary reason for reading this book: to heal your past and create a more fulfilling future for yourself. In nearly three decades as a practicing psychotherapist, I have come to learn that those who achieve the most durable peace and move through life with the greatest sense of contentment are those who transcend their own self-centered concerns.

A growing body of scientific evidence suggests that altruism, charity, and acts of kindness make for a more meaningful and healthier life. Medical research indicates that people who engage in regular service have more inner peace and personal fulfillment when compared to those who are self-absorbed. One study found that a selfless attitude made it 2.4 times as likely that an individual would be happy; selfishness made it 9.5 times more likely that he or she would be *unhappy*.[4] With regard to health, a study at the University of California at San Francisco Medical School found that self-centeredness may be a risk factor in coronary artery disease.[5] And a 13-year study of people between the ages of 60 and 94 concluded that maintaining a useful and satisfying role in society is a key factor in enhancing longevity.[6]

It is never too late to discover a calling and to commit time and energy to the endeavor. Finding your purpose may take some soul-searching. "Meaning is not something you stumble across, like the answer to a riddle or the prize of a treasure hunt," says John Gardner, professor of public service at Stanford. "Meaning is something you build into your life. You build it out of your own past, out of your affections and loyalties, out of the experience of humankind as it passed to you."

By breaking loose from the bondage of the past, you gain a sacred opportunity to let your vision of the future draw you to a life of dignity, meaning, and purpose. Look to what excites you. Revive the ideals of your youth, which may have been lost among the pressures and hardships of adulthood. Look to role models whose burning purpose, lasting impact, and exceptional qualities you would like to emulate. Look around and see who can use your help and what needs doing. Above all, listen to your heart; that is where your meaning and purpose reside. "Your vision will become clear only when you can look into your own heart," said Carl Jung. "Who looks outside, only dreams; who looks inside, also awakens."

HEALING OUR COLLECTIVE PAST

*To give of one's self; to leave the world a bit better, whether by
a healthy child, a garden patch, or a redeemed social condition
. . . to know even one life has breathed easier because you have
lived—that is to have succeeded.*

—RALPH WALDO EMERSON

Much of the pain of each individual's past is the product of our
collective past. When you take an unflinching look at the dark side
of human history, you see that we have taken turns murdering,
raping, and torturing one another. When we weren't going quite
that far, we were trying to dominate someone or beat the other
guy to resources we perceived to be scarce. It's been you against
me and us versus them, instead of you and me and us and them.
We don't have to continue that way. We have enough renewable
resources and technical knowledge right now to create a world
that can work for everyone. What is needed is the heart, wisdom,
and will to make it so. Whether or not we succeed depends upon
each of us, not just our leaders.

"The future never just happens," wrote historians Will and
Ariel Durant, "it is created." As you strive to create a future you
will be proud to have lived, you might pause to ask what you can
do to help heal our collective wounds. Earlier in this chapter, you
created a vision for your own future. What is your vision for your
family? Your circle of friends? Your workplace or profession? Your
community? Your planet? What would you like to leave behind as
your generation's legacy to future generations? What can you do
to help us correct our course, to not repeat the errors of our
ancestral past, and to fulfill humanity's highest destiny?

As heirs to a great but tumultuous past and custodians of
immense power worldwide, America suffers the tension of a
unique historical ambiguity. We are 5 percent of the world's population and consume 40 percent of the world's resources. We are
also the world's leading arms dealer ($50 billion annually). At the
same time, America is the beacon of freedom to the world's
oppressed and the heartland of hope for a peaceful planet. As

Americans, we are in a unique position to foster worldwide healing, yet here at home we still suffer from bitter social cleavages
that have torn the social fabric at various points in our history.
Slavery, segregation, and 400 years of racial enmity; the subjuga-
tion of women; the bigotry and resistance that greeted each new
wave of immigrants; the sacrifice and sorrow of the Great Depression and World War II; the divisiveness and destruction of Vietnam; the generation gap that burst open in the 1960s; the clash of
Victorian sexual attitudes and anything-goes hedonism; the persistent screaming match of conservatives and liberals; the tension
between ethnic pride and assimilation; the ever-widening gap
between rich and poor; the paradox of our gun-toting frontier heritage and the anguished cries to end violence; the conflict between
those who would protect the natural environment and those who
would exploit it; the ambiguous strain between spiritual and material values and between our ethic of rugged individualism and the
need to sacrifice for the common good—all these points of friction, carried by the collective national consciousness, are felt by
every one of us in the fabric of our being.

As a global civilization holding the fate of the planet in our
hands, it is time to put behind us an era of chauvinism, in which
relationships—between man and woman, parent and child, ruler
and ruled, boss and worker, human being and nature—were based
on a model of dominance and submission. If we are to live up to
our potential as a species and create a glorious new chapter in our
history, we have to adopt a more enlightened model, one based on
dominion and compassion.

Now is a good time to begin. "The dawning of the new millennium also brings with it the need for a new sense of universal
responsibility," implores the Dalai Lama. "We are responsible not
merely for our own happiness, we affect and are affected by the
concerns of all others on this globe. This is the nature of interde-
pendence. We are now faced with an opportunity to break down
barriers in the name of national, racial, ideological, or religious
identities. These narrow identities have often been destructive and
harmful and against the very spirit of a global family. We should
now look towards invoking the forces of peace and harmony, of
hope and strength, of renewal and responsibility."

Never before have conditions been so ripe for conscious, evolutionary change. Vast cultural shifts have occurred in the past, spurred by new technology, breakthroughs in knowledge, and social reorganization: the transformation of worldview wrought by Copernicus and Galileo, the age of global exploration, and the Industrial Revolution and urbanization, to name just a few. But not until the advent of our own Information Age has change of such magnitude taken place so rapidly that we can see a new era taking shape before our eyes.

Never before have human beings, individually and collectively, had so much power to transform our world quickly, and to direct the change with conscious intention. Never before has the elegant rule of mind had such potential to vanquish the brute rule of muscle. Never before have so many people had such easy access to the great wisdom traditions. The transformation taking place in the minds and hearts of large numbers of psychospiritual explorers has the potential to shape a new set of collective values, a new quality of collective consciousness, and a new form of collective being. Every loud cultural shift begins with quiet impulses in the hearts of individuals.

The atrocities, brutalities, and oppressive policies of the past were not perpetrated only by "them." It is not just "evil people" who shoulder the blame. As the cartoonist Walt Kelly famously observed through his character Pogo, "We have met the enemy and he is us." We all share responsibility because the dark side of human nature resides in each of us, not just the obvious villains. To the extent that we fail to be vigilant about our potential to do harm in our own families and institutions, we cannot expect to prevent the rampages of future Hitlers, Stalins, and Pol Pots. "It looks to me as if all of us must make our peace with these mean impulses within ourselves," wrote psychologist Abraham Maslow. "And my impression so far is that the best way to do this is to transmute envy, jealousy, presentiment, and nastiness into humble admiration, gratitude, appreciation, adoration, and even worship." To the extent that each of us can do that—and help others do it as well—we can turn the Information Age into the Age of Conscious Evolution.

How can you make a difference? How can you help us make peace with our collective past and redirect the tide of history?

Will you keep your focus close to home, making sure your children—or your nieces and nephews, or your neighbors' kids—have every chance to make it into adulthood without the heavy emotional baggage so many of us have had to bear? In the Preface, we saw that adverse childhood experiences lead directly to serious illness later in life. Statistics show that in America as well as the rest of the world, the well-being of children has actually gotten worse in this generation. Creating a world in which all children can be physically and emotionally safe and nurtured to reach their full potential is an imperative for the 21st century. We can prevent adverse childhood experiences by individually and collectively making peace with an era in which pain, shame, and blame were the principal means of child-rearing and by creating a world for all children where peace prevails.

Perhaps you will be moved to enlarge your domain and dedicate time and talent to helping mend some of society's wounds. Can you help create a world in which inner peace is as important as profits? Don't underestimate the potential value of your actions just because you don't have the fame or power to wield a large influence in the world. You may feel like just another tree in the forest, but we're all trees in the same forest and each of us profoundly affects the rest. Your future is your neighbor's future, your country's future, your planet's future. There's no one here but just us folks.

Like the rest of us, you have been wounded in the past. You can now become a wounded healer. There is powerful medicine in simply bringing love, kindness, and compassion to every interaction. However you decide to contribute, what matters most is this famous injunction from Mahatma Gandhi: "You must be the change you wish to see in the world."

KNOW THYSELF:
OUR QUINTESSENTIAL QUEST

Of all knowledge the wise and good seek most to know themselves.

—SHAKESPEARE

The questions we raised at the beginning of this book—Who am I? Where did I come from? Where am I going?—will always remain vital. The examined life requires that they be asked and answered anew throughout the course of one's lifetime. But it's the first question that matters most. It is for good reason that "Know Thyself" was inscribed on the oracle of Delphi in ancient Greece. "Who am I?" is the quintessential question because self-knowledge is our quintessential quest. It is the query that all other queries boil down to, the puzzle at the heart of all our science, art, and religion. And for each of us personally, it is the single most important reference point for living a full and happy life. Its power lies not in the answer but in the asking; simply by living inside the question, you open up to the awe and mystery of existence.

You can peel off answers to "Who am I?" in layers, as you would peel an onion. There are the historical facts: You are the woman or man who was born at a certain time in a specific location into a particular family; you went to these schools; you grew to this height; you settled on that career, had those victories and those losses. There are the roles you play: You're a wife or husband, a daughter or son, a mother or father, a butcher or baker, accountant or zookeeper. There are your personality traits: outgoing or shy, combative or conciliatory, adventurer or homebody, messy or orderly, easygoing or demanding. There is the makeup of your inner life: the things you believe in, your values, your needs, your desires and feelings.

While such attributes can't come close to defining who you really are, they command some attention as you chart your new course. One reason you may have had regrets in the past is that you did what you thought you *should* do, or what seemed "sensible" and "rational," instead of heeding the call of your heart. You may have been functioning under an erroneous definition of yourself. To answer the question "Who am I *now?*" it is imperative to tune in to the frequency of your soul. Deep inside you, the answer is always known. From that place, subtle, gentle voices are prodding you to live to your full potential. Now that you have quieted some of the harsher voices in your head and heart, you will be better able to hear them. "Whenever a mind is simple, and receives a divine wisdom," said Ralph Waldo Emerson, "old things pass away; it lives now, and absorbs past and future into the present."

SELF-REALIZATION

As important as they may seem, however, the layers of identity we usually think of—our labels, our stories, our values and beliefs—are, in the final analysis, too superficial and too transient to do justice to the question "Who am I?" What is permanent and unchanging about you is your existence itself. The essential nature of your Is-ness—the Self that transcends your personality and form—is your ultimate identity and that of everyone and everything else. In the Vedic tradition, this fundamental truth is captured in the famous statement, "I am That, thou art That, all this is That."

The true Self cannot be found by answering the question, "Who am I?" in words. It is the silent gap that lives between the words. It is that which witnesses the asking and the answering. It is the changeless screen on which the images of the mind are projected. The Self is to be found only in direct experience—or, more accurately, by transcending experience itself and coming to rest in the pure awareness and original bliss of Being.

Every great spiritual tradition, each in its own way, holds that the ultimate cause of human suffering is disconnection from our divine essence. That is why the wise have always beckoned us to realize the transcendent Self. The traditional name for this awakened state, enlightenment, is apt because it represents the illumination of our essential nature, and because it is accompanied by a lightening of the burdens of the past and a feathery lightness of being with which to unfold an optimal future. "When there is constant and unceasing remembrance of the Self," the *Upanishads* declare, "all bonds are loosed and freedom is attained."

Among my patients and seminar participants I note a powerful spiritual hunger. In many cases, their soul starvation is perpetuated by misconceptions about spirituality, usually rooted in a long-standing estrangement from the religion of their roots. Some link spirituality with superstition, old-fashioned morality, arbitrary lifestyle prohibitions, or airy-fairy escapism. But, as millions of people are discovering, authentic spirituality does not have to entail any of these.

Enlightenment is a spiritual awakening, the realization that we are one and that separation is an illusion. It confers an inner stillness in which you can experience the most unbounded, unconditioned aspect of your being. Far from a state of self-delusion, self-denial, or escapism, it represents the ultimate development of what are generally considered the most valuable qualities of human life: kindness, compassion, generosity, intelligence, creativity, freedom, and the capacity for spontaneous life-supporting responses to any circumstance. As suggested by scientific research on long-term TM practitioners, this quintessential growth process can be understood as a continuous integration of the nervous system that frees one from the stress of past experience.

While Self-realization is its own reward and represents, in itself, the ultimate fulfillment, each small step in that direction enables you more easily to fulfill the goals you set in this chapter: manifesting your vision for your personal future and contributing to some larger good. The chains of fear and inhibition loosen and the mind's din quiets down, making room for the wise voice of intuition. The barriers between inner and outer, me and you, us and them, dissolve into deep connection. As the petty needs of the small self fade into insignificance, it becomes easier to connect with people heart to heart; intimacy feels more natural and comfortable; and your innately generous, compassionate soul finds ways to heal, help, and serve.

The inner work of Self-awakening and the outer work of serving a higher purpose are not contradictory pursuits. On the contrary, they are natural complements. It is often overlooked that the brightest spiritual luminaries—Moses, Jesus, Mohammed, Buddha—were driven not only to know God but to teach and otherwise engage the world with vigorous action. In the *Bhagavad Gita*, Lord Krishna advises the reluctant warrior Arjuna to take up arms and fight the forces of evil—but first to turn inward and draw strength from the infinite energy and peace of the Quintessential Self. "*Yogastah kuru karmani*," reads the entreaty in Sanskrit: "Established in the transcendent Self, perform action."

That the combination of transcendence and service has trans-formative power for both the individual and society has been rec-ognized by sage and scientist alike. "When you are inspired by some great purpose, some extraordinary project, all of your thoughts break their bonds," declared the Indian philosopher Patanjali as many as 2,400 years ago. "Your mind transcends limi-tations, your consciousness expands in every direction, and you find yourself in a new, great, and wonderful world. Dormant forces, faculties, and talents become alive, and you discover your-self to be a greater person by far than you ever dreamed yourself to be."

Albert Einstein said it this way:

A human being is part of the whole, called by us the "Uni-verse," a part limited in time and space. He experiences him-self, his thoughts and feelings, as something separate from the rest—a kind of optical delusion in his consciousness. This delusion is a kind of prison for us, restricting us to our personal decisions and to affection for a few persons nearest to us. Our task must be to free ourselves from this prison by widening our circle of compassion to embrace all living crea-tures and the whole of nature in its beauty.[7]

CONSCIOUS EVOLUTION

Making peace with the past is a powerful catalyst for conscious evolution. Together, we can end the emotional ignorance of the past and treat ourselves and one another with greater understand-ing and dignity. The nightmares that terrified so many of us, and that at times shamed us into the depths of unworthiness, also made us seekers. At first with desperation, and later with determi-nation and persistence, we embarked on a search for the awareness and wisdom to heal and change both our inner course and outer circumstance. Once our presence no longer leaks or bleeds into the past, our consciousness, less encumbered, is free to fully grow. Our highest evolutionary path is the one that generates the least resis-tance and the greatest joy.

Now our very awareness can be transformed into a higher res-
onance—awakening. This awakening, like some cosmic pull of a
spiritual magnet, exerts a catalytic force over each of our lives and
all of humanity. Making peace with your past is a completely natural process. As Maharishi Mahesh Yogi once taught me, "The
purpose of life is the expansion of happiness." Evolution from the
past to the future is always a rich, amazing, self-transcending
process. The unstoppable power of evolution is helping you go
beyond whatever you were before, whether your shift is from fear
to love or fractured to whole. We human beings, fashioned out of
stardust millions of light years ago, are capable of remembering
and experiencing our universal birth in Original Bliss. With that
awareness, we can co-create with God a world that can work for
everyone—one that is fully worthy of our cosmic status as spiritual beings in human form. Then the human race can become
human grace and finally be at peace with the past.

APPENDIX A:
BIBLIOTHERAPY

A good book can be worth more than a dozen sessions. Many excellent self-help books can be used to facilitate progress in therapy.

—ARNOLD A. LAZARUS, PH.D.

Bloomfield, Harold, M.D. *Healing Anxiety Naturally* (New York: HarperPerennial, 1998).

———. *Making Peace in Your Stepfamily* (New York: Hyperion, 1993).

———, Melba Colgrove, Ph.D., and Peter McWilliams. *How to Survive the Loss of a Love* (Los Angeles: Prelude Press, 1996).

———, and Robert K. Cooper, Ph.D. *The Power of 5* (Emmaus, PA: Rodale Press, 1995).

———, and Robert K. Cooper, Ph.D. *Think Safe, Be Safe* (New York: Crown, 1997).

———, with Leonard Felder, Ph.D. *Making Peace with Your Parents* (New York: Ballantine, 1983).

———, with Leonard Felder, Ph.D. *Making Peace with Yourself* (New York: Ballantine, 1985).

———, with poetry by Natasha Josefowitz. *Love Secrets for a Lasting Relationship* (New York: Bantam, 1992).

———, and Robert B. Kory. *Inner Joy* (New York: Berkley, 1980).

———, and Peter McWilliams. *How to Heal Depression* (Los Angeles: Prelude Press, 1991).

———, Mikael Nordfors, M.D., and Peter McWilliams. *Hypericum (St. John's Wort) and Depression* (Los Angeles: Prelude Press, 1996).

———, and Sirah Vettese, Ph.D., with Robert Kory. *Lifemates* (New York: Signet, 1992).

Bradshaw, John., *Healing the Shame That Binds You* (Deerfield Beach, FL: Health Communications, Inc., 1988).

Campbell, Don. *The Mozart Effect* (New York: Avon, 1997).

Casarjian, Robin. *Forgiveness* (New York: Bantam, 1992).

Chopra, Deepak. *How to Know God* (New York: Crown, 2000).

Concept Synergy. *Making Peace with Your Shadow* (audiotapes and workbook) (Orlando, FL: Author, 1997). To order: 800-678-2356.

————. *Ending Shame* (audiotapes I–IV) (Orlando, FL: 1997). To order: 800-678-2356.

Cooper, Robert K., and Ayman Sawaf. *Executive EQ* (New York: Putnam, 1997).

Dalai Lama. *Ethics for the New Millennium* (New York: Riverhead, 1999).

Dossey, Larry. *Healing Words* (New York: HarperCollins, 1993).

Druck, Ken, with Jack Forem. *Strength of Heart: A Father's Journey through Love and Loss.* Forthcoming.

Dunas, Felice, Ph.D., with Philip Goldberg. *Passion Play* (New York: Riverside/Putnam, 1997).

Ferguson, Tom, M.D. *Health Online* (Reading, MA: Addison-Wesley, 1996).

Ferucci, Piero, Ph.D. *Inevitable Grace* (New York: Tarcher/Putnam, 1990).

Fritz, Robert. *The Path of Least Resistance* (New York: Fawcett, 1989).

Goldberg, Philip. *The Intuitive Edge* (New York: Tarcher/Putnam, 1983).

Goulston, Mark, M.D., and Goldberg, Philip. *Get Out of Your Own Way* (New York: Perigee/Putnam, 1996).

Harris, Rachel, Ph.D. *Twenty Minute Retreats* (New York: Henry Holt & Co., 2000).

Hoffman, Bob. *No One Is to Blame* (Palo Alto, CA: Science and Behavior Books, 1979).

Hubbard, Barbara Marx. *Conscious Evolution* (Novato, CA: New World Library, 1998).

Jampolsky, Gerald G., M.D. *Teach Only Love* (New York: Bantam, 1983).

Jeffers, Susan, Ph.D. *Feel the Fear and Do It Anyway* (New York: Fawcett, 1987).

Klein, Carole, and Richard Gotti, Ph.D. *Overcoming Regret: Lessons from the Roads Not Taken* (New York: Bantam, 1992).

Maharishi Mahesh Yogi. *Bhagavad Gita* (Fairfield, IA: Age of Enlightenment Press, 1967).

———. *The Science of Being and Art of Living* (Fairfield, IA: Age of Enlightenment Press, 1966).

Pennebaker, James W. *Opening Up* (New York: Morrow, 1990).

Shapiro, Francine, Ph.D., and Margot Silk Forrest. *EMDR* (New York: Basic Books, 1998).

Stoddard, Alexandra. *The Gift of a Letter* (New York: Doubleday, 1990).

Strohecker, James, and Nancy Shaw Strohecker, eds. *Natural Healing for Depression* (New York: Perigee/Putnam, 1999).

Thich Nhat Hanh. *The Long Road Turns to Joy* (Parallax Press, 1996).

Tutu, Desmond M. *No Future Without Forgiveness* (New York: Doubleday, 1999).

Vettese, Sirah, Ph.D. *What Happened to the Prince I Married? Spiritual Healing for a Wounded Relationship* (Fairfield, CT: Aslan, 1999).

Walsch, Neale Donald. *Conversations with God* (New York: Putnam, 1996).

Zweig, Connie, Ph.D., and Steve Wolf, Ph.D. *Romancing the Shadow: Illuminating the Dark Side of the Soul* (New York: Ballantine, 1997).

APPENDIX B:
SELF-HELP GROUPS

Alcoholics Anonymous
P.O. Box 459, Grand Central
  Station
New York, NY 10163
212-870-3400

Al-Anon Family Groups
  Headquarters, Inc.
P.O. Box 862, Midtown Station
New York, NY 10018
800-356-9996

Codependents Anonymous
P.O. Box 33577
Phoenix, AZ 85067
602-277-7991

Divorce Anonymous
2600 Colorado Avenue, Suite 270
Santa Monica, CA 90404
310-998-6538

Emotions Anonymous
P.O. Box 4245
St. Paul, MN 55104
612-647-9712

Families Helping Families
3636 Fifth Avenue, Suite 201
San Diego, CA 92103
619-294-8000

National Depressive and
  Manic-Depressive
  Association
730 North Franklin Street,
  Suite 501
Chicago, IL 60610
800-826-3632

National Foundation for
  Depressive Illness
P.O. Box 2257
New York, NY 10116–2257
800-248-4344

National Organization for
  Victim Assistance (NOVA)
1757 Park Road, NW
Washington, DC 20012
800-TRY-NOVA

Obsessive Compulsives
  Anonymous
P.O. Box 215
New Hyde Park, NY 11040
516-741-4901

Overeaters Anonymous
383 Van Ness Avenue, Suite
  1601
Torrance, CA 90501

Phobics Anonymous
P.O. Box 1180
Palm Springs, CA 92263
760-322-COPE

Sex Addicts Anonymous
P.O. Box 70949
Houston, TX 77270

Workaholics Anonymous
P.O. Box 66150
Los Angeles, CA 90066
310-859-5804

ACKNOWLEDGMENTS

My deepest gratitude to my wife, Sirah Vettese, for her radiant love, total support, and creative input. Her peace, wisdom, and compassion shine throughout. Heartfelt appreciation to our children, Shazara, Damien, and Michael, for their contributions to this book. Much love to my mother, Fridl, departed father, Max, sister, Nora, and brother-in-law, Gus.

I wish to express my heartfelt gratitude to Phil Goldberg for finding the right words and adding his own knowledge and insight. Ours was a brilliant, incisive, loving, professional, and joyous collaboration of the highest order.

Deepest thanks to my assistant, Molly Tulloch, whose help has been invaluable; to Dana Plant for typing and copyediting the manuscript; and to Lori Deutsch for her editorial assistance and for keeping Phil centered and sane throughout this project.

My appreciation extends to Bob Alderman, Steve Barthe, Ed and Nancy Bernstein, Kingsley and Leslie Brooks, Don Campbell, Ray and Patty Chambers, Bobby Colomby, Robert Cooper, Rabbi Laurie Cosky and Mark Lokhemper, Kathy Davison, Rebecca Drake, Dean Draznin, Ken Druck, Leonard Felder, Mike and Donna Fletcher, Russell Guess, John Hagelin, Ed Haisha, Rachel Harris, Christopher Hills, Paul and Barbara Hunter, Noel Johansen, Norman and Lyn Lear, Mike and Jackie Love, Peter McWilliams, Jach Pursel, Vince and Laura Regalbuto, Diane Roberts, Bob Roth, and Ayman and Rowan Sawaf.

I wish to especially thank all of my psychotherapy clients, with whom it has been my privilege to work, in Del Mar and throughout the world, for all they have taught me.

Special thanks to Joelle Delbourgo, my very dear friend and now my literary agent, who was a godmother over the inception of this book. I am grateful to Megan Newman, my editor, for her deep commitment to the highest vision for this book, her ready wit, and her astute editing; to Rose Carrano, who is the ideal publicist for this book because her sincerity and spirituality shine through; to Josh Marwell for a strong subtitle; and to Lynn Franklin for her friendship and her handling of foreign rights.

My profound thanks to Lazaris and Concept Synergy for ideas and experiences that have transformed my personal and professional life.

My appreciation to Bob Hoffman, Raz and Liza Ingrasci, and all the Hoffman Quadrinity teachers for a life-changing process that strongly influenced this book.

My deepest respect and profound gratitude to Maharishi Mahesh Yogi for the pure knowledge and experience of the peace that transcends understanding.

Finally, my thanks to my readers for the privilege of serving their healing and personal growth.

NOTES

PREFACE

1. Felitti VJ, Anda RF, Norenberg D, et al., The Relationship of Childhood Abuse and Household Dysfunction to Many of the Leading Causes of Death in Adults. *American Journal of Preventive Medicine*, 1998; 14(4):245–258.

2. Ruggiero J, Bernstein DP, Handelsman L. Traumatic Stress in Childhood and Later Personality Disorders. *Psychiatric Annals*, December, 1999; 29(12): 713–721.

3. Forge, W, Adverse Childhood Experiences: a Public Health Perspective. *American Journal of Preventive Medicine*, 14(4):354–355.

4. Weiss MJS, Wagner SH, What Explains the Negative Consequences of Adverse Childhood Experience on Adult Health? ibid, pp. 356–360.

5. Whitfield CL, Adverse Childhood Experiences and Trauma, ibid, pp.361–363.

6. Whitfield CL, *Memory and Abuse: Remembering and Healing the Wounds of Trauma* (Deerfield Beach, FL: Health Communications, 1995).

7. Thompson RF, The Neurobiology of Learning and Memory, *Science* 1986, 233:941–7.

8. Herman J, *Trauma and Recovery* (New York: Basic Books, 1992).

CHAPTER 1

1. Robert Pollack, *The Missing Moment* (Boston, Houghton-Mifflin, 1999).

2. Green EA, Walters ED, Voluntary Control of Internal States: Psychological and Physiological, *Journal of Transpersonal Psychology*, 2(1): 1–26 (1970).

3. The instructions up to this point should be used to begin each visualization exercise in the book.

CHAPTER 2

1. Robert Thayer, Ph.D., *The Biopsychology of Mood* (New York: Oxford University Press, 1989).

2. Matthew 18:3.

3. Sicher F, Targ E, Moore D, Smith H, A Randomized Double-blind Study of the Effect of Distant Healing in a Population with Advanced AIDS, *Western Journal of Medicine*, 169 (December 1998): pp. 356-363.

4. Byrd RC, Positive Therapeutic Effects of Intercessory Prayer in a Coronary Care Unit Population, *Southern Medical Journal*, 81, no. 7 (July 1988): pp. 826-829.

CHAPTER 3

1. Depression is a common, treatable illness, and nothing to be ashamed of. See pp. 221–225.

.2. Francis ME and Pennebaker JW, Talking and Writing as Illness Prevention. *Medicine, Exercise, Nutrition, and Health*, 1 (1) (Jan./Feb. 1992): 27–33.

3. Smyth JM, Stone AA, Hurewitz A, Kaell A, Effects of Writing About Stressful Experiences on Symptom Reduction in Patients with Asthma or Rheumatoid Arthritis, *Journal of the American Medical Association*, Vol. 281, No. 14, pp. 1304–1309.

CHAPTER 7

1. Van Biema D, "Should All Be Forgiven?" *Time*, April 5, 1999, pp. 55–58.

CHAPTER 8

1. For emotional literacy programs, contact Six Seconds at 650-685-9885, www.nexusEQ.com.

2. For more information about depression, see Bloomfield H, M.D. and McWilliams P, *How to Heal Depression* (Los Angeles: Prelude Press, 1994).

3. Sharma HM, Hanna AN, Kauffman EM, Newman HAI. Inhibition of Low-Density Lipoprotein Oxidation in Vitro by Maharishi Ayur-Veda Herbal Medicines. *Pharmacology, Biochemistry and Behavior*, 43: pp. 1175–1182 (1992).

4. Sharma HM, Hanna AN, Kauffman EM, Newman HAI. Effect of Herbal Mixture Student Rasayana on Lipozygenase Activity and Lipid Peroxidation. *Free Radical Biology and Medicine* 18 (4): pp. 687-697 (1195).

5. Scherwitz L, et al. Self-Involvement and the Risk Factors for Coronary Heart Disease. Advances 2(2): pp. 6-18 (Spring 1985).

6. Palmore, E.B. Physical, Mental and Social Factors in Predicting Longevity. *Gerontologist* 9(2): 103–108 (Summer, 1969).

7. Einstein A. *Ideas and Opinions* (New York: Bonanza Books, 1956).

ABOUT THE AUTHORS

Over the past 30 years, HAROLD BLOOMFIELD, M.D., has earned a reputation as "the psychiatrist America trusts." As a renowned psychospiritual educator, Dr. Bloomfield has been at the cutting edge of many important health and human development movements worldwide, and a champion of emotional literacy. Dr. Bloomfield has written 17 books, which have sold more than 7 million copies and have been translated into 26 languages. Dr. Bloomfield's bestsellers, *Making Peace with Your Parents* and *Making Peace with Yourself*, introduced personal and family peacemaking to millions of people. *How to Survive the Loss of a Love* and *How to Heal Depression* have become self-help classics. *TM: Discovering Inner Energy and Overcoming Stress* spent six months on the *New York Times* bestseller list. His most recent *New York Times* bestseller, *Hypericum (St. John's Wort) & Depression* and *Healing Anxiety Naturally* helped catalyze the herbal medicine revolution.

Dr. Bloomfield has appeared regularly on national television, including *20/20, Oprah, Larry King Live, Good Morning America*, and CNN. His work has been featured in *Time, Newsweek, U.S. News & World Report, People, Forbes, Cosmopolitan, Ladies' Home Journal, Prevention, American Health, USA Today*, the *New York Times*, the *Los Angeles Times*, the *Boston Globe*, and numerous other magazines and newspapers. In 1998 he was the Natural Law Party candidate for governor of California.

Dr. Bloomfield received the 1999 Theodore Geisel "Best of the Best" Book Award, the *Medical Self-Care Magazine* Book of the Year Award, the Golden Apple Award for Outstanding Psychological Educator, and the American Holistic Health Association's Lifetime Achievement Award. He is an adjunct professor of psychology at Union Graduate School and a member of the American Psychiatric Association and the San Diego Psychiatric Society. Dr. Bloomfield is frequently invited to speak at conferences and throughout the world. He brings a friendly, compassionate, inspiring presence to public seminars and professional meetings.

Dr. Bloomfield maintains a private practice of psychiatry, psychotherapy, and executive coaching in Del Mar, California.

Harold Bloomfield, M.D., offers a wide variety of seminars, public lectures, and educational programs, as well as private consultations. For further information, please contact:

Harold Bloomfield, M.D.
1337 Camino Del Mar
Del Mar, CA 92014
Phone: 858-481-9950
Fax: 858-792-2333
E-mail: harah@adnc.com

PHILIP GOLDBERG is the author or coauthor of 16 books, including *The Intuitive Edge, Get Out of Your Own Way, Passion Play*, and the forthcoming *Signposts on the Road to Enlightenment*. He has lectured widely on topics related to intuition, holistic health, and spirituality, and has appeared on numerous television and radio talk shows. A novelist and screenwriter as well, his first novel, *This Is Next Year*, is in development as a motion picture. He lives in Los Angeles.

MAKING PEACE WITH GOD

If you have found this book to be of assistance in your personal evolution, please consider making a contribution to my next book project, *Making Peace with God.*

My own personal experience, as well as my professional work with tens of thousands of clients, has shown me that once a person makes peace with the past, the next step on the soul's journey is often to make peace with God. I invite you to share a true story that you feel belongs in *Making Peace with God.* It may be an article from a magazine or newspaper, the story of a friend or relative, or a personal spiritual experience that touched you profoundly.

Have you deeply struggled to understand who—or what—God is? Were there times when you felt betrayed, abandoned, or forgotten by the Almighty? Did you ever hate, reject, or seriously question God? When was your faith most sorely tested? How have you been able to reconcile with God about the presence of evil in the world? What does making peace with God mean to you?

I would be grateful if you were to ponder these and other questions about God, and to share the results of your contemplation. Please write to:

Harold Bloomfield, M.D.
1337 Camino Del Mar, Suite E
Del Mar, CA 92014
Or E-mail me at: harah@adnc.com

Of course, both you and any source you contribute will be credited if your reply is used in the book. Thank you.